SEE BRITAIN AT WORK

by Angela Lansbury

UK: Exley Publications
USA: Two Continents/Exley Publications

By the same author:

ENQUIRE WITHIN UPON TRAVEL AND HOLIDAYS   1976 Barrie & Jenkins
The A to Z of SHOPPING BY POST   1978 Exley Publications

First published 1977
Second edition 1978
Copyright © Exley Publications Ltd, 63 Kingsfield Road, Watford, Herts WD1 4PP
Published simultaneously in the United States by Two Continents/Exley Publications,
The Two Continents Publishing Group Ltd, 30 East 42 Street, New York, NY 10017

ISBN 0 905521 19 6 (in UK)
ISBN 0 8467 0342 4 LCCN 77 76615 (in USA)

Front cover illustration: Dartington Glass Limited, Devon

Back cover illustration: Josiah Wedgwood & Sons Limited, Staffordshire

Printed in Great Britain by Morrison & Gibb Limited, PO Box 44, Tanfield,
Edinburgh EH3 5JT
Typesetting by Ardek Photosetters (Division of Mainline Typesetters), St Leonards, Sussex
and Beaver ReproGraphics Limited, Hawk House, 1a Sparrows Herne, Bushey, Herts
WD2 1AD

To my husband Trevor,
who likes to take things apart,
in the hope that he will visit Hoover
and find out how
to put the toaster back together.

Introduction

This book is a reference work listing 450 factories, workshops and small scale industries which the public can visit throughout Britain. These include small potteries and workshops where individual craftsmen will demonstrate handloom weaving, engraving on glass or the making of jewellery, as well as huge distilleries, breweries, nuclear power stations, textile manufacturers and glassworks, which sometimes accept thousands of visitors a year. The entries are divided into six main sections: The South (including London), the South West, the Midlands and East Anglia, the North, Scotland and Wales. Each region has its own character. For instance, the Midlands is the pottery region par excellence, the five towns known as the 'Potteries' boast some of the best tours of industrial scale china and glass making, including Wedgwood, Spode, Minton, Royal Doulton and other household names. In Scotland you can see whisky being made (and taste a dram), watch tweeds being woven, and sample highland cheeses. In Wales you can take a ride through slate caverns, watch Welsh weavers and a carver of love-spoons at work or stop to visit a huge hydro-electric scheme.

'See Britain at Work' is designed to help you, whether you are on holiday looking for places to visit, a teacher planning school trips or a club leader planning a day's outing.

If you are based in, say, Cornwall turn to the section on the South-West and look at the map to see which places of work are near you. There may also be some in adjacent counties near enough for a day trip.

If, on the other hand, you particularly want to visit a special type of factory — for example to show children how glass is made — look at the nationwide list of visits. This has an alphabetical list of categories of visits, so simply look under 'Glassworks'.

Planning Ahead

The key to a warm welcome and a successful visit is planning ahead. A telephone call in advance will save you from a possible disappointment. Even on a relatively unplanned holiday, it is usually advisable to make a local 'phone call to places you might visit the following day. Basically, factories are there to work and not as entertainers so very few are geared to receive trippers. The firms which have something to sell are the ones most likely to offer free visits at any time. The larger factories offer guided tours. In some cases these start at regular times and you can simply join at the appointed hour. Other tours are so popular that you need to book. In winter tours are often arranged according to demand for schools and clubs. Many firms allow individuals to join smaller groups when convenient.

The larger factories and mills with products to sell tend to welcome all kinds of visitors. Smaller firms and service industries are more inclined to encourage educational groups, particularly local school-leavers who might join the industry.

Owners of small craft workshops often like to see the general public in small groups but do not want to be overwhelmed by coach parties. Potters are particularly anxious not to have groups of schoolchildren arriving unannounced. There may not be an adult on hand to prevent children touching machinery and breaking pottery in the workshop when the potter is talking to the teacher in the showroom. People whose workshop is their home are often the friendliest to individual visitors. Naturally it is a courtesy to telephone in advance to check that your arrival will not interfere with their domestic arrangements. If you have a good reason for wanting to see around *any* place of work — because you are thinking of working in that trade — or already do so — many more doors will open to you. Many factories have long waiting lists. Yorkshire Television, for example, had a six-year waiting list for tours, though tickets for shows are available within weeks. So it pays to plan ahead, especially with popular places and big touring parties.

Several very popular factories are no longer accepting visitors. Some of the food and chocolate manufacturers who used to attract many thousands of visitors each year have now

become fully automated and there is very little
to see. The Post Office, the coal mines and
other businesses have discontinued mass
popular visiting for security reasons or to
comply with new safety regulations.
Then, children came in for a special mention.
A nationwide petroleum company put it in a
nutshell by saying that school parties were
'tolerated rather than encouraged'. No
wonder. Some firms mentioned incidents like
the protective guard that had been quietly
removed from a highly dangerous piece of
equipment. And then there was the story of the
scarf that was dropped into a sausage
machine. . . .

More Projects Please

If you should come across any other places
which would merit inclusion in a future
edition of this book, do let us know.
Meanwhile, Happy Visiting!

Photographic Credits

We would like to record our thanks to the
hundreds of firms, workshops and individuals
who sent in photographs to accompany their
entries in this book; without their help it
would have been impossible to choose such an
attractive selection of illustrations. We are
grateful to those who sent in pictures which
could not be included for space reasons and we
thank the British Tourist Authority, The
Heart of England Tourist Board and the
Welsh Tourist Board. We also owe special
thanks to the Central Electricity Generating
Board, who patiently answered all our
questions and lent us photographs.
Occasionally firms were not able to supply
illustrations and we had to seek additional
pictures elsewhere, and we record our thanks
to: Thames Television (page 114), Kevin
Redpath and Huw Evans (page 120), Elizabeth
Haines (pages 123 and 124), Arthur
Williamson (page 125), Tegwyn Roberts & *Y
Cymro* (page 128), Council for Small
Industries in Rural Areas (pages 136 and 144),
Derbyshire Countryside Ltd (page 91),
Birmingham Post & Mail Ltd (page 102).

Ideas for Other Visits

The main body of this book contains the
biggest and best in factory visits. It includes
the most publicised, the most famous, the
most popular places of work — in fact nearly
every factory that makes a speciality of visits.
But you or your child, or your group, may
have a particular interest in, say, farms or
lighthouses or crafts. Or you may want to take
your group to visit only local places of
interest. Or you may be interested in cheese-
making or an unusual career. Where do you
start in your search for your particular subject?
We have tried in this introductory section to
give some pointers.

Butter and Cheese Making

The Milk Marketing Board has creameries and
dairies in various parts of England and Wales.
These are open to groups such as secondary
school parties and adult education groups.
Visits are by appointment. Write in the first
instance to the Visits Officer, MMB, Thames
Ditton, Surrey (Tel: 01-398 4101).

Finding Farms

The Association of Agriculture acts as an
intermediary, finding farms to accept children
aged nine and over and adult parties. Demand
is heavy and they do not guarantee to find a
farm open to visitors in every area. A service fee
is charged and a questionnaire must be
completed. Adults can ask to be placed on the
monthly mailing list for programmes of farm
open days. Contact Miss Hilary Tinley,
Farm Open Days Officer, Association of
Agriculture, 16/20 Strutton Ground, London
SW1P 2HP. Tel: 01-222 6115/6.

The World of Entertainment

Theatres and opera houses sometimes admit
groups to dress rehearsals. The London and
Birmingham studios of Associated Television
are open to groups from recognised
organisations. Write to the Studio Controller,
ATV Studio, Eldon Avenue, Boreham Wood,
Hertfordshire or to the Studio Controller,

ATV Centre, Bridge Street, Birmingham B1 2JP. Tickets to watch shows are available from the same studios. Write to the Ticket Office. The studios of BBC television and radio are not open to the public but tickets for shows can be obtained by visitors aged fourteen and over.

For regions outside London write to the Ticket Unit of the BBC studio in that area. For London programmes write, enclosing an sae, to The Ticket Unit, Broadcasting House, BBC, London W1A 4WW. Applicants from outside London get priority for specific dates on any waiting list. Groups are accepted and audience seats are divided between large groups and individuals. State which show you wish to see or specify the type (eg comedy). Give the number in your party and offer a choice of dates.

The Independent Broadcasting Authority, at 70 Brompton Road, London SW3 1EY (Tel: 01-584 7011), has a gallery showing the history of television and radio. There are also models showing how programmes are put together nowadays and displays on future techniques such as videocassette recording.

Looking at Lighthouses

A list of twenty-seven lighthouses which are open to the public can be obtained from the Press Officer, Trinity Lighthouse Service, Trinity House, Tower Hill, London EC3N 4DH (Tel: 01-480 6601). These lighthouses are in England and Wales and on the Channel Islands. No charge is made and up to thirty people can be accepted on a visit. Lighthouses in Scotland are run by the Northern Lighthouse Board, 84 George Street, Edinburgh EH2 3DA, Scotland (Tel: 031-226 7051).

Learning More About Crafts

Those interested in crafts would enjoy reading 'Crafts and Craftsmen' before a visit. It is edited by Bruce Alexander and published by Croom Helm of London. A chapter is devoted to explaining the history and processes of each of several crafts. Working craftsmen in each field are listed at the back of the book, though most will welcome only prospective customers. The work of individual potters is described and illustrated in 'Potters', a directory of the work of full members of the Craftsmen Potters Association of Great Britain. It is sold by the Craftsmen Potters Shop, William Blake House, Marshall Street, London W1 (Tel: 01-437 7605). 'Craft Workshops in the Countryside' is published by the Council for Small Industries in Rural Areas, 35 Camp Road, Wimbledon Common, London SW19 4UP (Tel: 01-947 6761). (1977 edition 75p plus 17p postage.) This book lists craft workshops and retail shops which welcome visitors from home and overseas and which have craft goods for sale.

Seeing Lifeboats

The Royal National Lifeboat Institution has about 250 lifeboat stations. Times of opening are irregular but they will make special arrangements to open for schools and other groups. To obtain a map of lifeboat stations, and the address of the Honorary Secretary of your nearest one, write, enclosing an sae, to Mrs Heather Deane, RNLI, West Quay Road, Poole, Dorset (Tel Poole 71133). In addition to lifeboat stations there are several exhibition centres. There are displays, for instance, at Poole in Dorset (RBLI HQ); Southend in Essex; Shoreham and Eastbourne in Sussex; Sheringham and Cromer in Norfolk; Wales and Whitby (qv); Dunbar and Port Patrick.

Local Visits

Groups will often be able to arrange local visits to places that do not normally open to the public. For instance some post offices and water authorities arrange tours for local ratepayers or schools.

Specially for Tourists

Overseas visitors and business people will find that the tourist organisations in each region can put them in touch with relevant companies. Chambers of Commerce in every town maintain lists of members, and invitations will be given to people in the same business, which would not be extended to members of the general public.

The tourist boards of each region produce free and low-cost leaflets on places of interest. For example, 'Crafts and Rural Industries', 'Museums and Art Galleries' and a 'Disabled Visitors Guide' are sold by the Wales Tourist Board, PO Box 151, WDO Cardiff CF5 1XS. Literature from the tourist boards can help you plan a complete day out, taking in museums and monuments as well as places in this book.

Contact the English Tourist Board, 4 Grosvenor Gardens, London SW1 0DU (Tel: 01-730 3400); The Scottish Tourist Board, 23 Ravelston Terrace, Edinburgh EH4 3EU (Tel: 031-332 2433); The Wales Tourist Board, Llandaff, Cardiff CF5 2YZ (Tel: Cardiff 27281); or the British Tourist Authority, 64 St James's Street, London SW1 (Tel: 01-629 9191).

Mainly for Schools

How the Post Office Works

The Post Office issues free leaflets and posters. It is divided into two sections — postal and telecommunications. For details write to The Schools Office, Postal Headquarters Building, St Martins-le-Grand, London EC1A 1HQ and your enquiry will be passed on to the appropriate region. Apply to the local Head Postmaster for visits to local sorting offices. For telecommunications (telegrams, telex, telephone) write to the Telecommunications Manager at the above address, stating the age of pupils.

Police and Fire Brigade in Action

Junior schools usually find it easy to arrange visits from the local police or fire station. A Hertfordshire school reports, 'The police brought police dogs to the school playground and showed dogs chasing and catching a "criminal". This caused great excitement. On another occasion they brought fingerprinting apparatus and took all the children's fingerprints. Then the fire brigade came in the summer and soaked the children with water.' A school group can also visit the fire station to be shown fire engines, the alarm systems, different pipes and water hydrants.

Going Down a Coal Mine

There are twenty-two collieries in the National Coal Board's Western Area, which covers the coalfields of Lancashire, Cumbria, North Wales, Staffordshire and Shropshire. Visits are accepted from schools within reasonable travelling distance of the collieries and from organisations having a direct link with the mining industry. Normally numbers are restricted to twelve per group. Write to The Deputy Director (Mining), National Coal Board Western Area, Staffordshire House, Berry Hill Road, Fenton, Stoke-on-Trent, Staffordshire ST4 2NH (Tel: Stoke-on-Trent 48201).

City Life and Social Studies

Most offices of public services are listed in the telephone book. For information about gas, teachers should contact the Chief Home Service Adviser of the relevant gas region. County law courts are usually open to the public. Democracy in action can be seen at the Houses of Parliament. The public gallery of the House of Commons is open Monday to Thursday from 2.30 pm until late at night. Details are given in The Times and Daily Telegraphs. Use the St Stephen's entrance (Tel: 01-219 4324). Guided tours are held Saturday from 10 am to 4.30 pm. Go to the Norman Porch. There is no need to book. Waterworks tend to favour groups of local ratepayers. A useful book on early waterpower is 'Discovering Watermills' by John Vince, published by Shire Publications Limited at 50p.

Local Businesses—for School Leavers

Many businesses welcome local groups, especially school leavers. Look through the commercial classified section of the telephone directory or the yellow pages. Try local banks,

insurance companies, solicitors, accountants and estate agents.
Lists are often compiled by the Youth Employment Office, the Teachers Centre, the central County Library, or local authorities such as the GLC.

Ideas for Teachers

Teachers can plan lessons using the material in 'See Britain at Work' relating to the specific place they propose visiting. Some entries include general descriptions of processes. For instance, if the class is visiting a power station it would be helpful to read the long write-up of Fiddler's Ferry Power Station in the North. Dartington Glass in Devon has a good general description of glass-blowing, Glengarioch Distillery in Scotland has a description of the processes involved in whisky distillation, and so on. Consult the nationwide index for similar projects which might provide information.
Other sources of lesson material will be found in the 'Treasure Chest for Teachers' from Schoolmaster Publishing Co Ltd, Derbyshire House, Lower Street, Kettering, Northampton (Tel: Wadcroft 3407). It describes the films, wallcharts and other services available from museums and the PR services of industry. The latest edition costs 90p, post free.
Those interested in transport will find a wealth of places to visit in the annual 'Historic Transport', published by The Transport Trust, 18 Ramilies Place, London WC1.
British Airports issue a free booklet called 'Airport Information' which gives details about its airports, nearby places of interest, refreshments, spectators' terraces and arrangements for the disabled. The airports described are Aberdeen, Edinburgh, Glasgow, Prestwick, Heathrow, Stansted and Gatwick. Copies are available from British Airports Publications, Brochure Department, Wellington Road, Cheriton, Folkestone, Kent. British Airports head office is at 2 Buckingham Gate, London SW1E 6JL (Tel: 01-834 6621).

The nationwide list of visits

AGRICULTURAL MUSEUMS
Ashley Countryside Collection, page 35
Brympton d'Evercy, page 209
Lackham Agricultural Museum, page 210

AIRCRAFT MANUFACTURE
Scottish Aviation Limited, page 186

AIRPORTS
East Midlands Airport, page 90
Gatwick Airport, page 60
Glamorgan (Rhoose) Airport, page 117
Liverpool Airport, page 153
Luton Airport, page 213
Manchester International Airport, page 149

ANIMAL CENTRE
Little Creech Animal Centre, page 209

ARTISTS
Celtic Crafts Limited, page 124
George Garson — mural maker, page 222
Trevor and Valerie Green — tile painters, page 126
John Reilly — oil painter, page 79
Sheila Southwell — porcelain painter, page 58
George L Thomson — calligrapher, page 222

ARTISTS' SUPPLIES FACTORY
Winsor & Newton Limited, page 70

ATOMIC ENERGY
UK Atomic Energy Authority, page 223

BAKERIES AND BREAD BAKING
Greggs of Gosforth, page 173
S Moores, Goldencap Biscuit Bakery, page 41
Woodlands Craft Centre, page 74

BASKET WEAVING
The Royal Dundee Institution for the Blind, page 192

BATIK
Mary Potter Studio, page 58

BEE-KEEPING
Preseli Honey Farm, page 126

BIRD CENTRE
The Falconry Centre, page 109

BICYCLE MANUFACTURE
Raleigh Industries Limited, page 90

BLACKSMITHS
Bennett Ironwork (Dorset) Ltd, page 210
Cerne Valley Forge, page 210
Mr T D Davies, page 128
Hyders Limited, page 53
John M Price & Son, page 126
E Martin & Son, page 180
The Old Smithy, page 220
Wing & Staples, page 44

BOATS
Denis Ferranti Laminations Ltd, page 137
Halmatic (Scotland) Ltd, page 224
SS Great Britain, page 211

BOOKBINDING
Roger Powell, page 213

BREWERIES
Ansells Limited, page 101
Carlsberg Brewery Limited, page 88
Eldridge Pope & Company Limited, page 43
Fuller, Smith & Turner Ltd, page 213
Scottish & Newcastle Breweries Limited, page 184
Scottish & Newcastle Breweries Limited, page 173
Shepherd Neame, page 52
Vaux Breweries Ltd, page 220

BRICKMAKERS
Blockleys Limited, page 112

BUTTERFLY BREEDING
Worldwide Butterflies Limited, page 43

CANDLE MAKING
Candles in the Rain, page 136
Celmi Candles, page 142

CAR FACTORIES
Ford Motor Company Limited, Dagenham, page 50
Ford Motor Company Limited, Halewood, page 153
Vauxhall Motors Limited, page 75

CARPET MANUFACTURERS
Axminster Carpets Limited, page 33
Blackwood, Morton & Sons Ltd, page 222
Wilton Royal Carpet Factory Limited, page 44

CHEESE MAKING
Highland Fine Cheeses Limited, page 204
Islay Creamery Co Ltd, page 224
J M Nuttall & Company, page 93
Overton Hall Cheshire Cheese Dairy, page 218
Scottish Milk Marketing Board, page 224
Swannay Farms Limited, page 208

CHILDREN'S VILLAGE
Pestalozzi Children's Village, page 212

CHINA CLAY
English China Clays Limited, page 24

CIDER MAKING
H P Bulmer Limited, page 110
R J Sheppy & Son, page 37

CITY COUNCILS
The Guildhall, London, page 65
The Town Hall, Liverpool, page 153

CLOTHING MANUFACTURERS
Bernat Klein Designs Ltd, page 208
Damart Thermawear (Bradford) Ltd, page 219
Hector Russell (Highland Industries) Ltd, page 223
Kagan Textiles Limited, page 159
Pandy Garments, page 137
Richesse Furs, page 57

CORN DOLLIES
Betty Loughborough, page 123

COSMETIC FACTORIES
Columbia Products Company Limited, page 78
Max Factor & Co, page 214

FLOUR MILL
Booker Health Foods Limited, page 57

FOOD MANUFACTURE
Colman Foods, page 82

FRUIT PICKING
Peter Bossom, Glyn-y-fran, page 125
Rosemount Farms, page 193

FUR FABRIC MANUFACTURER
Richesse Furs, page 57

FURNITURE RESTORATION
Aruncraft Workshops, page 55
Keith Durrant, Celtic Crafts Limited, page 124

GARDENS
*Cornwall Education Committee
Demonstration Garden, page 21*
The Scottish White Heather Farm, page 205
Trentham Gardens Limited, page 97

GEMSTONE WORKSHOPS
Creetown Gem Rock Museum, page 177
Lapidary Workshops Company, page 197
Sutherland Gemcutters, page 203

GLASS CRAFTSMEN
Raymond G Adnitt, page 52
The Glasshouse, page 68
The Glass Workshop, page 88
Harold Gordon, page 200
Island Glass, page 79
Isle of Wight Studio Glass Ltd, page 214
North Glen Gallery, page 178

GLASS FACTORIES
Caithness Glass Limited, page 204
Cumbria Crystal Limited, page 175
Dartington Glass Limited, page 30
Dent Glass, page 220
Edinburgh Crystal Glass Company, page 182
Oban Glassworks, page 205
Royal Brierley Crystal, page 105
Strathearn Glass Limited, page 188
Stuart & Sons Limited, page 104
Thomas Webb & Sons, page 100
Webb Corbett Limited, page 102
Webb Corbett Limited, page 98

Wedgwood Glass, page 85
Whitefriars Glass Limited, page 69
Wood Brothers Glass Co Ltd, page 219

GOLD AND SILVERWORK
Clevedon Craft Centre, page 45
Ortak Silvercraft, page 208
Clare Street, page 73
Thomas Fattorini Limited, page 100
Workshop Wales, page 125

GRAPHIC DESIGN
Old Rectory Design, page 224

GROG BOTTLES
Grogport Old Manse, page 206

GUNPOWDER MILLS
Chart Gunpowder Mills, page 211

HERB PRODUCTS
Carlton Crafts, page 172

HORNWORK
Glenroy Horncraft, page 194
St Inan (Products) Limited, page 185

HORSES
Courage Shire Horse Centre, page 54

INDUSTRIAL MUSEUMS
Abbeydale Industrial Hamlet, page 162
Admiral Blake Museum, page 209
Ark Museum, page 219
Avoncroft Museum of Buildings, page 216
Beamish Museum, page 219
Bradford Industrial Museum, page 161
Bridport Museum, page 210
Bury Transport Museum, page 218
Castle Museum, York, page 65
Craven Museum, page 219
Dodyke Pumping Station Preservation Trust, page 215
George Leatt Industrial & Folk Museum, page 219
Haxted Mill, page 211
Herefordshire Waterworks Museum, page 111
Horsham Museum, page 212
Ironbridge Gorge Museum, page 111
Monks Hall Museum, page 218

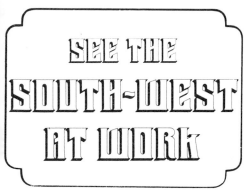

THE SOUTH WEST

Cornwall, Devon, Dorset, Somerset Avon, Wiltshire

1   Textured Pottery

Tremaen Pottery Limited
Newlyn Slip, Penzance, Cornwall
Tel: Penzance 4364

The pottery is sited in a large old fish loft overlooking the busy harbour of Newlyn. It specialises in asymmetric stoneware decorated with textures and glazes inspired by the natural weathered beachstones that surround the Cornish coast. From the showroom, or on a guided tour you can see the clay being prepared, and slip casting and pot finishing. It is certainly worth a visit. Princess Anne called here in 1972 during her official visit to Cornwall.
Practical details: The workshop and showrooms are open all year Monday to Friday, from 9 am to 1 pm and 2 pm to 5.30 pm. They are closed on bank holidays. Individuals and groups of up to 20 people, including school children, can observe work in progress, and guided tours can be arranged. Advance notice is essential. Contact Peter Ellery a week ahead.

2   Craft Workshops

Wendron Forge
Helston, Cornwall
Tel: Helston 3531

Wendron Forge is a four-acre complex with craft workshops producing clocks and pictures etched on metal.

It also houses a major collection of antique machines arranged around the entrance to old mine workings which date back to 1725. The whole family can go underground. There are children's amusements, craft workshops, a large restaurant and adequate free car parking.
Practical details: The complex is open seven days a week from March 1st to November 1st, between 10 am and 6 pm. There is an admission charge, with reductions for

Textured ware from Tremaen Pottery

children. A visit to Wendron Forge is likely
to take several hours — it is a good family
outing, with a lot to see.

3   Tin Mine

Tolgus Tin Company
Portreath Road, Redruth, Cornwall
Tel: Redruth 5171

This is both a place where tin is produced
commercially and a working museum. The
Tolgus Tin complex covers an area of 20 acres,
and looking at the car parks for 800 cars one
wonders whether the tourist industry is more
profitable than tin mining. The company
plans to preserve the whole area of the
Portreath valley and is restoring more of the
old plant each year. A guided tour takes about
half an hour, and the route starts at the
museum with an excellent slide presentation
which tells you a great deal about the history
of tin mining in the county.
The original workings are in a series of sheds
and the whole process is something like the
method of gold panning. As you walk round
you see how water power was used; tin ore is
shaken into a trough, combed with an arm of
heather brushes, carried away by water, and

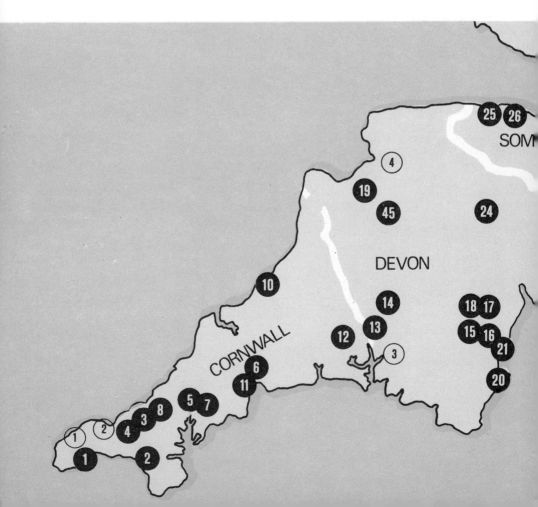

pulverized with heavy stamps. Parties can try their hand at some of the old devices in the prospecting and tin dressing area, where equipment can be hired for an hour, and you can keep any tin you get.

Practical details: The tin mine is open all year from 10 o'clock in the morning. It remains open on bank holidays with the exception of Christmas week. There is no need for individuals and families to give notice, but groups should book in advance. Coach parties are welcome and there are special admission rates for groups of twenty or more people. Articles made of tin are sold in the large craft centre and mineral shop which shares its

building with a restaurant. There is also a picnic site. As you can tell, the place is very well organized for tourists, and you will find it 2 miles from Portreath on the B3300.

4   Mining Museum

CompAir Construction & Mining Limited
Camborne, Cornwall TR14 8DS
Tel: Camborne 712750

The Holman Museum covers mining from the early days to the present and there is something to interest all ages, including

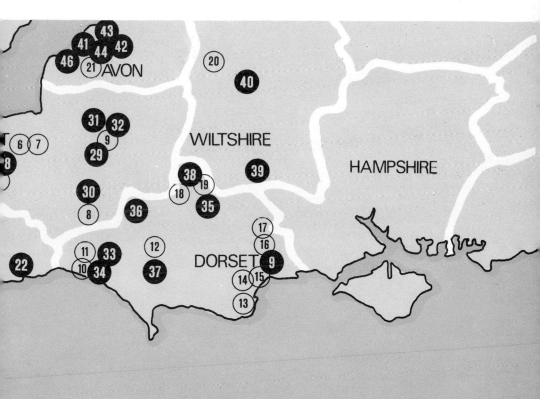

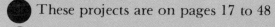

These projects are on pages 17 to 48

These projects are in the addendum, pages 209 to 211

working models of some machines. Mining in Cornwall dates back to Phoenician times, and by the 19th century it was highly organized. In 1862 there were 340 mines employing 50,000 people — men, women and children. The 'widow-maker', a Holman ore extracter, is one of the exhibits. Its nickname comes from the fact that it caused dust to fall on the operator who breathed it and developed silicosis, the disease from which hundreds of Cornishmen died. Exhibits include mining lifts and the Clanney safety lamp, which was less effective than the Davey's lamp, because it had glass which was liable to break, exposing the dangerous flame. You will also see a drill sharpener (which was used in small smithies, until tungsten carbide tipped bits were introduced in the 1940s), a mine director's carriage, and an old Cornish kitchen range.

Postcards and catalogues are on sale. Entry to the museum is free. There are more than 90 items in the museum, and more are being added.

Practical details: This is a private museum open to the general public during working hours, Monday to Friday from 10 am to 4 pm, except for works' holidays. It is best to contact the Public Relations Department in advance to arrange a visit. Individuals and groups can be catered for. The company prefers groups of less than 12 unless special arrangements are made.

5   Ancient Handcraft Pottery

W H Lake & Son Limited
Truro Pottery
Chapel Hill, Truro, Cornwall
Tel: Truro 2928

Before the days of the Staffordshire potteries small rural potteries provided for local needs, and these little potteries sprang up in areas where there was suitable clay and a supply of fuel. As kilns were wood-fired, areas near forests were often chosen and remains of Roman potteries have been found in such places. The Chapel Hill pottery is above the clay seam which runs through Truro. The city of Truro was built over the clay area and the clay now comes from Devon. But the nearness of the clay seam probably suggests that the pottery dates back several hundred years, especially as the pitcher design which is unique to this pottery dates back to Tudor times.

There are now only two ancient handcraft potteries left in Great Britain (which were in production before the days of mass production), and which still make the majority of their wares entirely by the old methods — and Lake's is one of them. Visitors are given a brief history of the pottery and are shown articles made in the early days, and the Ancient Cornish Cloam (meaning clay) Oven. These ovens used to be built into cottages for household baking, before the days of the iron stove, and thousands were made here. In recent times one was ordered for the British Museum.

The potters (about 7 of them) can be seen at work, hand throwing pottery on electrically driven wheels. Pots are seen at the various stages. Coffee-sets, mugs, jugs, slipware dishes, garden vases, candle holders, traditional pitchers, and outsize bread pans are some of the interesting items that are made here. The kilns are shown to visitors and a description is given of the amazing changes that take place during the firing at different temperatures. The tour ends in the large, pleasant showroom where the history of some of the pots and the uses of many more are described. Souvenirs (seconds) are sold at greatly reduced prices.

After belonging to the Lake family for four generations the pottery has now become part of the Dartington Trust.

Practical details: The showroom is open Monday to Friday from 9 am to 1 pm and 2 pm to 5 pm. Guided tours are held Monday to Friday between 10 am and 12 noon and 2 pm to 4 pm, with the exception of bank holidays when no tours are held.

Individuals and groups are catered for and advance booking is not necessary although it is preferable in the case of large parties or coaches.

6   Mining Museum

Wheal Martyn Museum
Carthew
St Austell, Cornwall
Tel: Stenalees 850362

Wheal is a Cornish word meaning a mine.
Wheal Martyn Museum is a restored open-air
100-year-old clay works. It has working
waterwheels, one of them 35′ in diameter,
working machinery, an introductory slide
show, other indoor displays and a blacksmith.
A small working craft pottery produces stoneware and porcelain made from West Country
clays.
The pottery products are sold in the museum
shop.
Practical details: The museum is open from
April to October, 10 am to 6 pm. The last
admission is at 5 pm. A small charge is
made, with reductions for groups of twelve
or more. It is open to groups all year,
by prior arrangement only. Most of the
site is suitable for the disabled.
Refreshments and souvenirs are on sale.

7   Demonstration Garden

Cornwall Education Committee
County Demonstration Garden
Probus, Near Truro, Cornwall

The garden was officially opened in 1972. It is
divided into 41 sections and if you follow the
numbers you start at the labour-saving garden
— then see herbs grown for use in medicines
and food, a children's garden, fruit, ferns,
vegetables, pruning, plants for shade,
windbreaks, a nature trail, pavings and front
garden designs. There is even an apiary for
would-be bee-keepers.
Demonstrations show how soil can be
improved, how shrubs and trees should be
cared for and how they can be used to create
shelter, and how lawns can be improved. The
garden is intended to interest both the public,
and architects and planners, whose work
involves landscaping.

Practical details: The Demonstration Garden
is open to the public from October to April on
Thursday from 2 pm to 5 pm; and from May to
September on Monday, Tuesday, Wednesday
and Friday from 2 pm to 5 pm, and until 8 pm
on Thursday and 6 pm on Sunday.
Groups with a minimum of 15 members can
apply for general or specialized demonstration
tours during afternoons and evenings (with
the exception of Thursday and the weekend).
Tours last 1½ hours. Application forms and
further details can be obtained from P Blake,
County Horticultural Organizer, County
Hall, Truro TR1 3BA, Tel: Truro 4282. The
cost is 20p per person.

8   Large Popular Pottery

Foster's Pottery Company
Tolgus Hill, Redruth, Cornwall
Tel: Redruth 215754

Some places merely tolerate tourists but here
they are really welcomed. The well-organized
tour shows you every aspect of making
pottery, and one of the enthusiastic guides
(there are 11 of them) may tell you that at the
height of the season they get 1,000 visitors a
day!
Fifty craftsmen and women are at work using
old traditional methods of pottery-making
such as handthrowing, or newer methods such
as slip casting in moulds, and jigging and
jolleying with machinery. Large electric kilns
are used to fire the pots, and all sorts of
practical pieces — cups, saucers, butter dishes
and so on, emerge from them. You can watch
the pottery being decorated, some of it in a
distinctive mottled green glaze. You may also
see row after row of identical teapots being
made to go into 'Teasmaid' machines — at the
rate of 3,000 a week. The showroom has a
range of colourful gifts including slight
seconds at reduced prices. 'Try not to leave
your visit for a wet day,' they say. Wet days are
usually the busiest.
Practical details: In Summer (April to
September) the pottery is open Monday to
Friday from 9 am to 3.45 pm. The showroom is

Visitors watching 'throwing' at Fosters

open Monday to Friday from 9 am to 5 pm, and also on Saturday from 10 am to 12 noon. In Winter (October to March) the pottery and showroom are open for tours Monday to Friday from 10 am to 12 noon and 1.30 pm to 3.45 pm. The pottery is closed on bank holidays and Sundays. Large parties can make arrangements for tours at any time of year. Coach parties (maximum size of group 50) should give at least 24 hours notice. There is a small charge for tours. The pottery is on the A30 Redruth by-pass and there is a free car park.

9   Modern Pottery Factory

Poole Pottery Ltd
The Quay, Poole, Dorset BH15 1RF
Tel: Poole 2866

A trained guide shows you behind the scenes at a quayside pottery overlooking Poole harbour.
They make mass produced and other pottery by a variety of methods. The tour through the three-floor craft section

Ashtrays being made at a large pottery

follows all the craft processes. You will
watch throwers at work on the wheels and a
'turner', with enviable precision, making the
thrown pot smooth and finished on a lathe.
You will also see birds and animal figures
being turned out of moulds.
The pottery will then be ready for its first
firing in gas kilns. Firing lasts about 34 hours
and takes place at a temperature of 1150°C.
This is more than four times the heat of your
oven at home, which reaches about 250°C.
Then you will look at just a few of the many
ways of decorating vases, bowls etc — all hand
painted using different techniques and skills.
The 'Traditional' range has changed little
since its beginning in the 1920s, with its flower
patterns composed of single brush strokes.
Modern brightly coloured 'Delphis' ware is
decorated with startling reds and oranges.
Their 'Aegean' line has similar standard
shapes painted in more sober colours. You
will also see a faience section where large
wall plaques are made for mounting in homes
of the famous.
A stained glass window technique is used for
limited edition plates. Each one has to be very
carefully made — one mistake and the plate
has to be smashed. There are no seconds in
limited editions.
All the decorated ware is now fired for the
second time, this time in electric 'Top Hat'
kilns. These, installed in the 1960s, have
top hat covers which are moved from base to
base by an overhead gantry. After each firing
the top hat is lifted and moved to the next
base which has been filled with ware for
firing.
The second firing process takes 24 hours at
1050°C. At the end of this firing the pottery
emerges as the finished product.
Finally, glimpse the past with a look at a small
selection from their previous productions in
the miniature museum. Pieces dating back to
the 1900's are on view. The pottery was
founded in 1873. After the Second World War,
when white utility ware was produced, they
went back to producing tableware in the
flowing curves of the 1930's era, in glazes with
an eggshell or satin matt surface. It is still
popular today on British breakfast tables — in

icegreen/seagull, mushroom/sepia, sky blue/
dove grey combinations.
At the end of the tour you can browse at
leisure in the spacious showroom shop (open
to the public without booking a tour) which
has open shelves, dinner sets laid out on
tables, and supermarket-style wire baskets
in which you can collect your bargains. All
the ware shown is seconds.
Practical details: Tours at intervals from
10 am until 12.30 and 1.50 pm to 4.15 (last
tour Friday at 3pm). Closed weekends. Small
charge. Booking essential. Showroom also
open on Saturdays.

10   Quarry and Slate Splitting

Old Delabole Quarry
Delabole, Near Camelford, Cornwall
Tel: Camelford 2242

Slate splitting demonstrations using the
traditional bettle and chisel are arranged from
11 am to 4 pm. A small museum and craft shop
are open to the public. The charge is 15p with
reductions for children and old age
pensioners.
The old quarry which has been worked
continuously for more than 400 years is $1\frac{5}{8}$
miles around and it can be seen from a viewing
terrace.
Practical details: The quarry is open during
Easter and the season from May to September,
seven days a week from 10 am to 6 pm. Both
individuals and parties of any size are welcome
and no advance notice is required.

11   China-clay Pit

English China Clays Limited
John Keay House, St. Austell
Cornwall PL25 4DJ
Tel: St. Austell 4482

Ask most people what china-clay is used for
and they will just say 'for pottery'. But china-
clay is used in making dozens of other
everyday articles — pills, stomach powders,

kaolin mixture, bathroom tiles, plastics, rubber soles for shoes and the coating of glossy pages in magazines and books. China-clay is a fine white powder which is chemically inert, so it is used as a filler or extender in many products.

Surprisingly it is papermaking which uses 80% of all clays. Clay is used in paper as a filler and as a coating for the surface. A good quality magazine paper may contain up to 30% of clay. As china-clay is much cheaper than pulp, it lowers the cost of finished paper as well as improving the quality. The white coating improves the feel of the paper and enables the printer to reproduce the print and pictures in sharp detail.

China-clay is also used in the ceramics industry in bone china, earthenware, tiles, sanitary ware and electrical porcelain. Clays differ greatly in quality, even clay taken from only one pit. In order to produce goods of consistent quality, as many as six or more clays are blended to a standard specification. It would be uneconomical and impractical to make most rubber articles out of purely natural or synthetic rubber. By adding china-clay, the cost is reduced and the article has greater resistance to wear; so china-clay is often used in products like Wellington boots and hot-water bottles.

China-clay is also used in the more expensive prime colour pigments in paints. It disperses easily in a mix and does not quickly settle on the bottom. It flows well and spreads evenly when it is applied.

China-clay is used in pharmaceuticals, too, where it acts as a carrier for the active ingredients. Insecticides in dust form are mixed with china-clay which acts as a bulk carrier. Fertiliser in granular form tends to cake together, so china-clay is used as an anti-caking powder on the granules. Fine quality leathers are dressed with a preparation containing china-clay, which fills the surface pores and helps to produce a smooth surface; and textile manufacturers use china-clay to help strengthen the fibres during weaving. The list of uses is almost endless!

English China Clays Group is the largest single producer of china-clay in the world. Over 75% of the clay is exported and the company won the Queen's Award to Industry in 1966, 1969, 1971 and 1975. It exports about $2\frac{1}{2}$ million tonnes a year.

In the United Kingdom china-clay is found only in Cornwall and on Dartmoor in Devon. The old Cornish method of extracting china-clay was to wash it out of the kaolinised granite, which was broken up with hand tools. The china-clay, suspended in water, was allowed to settle in tanks. The sediment at the bottom was sliced into lumps which were then dried in the air.

Modern methods still rely on water for extracting the china-clay. Very powerful remotely-controlled water hoses are directed at the pit face (the stope). They are strong enough to disintegrate the rock and wash out the china-clay in one operation.

China-clay and quartz sand are now suspended in water and this claystream flows to the bottom of the pit where it is pumped to a sand separation plant. The coarse sand is carried away by a conveyor to large tips. The china-clay and water mixture (called slurry) is pumped out of the pit and passed through a series of tanks which remove the water. The china-clay is then passed through fine mesh screens and enters a drying plant, where it is pressed into a putty-like consistency ready for drying.

Throughout the process samples of clay are tested in laboratories, and computers select the proportions of different clays to be blended for specific grades of clay. Dried clays are transported in bags or in bulk. Special bulk carriers are used to carry china-clay in slurry form by rail to customers in the United Kingdom, and the company has a transport fleet of more than 700 lorries.

The Blackpool pit is 300 ft. at its deepest point and covers more than 120 acres of the surface. At this pit, you see sand being extracted from the clay and dewatering and refining taking place. Because the company cannot get rid of the sand tips at the moment, it has set up a landscaping section to see what can be done to improve their appearance. Experiments are being made to find ways of growing plants on the tips. In a tree nursery 100,000 trees are being brought on for planting in the works areas.

China-clay from the Blackpool and Goverseth refining plants is received at the Blackpool Drying Plant and held in storage tanks. The solid content of the china-clay is increased from fifteen per cent to seventy per cent by screening and then filter pressing. It is then passed to the driers.

Blackpool is one of English China Clays'

Thirty-two-foot waterwheel—Morwellham

largest drying plants, producing about ten thousand tonnes of china-clay every week. But probably the most striking thing you will see is the complex of eighteen silos. They are one hundred and twenty feet high, twenty feet in diameter and can each store six hundred tonnes of china-clay.

Practical details: Conducted tours of the Blackpool open china-clay pit and the drying plant can be arranged from Monday to Friday at any time of year except on bank holidays provided that you book in advance. Write to the information officer at the address above, quoting two or three convenient dates for a tour. Young children under the age of seven cannot be accepted. Up to 25 people are allowed on any one tour.

Tours start at 10 am, 10.30 am and 2 pm and consist of a tour of the Blackpool pit and the

drying installations. Route maps to the pit are provided and there is a limited amount of free parking.

12   Reproduction Armour and Antiques

Calcraft Products
Wheal Arthur, Gunnislake
Cornwall PL18 9AB
Tel: Gunnislake 832648

Calcraft Products make reproduction antique pistols, muskets, armour and other articles for interior decoration.

You can watch the different stages in the manufacture of a suit of armour — cutting and shaping metal, rivetting, hammering, assembling and so on, and also preparation of woodwork, metalwork, and assembly of 'antique' firearms. All the products are hand-made and bench fitted, and are on sale.

Practical details: The factory is open all the year round but visitors should contact the proprietor, Mr. W. Michael Davies, a few days in advance. Small groups of up to 8 persons can be shown around.

13   Open Air Industrial Museum

Morwellham Quay Centre
Near Tavistock, West Devon
Tel: Gunnislake 832766

The Tamar river port lies at the foot of steeply wooded hills. Valuable copper ores were brought from the mines to its quays in the 1800s and the area has so much of interest that it was turned into a visitors' centre by the Dartington Hall Trust in 1970. An audio visual show called 'Introduction to Morwellham' is given in the slide theatre which includes local history and what there is to see.

Visitors can then follow short or long self-

A powerful water-jet blasts China Clay

guided trails round the quays and docks, and
see waterwheels, a water-powered thresher,
farm buildings containing old agricultural
implements, lime kilns, inclined railways, the
local history museum and trailside displays. A
souvenir and craft shop sells trail leaflets
including a guide for teachers, and, inevitably,
Dartington glass and textiles.
Practical details: Open all year round
including bank holidays from 10 am to 6 pm
in summer and 10 am to dusk in winter.
There is an admission charge, children half-
price. There are price reductions for coach
parties and groups arriving by river from
Plymouth. School parties and other groups
can contact the warden at the above telephone
number to make special catering and
educational arrangements.
If you'd like to come by river, the Millbrook
Steamboat Company runs regular sailings on
the afternoon tides from Plymouth. Tel:
Millbrook 202. By road: On the A390
travelling from Tavistock to Liskeard, turn
left 2 miles west of Tavistock. Travelling from
Cornwall turn right 2 miles east of
Gunnislake.

A turbo-generator at Mary Tavy

Quay and a combined visit to waterwheel and
power station can be arranged.
More details about power stations can be
obtained from The Public Relations Officer,
Central Electricity Generating Board, South
Western Region, 15–23 Oakfield Grove,
Clifton, Bristol BS8 2AS. Tel: Bristol 32251.

14   Hydro-electric Power Station

Mary Tavy Power Station
Tavistock, Devon PL19 9PR
Tel: Mary Tavy 248

Hydro-electric power stations are the ones
which most people find easiest to understand.
Just as water turns a waterwheel, waterpower
moves the turbine, or power generator, which
creates an electric current. Free literature is
provided.
Practical details: As the power station is in
more or less continuous operation visitors can
arrange to see it at any time. Groups of up to 50
people can be taken around, but only small
groups at evenings and weekends. Telephone
or write to the station manager.
Another hydro-electric power station in the
Mary Tavy group is at Morwellham.
Dartington Trust has a nature trail and
waterwheel at the adjoining Morwellham

15   Wool Mill and Tweed Shop

Dartington Hall Tweeds Limited
Dartington, Totnes, Devon
Tel: Totnes 86 2271

Dartington Hall itself is a thriving
community. The main buildings dating from
the 14th century are built around three sides of
a square, and house the Dartington art and
music college. More details about the
philosophy behind Dartington projects are
mentioned under Dartington Glass Limited of
Torrington, Devon, on page 30.
Practical details: The mill is open all year
Monday to Friday except on holidays. Visitors
arriving between the hours of 9 am and 4 pm
can walk around seeing how raw wool is
transformed into finished cloth. Educational
and other parties may book a guided tour by
arrangement with the mill office, for which a
fee is charged. Tel: Totnes 862271 Ext: 247.
The mill is situated on the Dartington to
Plymouth road and has ample car parking, off

the public highway.

16   Large Farm and Self-Sufficiency Exhibition

Riverford Farm
Staverton, Near Totnes, Devon TQ9 6AE
Tel: Staverton 636

Riverford is a typical British large mixed farm set in some of Devon's most beautiful countryside, with old local stone buildings, rolling fields and woodland. When you arrive you will be taken on a tour of the 500 acres on a specially converted farm trailer towed by a tractor. The guide explains how the farm produces milk and barley and shows you the work in progress — which could be feeding the pigs, sowing, ploughing, harvesting or haymaking, or milking the 100 black and white Friesian cows.

The cows are outdoors in summer. In the afternoon they are milked and you can watch through a glass panel in the milking parlour. Milking takes most of the afternoon. The 100 cows are milked six at a time, by machine. They produce about 11,000 gallons a year. The milk goes by tanker to a factory in Totnes where it is pasteurised. Part of it is turned into Devonshire cream. The rest is distributed as liquid milk.

The herds are calved in spring and autumn which ensures a regular supply of milk. Winter milk fetches a higher price because of scarcity but it is more expensive to produce. The cows are fed on grass, silage, hay and dairy cake (compressed barley with added protein for dairy cattle).

You can stroke the young calves, hold small piglets, and look at the sheep, cows, chicken or ducks. The sounds and smells of the farm, the things you can see and do, change from month to month.

In addition, a viol maker, a woodworker and a weaver are usually busy demonstrating local crafts. You will see bowls and boxes made in many shades of local and foreign wood polished with natural oil, and woollen bags and blankets being woven in intricate patterns. Some of the wool is dyed here in soft colours from natural dyes. You can buy these and other farm-made goods along with local products.

Practical details: Riverford Farm is open for conducted tours from April to mid-September. Tours start at 2.30 pm lasting 2 to 2½ hours, or at other times by arrangement.

Individuals and groups are recommended to book in advance at crowded times. Evening tours with a barn dance or barbecue can be arranged for parties. School visits should be arranged in advance and pupils can be given a special tour. Although the visits organiser tries to keep the tour to clean, dry areas, in wet weather visitors are recommended to bring waterproof boots. Entry to a small farmyard exhibition is included in the farm tour.

There is a riverside picnic area where you can eat your packed lunch.

Riverford Farm is on the regular Paignton-Totnes-Buckfastleigh bus route, ½ an hour from Torquay, 15 minutes from Totnes.

17   Leather Goods Manufacture

Devon Leathercrafts Limited
Kingsteignton Road
Newton Abbot, Devon TQ12 2QB
Tel: Newton Abbot 4262

Wallets, purses, shopping list pads in cases, and bookmarks are made here. The leathers used are mainly cow skins and goat skins. Both are tanned with vegetable matter, usually bark, to preserve the skin. Unlike cloth, which can be cut in several thicknesses at once, leather must be cut one thickness at a time to avoid flaws. The more pieces that an article can be made from, the more economical is the use of the skin. But an article made from several parts needs more work done to assemble it.

You will see leather being pared to thin it for hemming and folding. Then it is machined, attached to purse frames, welded with synthetic linings, and stamped in gold lettering.

Practical details: Guided tours are held from early April to late October, Monday to Friday, 9.30 am to 12 pm and 1.30 to 5 pm. The last tour starts at 4.30 pm. During the lunch hour the shop remains open but the factory itself is closed. There is an admission charge, but a joint ticket allowing you to visit the nearby New Devon Pottery as well, is good value. There are party rates for groups of 25 or more people. Children under 14 who are accompanied by adults are not charged, and school parties are accepted by special arrangement. Winter bookings, too, can be made by prior arrangement.

Visits to the showroom are free, and seconds and discontinued lines are on sale at reduced prices. There is a picnic area where drinks and ice cream can be bought. Parking is free.

18   Devon Pottery

New Devon Pottery Limited
Forde Road, Newton Abbot, Devon
Tel: Newton Abbot 4262

Seventy-five per cent of the clay used here comes from the West Country. The clay is a mixture of China clay, which is relatively pure, and ball clay which has impurities. The impurities make the clay more malleable, though it does not fire as white. Much of the pottery produced is glazed with a semi-matt or vellum, off-white glaze. One process you will see is jolleying on to a revolving wheel with a semi-automatic cup-making machine.
Another process is casting with slip (liquid clay) into a Plaster of Paris mould. The pottery is dipped in glaze, or sprayed, and loaded on to kiln trucks. The kilns are fired at night when electricity is cheaper.
Decorative transfers are applied and these sink into the glaze after firing. Finally the pottery is sorted and seconds are picked out for sale in the factory shop.
Practical details: Guided tours are held from Easter to October 9.30 am to 12 noon and 1.30 pm to 4.30 pm. The factory closes at 5 pm, and during the lunch hour. The shop is open during lunch time. There is an admission

charge to the pottery, but a joint ticket, admitting you to the nearby Devon Leathercrafts, is good value. Children are admitted free of charge if accompanied. For party rates (groups of 25 or more) and school visits, telephone Mrs. Phyl Johnson. Parking is free.

19   Hand-blown Glass Factory

Dartington Glass Limited
Great Torrington, North Devon
Tel: Torrington 2321

Most people have seen Dartington glass — the avocado dishes, the Irish Coffee glasses and modern drinking glasses — even if they do not know the name. Dartington makes unusual modern glassware such as candle-holder vases which are featured at the Design Centre, London. In fact Dartington Glass has won a Design Council award and in 1972 Frank Thrower, the designer, won the Duke of Edinburgh Design Prize for a collection of kitchen and table glass.
The story about how Dartington Glass came to be produced is as pleasing as the glassware itself. For the past 50 years projects undertaken at Dartington, 40 miles away in South Devon, have been concerned with the quality of life. Leonard and the late Dorothy Elmhirst settled at Dartington on a large estate. Together they and their trustees developed Dartington's woodlands and pioneered selective cattle-breeding. The people who worked on the estate were given the opportunity of learning new skills. Cultural activities were started for the benefit of the community and Dartington Hall School was founded to provide an education for children of people who worked on the estate.
In 1963 the trustees of Dartington Hall decided to repeat the experiment by setting up a small community in North Devon. Ever since the decline of the wool trade, the numbers of people living and working in North Devon had fallen by 6% every 10 years, and North Devon is designated as a development area. It was decided by the Trust that the

A glass-blower at Dartington Glass

manufacture of glassware by the traditional Scandinavian method would be an ideal craft for young people in the area to learn, so workers were brought over from Scandinavia. When the glass works was opened in 1967 there were 16 people from abroad and 30 learners. There are now 185 local employees and 20 from abroad.

The main raw materials used for making glass are sand, soda and lime. Red lead, potash and other chemicals are used to give the glass better quality. Arsenic, barium and antimony are used for purifying the glass. Colouring agents for other types of glass include copper oxide, iron oxide and potassium permanganate.

Factory furnaces contain ovens known as pot arches. Before melting in these pots, the chemicals are weighed and carefully mixed together to make up a batch. Clean broken glass, called cullet, is added. A new batch takes 10 hours to melt, at a temperature of about 1450°C.

The glass blowers work in teams around each pot. A full team consists of a master blower, the deputy master blower, the blower, three gatherers and assistants such as mould holders and carriers.

This is how a wine glass is made: a gatherer

takes the melted glass from the furnace on a blow pipe which he passes to the blower who blows down the pipe forming the first bubble in the glass. The molten glass is then rolled evenly on a smooth plate. The pipe is then passed to the next blower who points it downwards and blows the bowl for the wine glass in a water cooled mould which gives the glass its shape and pattern. The glass then passes on to the master blower who shapes the stem with extra glass brought from the furnace by another gatherer. The master blower makes the foot of the wine glass by adding another piece of melted glass which is shaped, as the glass is turned, to make a flat base. The piece of glass is now ready for the lehr, which is an extremely slow conveyor belt which takes the glass through a cooling tunnel. This process takes about 4 hours. When they emerge open mouthed articles go to the cracking off machines where the tops are removed by propane jets which burn at the correct height as the glass is revolved on turntables. The top edges are ground by belts. Then the glass is placed on another turntable and propane jets melt the top edge to finish it off. After a final inspection, first quality glassware is sent to British retailers (about 1,200 of them) or to any one of 55 countries.

Practical details: The factory is open Monday to Friday from 9.30 am to 10.30 am and from 12 noon to 3.30 pm (closing at 3 pm mid-July to mid-August). There is a small charge for adults and children over 12. Party rates by prior arrangement only. The glass shop is open from 9 am to 5 pm on weekdays and from 10 am to 4 pm on Saturdays.

20   Local Clay Pottery

Brixham Pottery Limited
The Old Pound House
Milton Street, Brixham, Devon
Tel: Brixham 2262

The Old Pound House buildings, believed to be 16th or 17th century, were once used as a cider factory. The pottery's showroom was originally the loading bay for horse-drawn carts carrying cider barrels. Ring bolts, to which the horses were tethered, can still be seen set into the wall.

The clay used in the pottery comes mainly from the nearby Newton Abbot clayfields and you can watch the potters making earthenware and stoneware. There is no guarantee that you will see 'hand throwing' on the wheel, but, at most times during the height of the summer season, someone is working on the wheel. About 20 people are busy throwing, casting, fettling (cleaning up rough edges), decorating, glaze dipping, and firing the pottery in the electric kilns. In the showroom handthrown pottery and stoneware, including many seconds, are on sale.

Practical details: The pottery is open Monday to Friday from 9 am to 12.30 pm and 1.30 pm to 5.30 pm. Only the showroom is open on Saturdays 9 am to 12.30, and on bank holidays. There is a free car park, but because of limited space, visitors in organised groups and coach parties should give advance notice of at least 3 days. Individual visitors are welcome to arrive without prior notice during working hours and walk around the pottery. There is no charge. The staff will gladly answer questions. Young children should be accompanied by an adult.

The pottery is on the Brixham to Kingswear road, about ¾ of a mile from Brixham town centre, opposite a garage.

Throwing a pot at Brixham Pottery

The weaving shed at Axminster Carpets

21   Babbacombe Pottery

Babbacombe Pottery
Babbacombe Road, Babbacombe, Devon
Tel: Torquay 38757

A flag-bedecked entrance welcomes you to
Babbacombe pottery with its ornamental
gardens, fish ponds and dovecot. You can
watch the potters at work, throwing clay,
casting, jolleying and decorating the pottery
by hand. Seconds, experimental items and
discontinued lines are sold at a discount.
Practical details: The pottery is open all year
(including bank holidays), Monday to Friday
from 9 am to 5.30 pm, and on Saturday
morning in the summer season. All visitors are
welcome and no advance notice is necessary.
Admission free.

22   Carpet Manufacturers

Axminster Carpets Limited
Gamberlake
Axminster, Devon EX13 5PQ
Tel: Axminster 32244

The first Axminster carpet was woven in 1755
by a local man, Mr. Thomas Witty. The
buildings which housed his factory can still be
seen in Silver Street. Those early carpets were
hand-knotted. But today's are completely
machine produced and the pile tufts are held
in place by the threads in the base of the carpet.
Axminster carpets are made from three raw
materials — wool, jute and cotton. The wool
comes from Scottish and Irish blackface sheep

and Devon and New Zealand sheep. After the wool has been blended it is scoured, carded, twisted, spun and dyed at Buckfastleigh by a subsidiary of Axminster carpets called Buckfast Spinning Company Limited. Jute is grown in India and Bangladesh and is spun into yarn in Dundee. Cotton is grown in America and spun into yarn in Lancashire. At this factory the first stage you see is coils of wool being wound on to bobbins. The bobbins are placed on 'creels' at the back of the loom and the ends of the wool are fed through to the front of the loom. Then the actual weaving begins. The pile of the carpet is inserted and held in place at the same time as the back of the carpet is woven. Carpets are inspected for small machine faults. This inspection is called picking. The next process is steaming to 'burst' the yarn to make it cover the base. Then the carpet is sheared to give it an even surface. It is then inspected for the last time. Finally each carpet is rolled and measured.

In the showroom there is a variety of carpets on display in patterns ranging from the traditional to modern, from rugs to broadloom carpets. Broadloom carpets, as the name suggests, are made on large machines and so provide a large area of luxury carpet with a minimum of seaming. The showroom manager answers questions and can give information to anyone who wants to know about retail suppliers.

Visitors must observe the factory's rules. No photography is allowed. Do not talk to the people operating the looms, and take care when walking past machinery which has moving parts, because although the machinery is guarded much of it is close together and the company is not responsible for accidents caused by carelessness. Finally, no smoking — a fairly common rule in factories, which applies here even though wool does not flare up like some other fibres. **Practical details:** Individuals are welcome without prior booking between 10 am and 12.30, and 2 pm and 4.30 Monday to Friday, and they can walk around the factory on their own. Groups should make an appointment with Mrs. M. Price, Works Management. The

guide accompanies groups of between 12 and 35 people, and a guided tour lasts about 1½ hours. School parties are welcome provided that the children are aged 10 or over. There is no charge.

23 Honiton Pottery

Honiton Pottery Limited
30-32 High Street, Honiton, Devon
Tel: Honiton 2106

There are no conducted tours. Just walk round at your leisure. Notices in every department explain the processes. A handout leaflet and children's question paper are available on request.

Pottery making has been carried out in Honiton since the 1700s. The original products were things like bread crocks and milk coolers — made on the potter's wheel but rarely decorated. Local clay was used until about 1947 and it all fired to a red-brown colour. Nowadays the cost of land in the High Street is so high that it is not economic to take the coarse clay from the seam behind the factory, so blends of clays from Devon and Cornwall are used. Traditional vases and jugs are hand-painted on a cream glaze.

You will see the Making Department where clays are mixed into the creamy liquid slip. This is poured into plaster of Paris moulds for vases or jugs. The shapes of the pieces are designed here, and the moulds are made as well. It must be sound economics to use a mould for a range of pottery in the same shape but each piece looking very different because of the pattern.

In the sponging department pots and vases are 'fettled' to remove the seam line and sponged smooth. The clay pieces are fired in electric kilns and removed in the biscuit state (so called because they have the brittle texture of biscuits). The porous pottery is sealed with a glaze, which is sprayed onto it in powder form. After hand painting with metal oxide colours, the pottery is returned to the kilns where the glaze is fused.

The resident designer can be seen at work in

his studio, creating designs on the drawing board or hand-throwing, turning, modelling, hand-painting, decorating or glazing. In the showroom you can see the products and buy export rejects at reduced prices.

Practical details: The *showroom* is open Monday to Saturday from 9 am to 5.30 pm. The *pottery* is open Monday to Thursday from 9 am to 12 noon and 2 pm to 4.30 pm, and on Friday from 9 am to 12 noon and 2 pm to 4 pm. The pottery is closed on bank holidays. Please contact the pottery if you have a party of more than 20 people.

24   Sheep Farm and Countryside Museum

Ashley Countryside Collection
Ashley House, Wembworthy
Near Chulmleigh, Devon EX18 7RH
Tel: Ashreigney 226

If you have always thought that one sheep looked pretty much like another you will probably change your mind after visiting this farm and seeing the 40 breeds of sheep. You drive up past a large open-fronted shed, full of equipment from the 'horse and open fireplace' era. Having parked your car in the farmyard and paid your admission you are free to wander around looking at the 600 items from days gone by. Catalogues are available. You can usually see baby calves in the shippons, 40 different fleeces of wool, and a spinning wheel and small loom used for making woollen goods.

When you have finished looking at these you will be able to see the 40 breeds of sheep in the adjoining field. From the field you can see across the valley to Eggesford Fox Hounds Kennels and the Wembworthy Centre where Devon schoolchildren stay for field studies. The visit is suitable whatever the weather because most of the exhibition is under cover and there is a wet weather picnic shelter.

Practical details: The farm and museum are open to the public from 10 am to 6 pm on Wednesday, Saturday and Sunday, including bank holiday weekends from Easter to October, and every day in August

except Thursdays. Schools, coach parties and other groups are welcome by arrangement with Mr. T. R. Blackford. Overseas visitors are particularly welcomed.

Ashley Countryside Collection is halfway between the A337 and the B3220 in North Devon. Those coming off the A387 at Eggesford Station will cross over the river Taw. Then turning right, drive past the first plantings of the Forestry Commission on your left, and the entrance to the mile-long drive of ruined Eggesford House on your right. RAC signs direct you around Wembworthy downhill then up to Ashley.

25   Small Remote Pottery

Waistel and Joan Cooper
Culbone Lodge Pottery
Porlock, Minehead, Somerset TA24 8PQ
Tel: Porlock 862539

Culbone Pottery is usually approached on foot along the public footpaths from Silcombe Farm (½ mile), or from Porlock Weir, past the

Ashley Combe Toll Gate (where there is a car park). This second route is 2 miles long, but very beautiful. The visitor walks up a slowly winding cliff-path from the toll gate, perhaps stopping occasionally to sit and admire the breath-taking views, until — 450 feet above sea-level — he or she arrives at the opening into Culbone combe. This is a tiny world of its own, filled with peace and tranquillity.

A few yards up the public path, beyond the 12th century Culbone Church, is the Culbone Lodge Pottery, where Waistel and Joan Cooper make stoneware pottery and sculpture. Culbone Lodge, formerly a keeper's lodge, is a striking building, built of local stone and 4 floors high. Part of it is thought to be 300 years old. The terraces and gardens on the wooded hillside are filled with unusual pottery shapes.

All the pottery is hand-thrown stoneware. Some pieces are repeatable but the Coopers are continuously trying to explore new forms. The pottery is rough-textured and decorated with a variety of oxides, ranging from startling near-white through reddish-brown tones to charcoal-black. Many pieces are glazed with natural wood ashes to produce green-blue to rich gold tones. Bowls, jugs, mugs, vases, table lamps and larger pieces are displayed, and pieces have been acquired by several museums including the Victoria and Albert.

Practical details: The pottery is open every day, including weekends and bank holidays, March to November, from 10 am to 7 pm, and in winter at the weekend or by appointment. Individuals are always welcome, but parties of schoolchildren or groups of 10 or more should write or telephone in advance.

26   Sheepskin Products

John Wood & Son (Exmoor) Limited
'Linton', Old Cleeve
Minehead, Somerset TA24 6HT
Tel: Washford 291

Visitors are given a potted history of the firm which started its activities about 100 years ago

De-fleshing a sheepskin at John Wood's

with the great-grandfather of the present owner. Then the guide explains how the skins are bought in the raw state and processed — the skins are scoured, the flesh is removed, the leather is tanned, the pelt is sueded, natural greases are removed, the wool and leather are dyed in some cases, and the wool is finished ready for the skins to be made into various products.

In the cutting department visitors see the skins being cut up for two different styles of moccasins and items such as gloves, mitts, seat covers, soft toys, footmuffs and hats.

Practical details: Visitors are welcome to the factory from April to October. There is a 40-minute guided tour Monday to Friday at 11 am, and in addition on Thursday afternoon at 3 pm. There is no charge.

Schools and groups can make appointments to have a guided tour of the factory at any time of year during the day, although these visits are limited as they tend to interfere with production. A limited number of parties can be taken around in the evenings at any time of year — groups can make appointments. The factory seconds shop is open all year round Monday to Friday from 9 am to 4.30 pm, and on Saturday from March to December only, from 10 am to 4 pm.

27   Somerset Cider Farm

R. J. Sheppy & Son
Three Bridges, Bradford-on-Tone, Taunton,
Somerset TA4 1ER
Tel: Bradford-on-Tone 233

Somerset has been 'The Cider County' for generations and until the 1930s most farms of any size produced their own cider. Since the Second World War large centralised factories have been set up and nowadays most farms send their apples to these factories. But Sheppy's, who have been making cider since 1925, still produce their own cider from more than 20 acres of orchards. Visitors can see the orchards, cider-making plant and museum. There is a shop on the farm which sells cider, honey, other produce and cider mugs.
Just to tempt you, here are some lines from a poem on their leaflet: 'The juice is extracted like wine. The product—Pure Somerset Cider, de-lightful, de-licious, di-vine!'
Practical details: The farm and cider museum are open to visitors Easter to Christmas, from 8.30 am until dusk Monday to Saturday, and on Sunday from 12 noon until 2 pm. Visitors may wander around as they wish. Coach parties can make prior arrangements for a conducted tour, if the proposed time is convenient to the farm's staff. The farm is on the A38, between Taunton and Wellington.

28   Telecommunications Museum

Post Office Telecommunications Museum
38 North Street, Taunton
Somerset TA1 1LY   Tel: Taunton 3391

The Post Office Telecommunications Museum at Taunton is the largest museum specialising in telecommunications in the country and the only one which is regularly open to the public. The exhibits consist of telephone, telegraph and transmission equipment showing the history and development of one of Britain's most important industries.
Visitors are usually particularly interested in the old manual telephone exchange of 1900 which is reconstructed in the setting of a contemporary private house. The more technically-minded can study the intricacies of automatic exchange equipment and displays including a complete working automatic exchange of 1929. The telegraph section has some of the oldest equipment in the museum.
There is also test equipment used by telephone engineers. You can dial a call through a working exchange, using an old telephone, and there are several other working exhibits.
Practical details: The museum is open on Saturday from 1.30 pm to 5 pm and at other times by arrangement. Advance notice is needed for mid-week visits. Write to the curator, Mr. P. J. Povey.

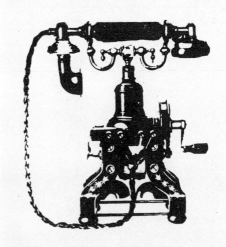

29   Shoe Manufacturers

C & J Clark Ltd
Street, Somerset
Tel: Street 3131 extension 2321

The museum has documents and photographs showing the early history of C. & J. Clark from the founding of the firm in 1825. Shoes and machinery are displayed in the oldest part of the factory built by Cyrus Clark in 1829. Sole-cutting presses and sewing machines can be seen and there is a collection of slippers, boots and shoes from Roman to modern times, including some high ones which must have sorely tried a lady's sense of balance. Silly shoes are not merely the products of the age we live in. (Clark's, however, have been making children's shoes in a choice of half-sizes and multi-fittings for 100 years. One of their original advertising posters of 1883 advocates correct fitting footwear for children.)

The story of Clark's beginning is of interest. Young James Clark was apprenticed to his older brother in the 1820s. He was bound not to gamble or marry for 5 years. At that time the factory made sheepskin products like rugs and mops and to while away his evenings, and make some extra pocket money, James started using short wool skins to make warm slippers. The sideline was soon so successful that it overtook the main business and the younger Clark became a partner.

In those days the work was largely done by outworkers, who were fined 1d. if they brought in work with soiled linings or tied odd shoes together! Today there are 2,500 employees at these headquarters alone, and Clark's has grown into a world business.

Practical details: Clark's Shoe Museum is open to the casual visitor in the summer months, Monday to Friday from 10 am to 1 pm and 2 pm to 4.45 pm and on Saturday

One of Clark's early posters—1883

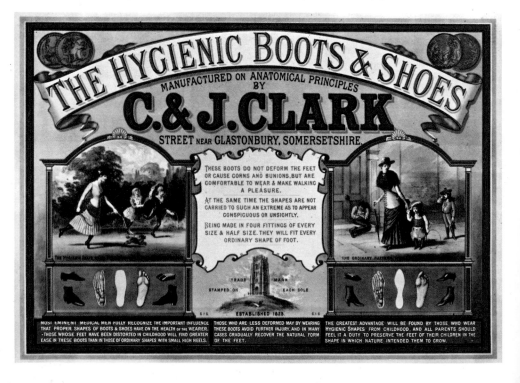

mornings. No pre-booking is necessary. It is closed on bank holidays.

The shoe factories accept pre-booked organised trips. Write well in advance because the demand is so great that these tours are usually fully booked a year ahead. The factory is closed at weekends and at holiday times. Schools, colleges, clubs and so on are welcome. The maximum number allowed in a group is 40 and the lower age limit is 11 years.

30   Naval Air Station

Fleet Air Arm Museum
Royal Naval Air Station
Yeovilton, Yeovil, Somerset
Tel: Ilchester 551 Ext: 521

The models and photographs in the museum explain how Naval Aviation has developed since 1903 via the Royal Naval Air Service to the Fleet Air Arm of today. The museum has a collection of more than 40 historic aircraft; many are unique and some are still flying. A museum exhibition 'The Modern Navy' shows life at work, afloat and in the air. There are photographs, a life-size model of the controls of a helicopter and a special section on careers (for girls too).

Outdoors you can picnic in the grassed public viewing area while watching the Navy fly. Concorde 002, the first British built prototype can be seen next to the museum and for a small extra charge you can go inside.

Parking is free and coaches and caravans are welcome. Refreshments are available, and there is a shop with books, charts and models on sale. There is a small admission charge

which is reduced for children and schools. **Practical details:** The museum and Concorde are open daily (except Christmas Eve and Day) from 10 am to 5.30 pm weekdays, on Sundays from 12.30 to 5.30 pm (or dusk, if earlier). The museum is 2 miles east of Ilchester on the B3151, reached by bus 478 from Yeovil.

31   Hand-made Paper

The Caves and Mill
Wookey Hole, Wells, Somerset BA5 1BB
Tel: Wells 72243

Many people have heard of the famous caves at Wookey Hole, but do not know about the interesting things you can see in the nearby mill. The entire site is now owned by Madame Tussaud's and the tour takes you first to the caves, then to the mill.

The caves are impressive, rather than pretty, and legends surround the witch who once lived here.

The mill, where hand-made paper used to be made in large quantities, is still producing high quality hand made paper on one vat for sale to the paper trade and to visitors. Two or three men can be seen at work and other trained mill staff will answer questions on papermaking and the other exhibits.

Wookey Hole — making paper by hand

Elsewhere in the drying lofts is the collection of fairground relics, recently bought by Madame Tussaud's from Lady Bangor. There are coloured cats and ostriches, wild gold men and other fantasy figures. On your way you walk through the Madame Tussaud storeroom, where the heads of famous people are kept in case they suddenly come into fashion again. You may spot the head of a pop singer, or a British MP awaiting re-election.

Practical details: Wookey Hole is open every day of the year except Christmas Day, from 10 am. The last visitors are admitted at 4.30 pm in winter and 6 pm in summer. There is an admission charge, with reductions for children and pensioners — a cost which covers the combined tour to caverns and mill. Parties of 20 or more people can obtain reduced prices by writing in advance to the party booking officer. Parking is free. There is a shop, a picnic area and a cafeteria which is open all year round.

32   Steam Railway Centre

East Somerset Railway
Cranmore Railway Station
Shepton Mallet, Somerset
Tel: Cranmore 417

Steam engines fascinate everyone and at Cranmore they have locomotives of all sizes from the smallest (class one) up to the largest — like huge, powerful Black Prince, a British Rail class 9F (freight). Owned by the famous artist David Shepherd, who is one of the directors and a founder of the railway, Black Prince has appeared in the film 'Young Winston' and the film 'The Man Who Loves Giants' about David Shepherd's life.
Green Knight, a class 4MT (mixed traffic) engine was one of the first modern engines designed to be powerful enough for main line traffic, yet light enough not to damage old bridges on branch lines. Also see wildlife and railway prints by David Shepherd in the Signal Box Art Gallery.
Practical details: The railway centre is open daily from 9 am to 3.30 pm November to March

and from 9 am to 5.30 pm April to October. Steam trains run for brake van rides on Sundays and bank holidays from April to October. The admission price is small and there are reductions for children.
Light refreshments are available and you will find free car parking space. Cranmore is on the A361. For further details telephone the above number.

33   Custom-made Furniture

The John Makepeace Furniture Workshops
Parnham House, Beaminster, Dorset
Tel: Beaminster 862204

Both individuals and groups are welcome to the cabinet-making workshops of John Makepeace and his assistants. Fine furniture is

designed and made here, using solid woods like oak, cherry, walnut, rosewood, satinwood and ebony. Suede, ivory, perspex and other materials can be incorporated. Usually only one of each design is ever produced, and furniture is made on commission for private customers or corporations in the UK and abroad.

Parnham itself is a fine Tudor manor house, built around 1400 with later extensions by John Nash. It is romantically set in a secluded valley with the river Brit running through the grounds. Oaks and cedars, woodpeckers and wild deer form the setting.

Practical details: The principal rooms of Parnham House, the gardens, gallery and workshop are open Easter to October, on Wednesdays, Sundays and bank holidays from

John Makepeace: working with satinwood

Dorset Knobs being made at S. Moores

10 am to 5 pm.

Tea is served in the 17th century dining room from 3 to 5 pm. Car parking is free. Western National buses 400 and 401 from Bridport to Beaminster stop at the entrance.

34 Biscuit Bakery

S. Moores
Goldencap Biscuit Bakery
Morcombelake, Bridport, Dorset DT6 6ES
Tel: Chideock 253

This is a mouthwatering visit, and something a little bit different. Moores make speciality Dorset biscuits — Dorset Butter Biscuits, Dorset Shortbread, Dorset Gingers, Easter Cakes (January 1st to April 30th) and Dorset Knobs (in the winter).

Moores' Dorset Knob Biscuits — rusks shaped

like a small bun — originated about 150 years ago at the old Moores homestead of Stoke Mills in the Marshwood Vale, West Dorset. Homegrown wheat was ground by the watermill and the knobs made from this flour were cooked in a faggot heated oven. Dorset Knobs, with early tea, made a traditional meal for local farm workers at the start of the day. The business is still carried on by the Moores' family and Dorset Knobs are made about three days a week at the rate of about 25,000 a day, in much the same way as they always were. Each biscuit is individually moulded by hand and has three separate bakings lasting a total of four hours. The whole process takes at least 8 hours, starting with the making of the dough at 6 am.

There is no charge for visits but only the most strong-willed will be able to resist the temptation to buy some of the company's products which are sold in the retail food shop on the premises.

Practical details: The bakery is open on Monday to Friday from 9 am to 5.30 pm except on public holidays. The person to contact is Mr. Keith Moores who writes, 'The bakery is open to the public who are welcome to see whatever production is in progress. We like at least three days' notice for parties. A tour takes only 10 to 15 minutes and because of limited space we have to restrict groups to not more than 20 people at a time. We try to give a guided tour but cannot guarantee one. Depending on the time of day visitors will see the production and perhaps baking and packing of one or two of six lines of biscuits.' Moores' Biscuit Bakery and Dorset Shop are on the south side of the A35 road in Morcombelake, 4 miles west of Bridport.

35   Hand-made Furniture

Pilgrims Craftsmen (Shillingstone) Limited
Shillingstone, Blandford Forum
Dorset DT11 0SA
Tel: Child Okeford 673

In these country craft workshops you can see skilled men making solid wood furniture in the old tradition. The furniture is hand-made with the minimum of modern machinery from English Oak, Kauri Pine and Mahogany. Half the pieces are one-off items built to customers' own designs, although there are a number of standard designs exhibited in the showroom.

'Our range is limitless, stretching as far as the imagination will go,' they say in their brochure. The customer might want 'a single coffee table or a whole roomful of furniture with matching wall cladding, doors and fittings. No job is too big or too small. Each piece is signed by the man who makes it. It is our aim that anything made by our craftsmen will be a delight for generations to come and should eventually become an antique.' Pilgrims stain oak to match their customers' existing furniture in colours ranging from

A one-off hand-made piece from Pilgrim's

very pale yellow, through pinky brown, to
deep brown. They upholster customers' own
materials in vinyls, dralon, Sanderson fabrics,
or arrange for leather upholstery or cane
seating. They also do complete kitchen
fitments, corner units, four poster beds and
carriages to be drawn by ponies and horses —
with all the springing, undercarriage and
metal trimming prepared in the Pilgrims
metal workshops.

Practical details: Visitors are welcome to the
workshops and attached showroom seven days
a week between 10 am and 4 although nobody
is working in the workshops on Saturdays and
Sundays. Parties of up to 20 people are also
welcome, by appointment, and a guide will
explain what is going on. Contact Julia Ellam
or Robert Laing.

The Pilgrims workshop is in the old station
yard at Shillingstone on the A357.

36 Butterfly Farm

Worldwide Butterflies Limited
Compton House, Sherborne, Dorset
Tel: Yeovil 4608

Living butterflies can be seen flying and
breeding in the indoor jungle. There are
brilliantly colourful displays of butterflies
and collections from every continent and a
breeding hall for both butterflies and moths.
In Summer there is more to see, as an outdoor
section is open. In fine weather butterflies can
be seen flying in the Butterfly House and
sleeves of caterpillars are on the trees. Apart
from butterflies, you can see green, pink and
brown stick insects, scorpions and locusts, and
the Giant Atlas Moth with a wingspan of
nearly 1 foot.

The farm was started in 1960 by Robert
Goodden when he was 20 years old. With the
encouragement of all the family, he expanded
it from an attic collection, bought a printing
press to produce catalogues, and toured the
Far East. Now the farm supplies live and
mounted butterflies to museums, schools,
photographers, film-makers and gardeners
throughout the world.

As many butterflies live for only 7 to 14 days
there are different things to see each time you
visit the farm. You can walk through the new
Palm house which looks like an equatorial rain
forest, and Compton House has lawns.

Practical details: The butterfly farm is open
from 10 am to 5 pm, including weekends and
bank holidays, from Easter to the end of
October. Individuals and groups can visit the
farm during these hours without an
appointment. There is an admission charge to
the farm, with half price for children.
Entry to the showroom is free. There is a
discount for booked groups of 30 or more
making one payment for everybody. Groups
need not book, 'though it helps if you do'.
Visitors can picnic in the grounds and buy
refreshments. Meals are obtainable from the
Little Chef Restaurant just outside.
Groups telephone Yeovil 23890 to book seats.
Worldwide Butterflies is on the A30 and there
is free parking space for cars and coaches.

37 Old Ale Brewery

Eldridge Pope & Company Limited
Dorchester Brewery
Dorchester, Dorset DT1 1BR
Tel: Dorchester 4801

Huntsman Ales are brewed here by a family
firm which has been independent since 1833.
The brewery and wine merchants have unique
Victorian premises, built in 1897, and they
still brew beers similar to those made at that
time — as the old 'Brewing Book', which you
can inspect, will prove. The tours include the

brewing process, bottling, and Maltings
Conference Centre museum.
Practical details: The brewery welcomes
individuals and groups of up to 30 people,
aged over 18, to take a general tour on a
Tuesday, Wednesday or Thursday, between
2.30 pm and 5. Telephone or write to the
Marketing Director.

38   Wrought Iron Work

Wing & Staples
The Forge, Motcombe
Shaftesbury, Dorset SP7 9PE
Tel: Shaftesbury 3104

Mr. Staples writes, 'Visitors can see
blacksmiths at work, and occasionally horse-
shoeing at the forge. Through many centuries
the blacksmith has played an important role
in his country's heritage. He has forged, bent,
twisted, rolled, shaped, cut and welded metals
into rugged shapes or beautiful works of art.
'You are welcome to visit our showroom and
see for yourself where hand-made pieces are
produced for you. The showroom has a few
items available for sale but the majority of
work is made to customers' specifications.'
The forge produces flower pot holders, door
knockers, lanterns, wall-light fittings, fire
screens, gates, boot scrapers, adjustable flower
pot stands, paper knives, balustrades, weather
vanes and pokers. Something for everyone.
Practical details: Individual visitors and small
parties are welcome to watch work in progress
and browse in the showroom on Monday to
Friday from 10 am to 4 pm, except lunchtime.
Please give at least one week's notice.

39   Carpet Manufacturers

Wilton Royal Carpet Factory Limited
Wilton, Wilts. SP2 0AY
Tel: Wilton 2441

This is the oldest carpet factory in the world. A
history of the factory is given and the different
types of carpet are explained. Four hundred

people are employed here and the old
buildings are still in use together with new
purpose-built ones. Carpet seconds are
available at the shop on the premises.
Practical details: A complete tour of the
factory is given at 10 am and 11 am each
weekday, with the exception of bank holidays.
Up to 10 people can be taken round at a time.
Visitors are advised to book in advance,
especially during the summer months. The
tour lasts 45 minutes and the charge is 30p per
person with reductions for schools.

40   Stone Carving

Bedwyn Stone Museum
Great Bedwyn, Marlborough, Wiltshire
Tel: Great Bedwyn 234

Mr. Lloyd is a local stonemason who carves
monuments and fireplaces and does repairs to
churches and other buildings. The museum,
which he inherited from his father, is his
hobby. He writes that a visit here is
'Humorous — very. Educational — in a way
that you had never thought of before.
Religious — in a strange and rather vulgar
sort of way.'
But it is his theories about the symbolism of
carvings which attract coach parties to the
museum. At a time which most of us would
regard as the Dark Ages, the local villagers
believed that learning reading, writing and
grammar was dangerous. The mason, often
himself illiterate, would carve messages in
stone on church buildings and gravestones.
Mr. Lloyd, who claims he can crack any code,
interprets the moral tales from symbols on the
carved and painted headstones which he has
restored. Baskets of flowers, surrounded by
certain numbers, indicate that the soul had
gone to a happy place. A bad man had
cherubims on his memorial which showed,
says Mr. Lloyd, that sexual experience was his
highest ideal.
The local church of St. Mary's is famous for its
carvings, and associations with Jane Seymour,
wife of Henry VIII. The church authorities,
while not agreeing with Mr. Lloyd's
interpretation, have no objection to members

Gravestone of a good woman from Bedwyn

of the public visiting the church, either guided by Mr. Lloyd or on their own.
Practical details: The museum is out of doors and so it is always open. Visitors are accepted at any time. A guide will be supplied by appointment.

41   A Variety of Crafts

Clevedon Craft Centre
Newhouse Farm, Moor Lane (off Court Lane), Clevedon, Avon BS21 6TD
Tel: Clevedon 872867

Clevedon Craft Centre is housed in what was formerly a farm on the Clevedon Court Estate. The outbuildings, some of them up to 300 years old, have been turned into studios where you can see craftsmen and women at work. There is quite a variety. Gold and silver jewellery and silverware are made by silversmiths, Stear and Bright; tile and marble-topped tables and trolleys are made by D. and J. Bettens, and custom-built kitchens and furniture in pine and oak are produced by Castle Woodcrafts. There are photographs by James Davis, landscape paintings by Margaret Kelsey, and pressed flower pictures by Jenny Shuttleworth. You might also see somebody sewing soft toys and doing macramé work. Carving and woodturning demonstrations are held on Sunday afternoons.
One of the old barns has been made into a countryside museum where you can look at old farm implements, craftsmen's tools, early household equipment and a unique collection of remedial horseshoes. An open-ended wagon house, with the original stone walls, has been converted into a licensed restaurant which serves morning coffee, lunch and tea. Telephone 872867 to book a table for a traditional Sunday lunch. Attached to the restaurant is a craft shop selling local work including wrought iron, pottery and turnery. The farm buildings are picturesque, many of them having preservation orders, and colourful birds will keep the children amused. Admission is free throughout the centre and there is plenty of parking space.
Practical details: The craft centre is open every day of the week. The museum and restaurant are closed on Mondays (but stay open on bank holiday Mondays). Individuals are welcome without notice. Groups should contact Mrs. Pam Huxtable 2 days in advance.

42   Printers and Publishers

The Abson Press
Abson, Wick, Bristol, Avon BS15 5TT
Tel: Abson 2446

Visitors can see a Heidelberg press working and, according to what is going on, a variety of jobs such as typesetting, which lead up to the final printing. An explanation will willingly be given of the mechanics of publishing with visual examples of making a book at all stages from the author's manuscript, designs for covers and proofs, through to the finished book. This small publishing house produces recipe books and dialect books, like American/English and Scottish/English glossaries.
Tourists and overseas visitors are particularly intrigued by humorous local interest language glossaries like 'Krek Waiter's Peak Bristle' (Correct Way to Speak Bristol).
All Abson books are on sale at the normal retail price.
Practical details: Heidelberg letterpress printers operate 7 days a week from 9 am to 5 pm and visits — for groups or individuals — are by appointment.

43 Nuclear Power Station

Oldbury-on-Severn nuclear power station

Oldbury-on-Severn Power Station
Thornbury, Bristol BS12 1RQ
Tel: Thornbury 416631

Oldbury-on-Severn Power Station is on the east bank of the River Severn, about 15 miles north of Bristol. The site covers 175 acres of land on the bank of the Severn, and a 380-acre reservoir has been excavated in the river bed to ensure that cooling water is available at all states of the tide. It can provide 416 million gallons of cooling water during low-tide.
The station buildings consist of three major blocks housing the two nuclear reactors, the turbine house and the main 132,000 volt switchgear. The appearance of the buildings was carefully designed to blend with the surrounding open countryside, and semi-mature trees have been planted.
This is the Central Electricity Generating

Board's first station where each of the nuclear reactors is housed in a cylindrical pressure vessel of pre-stressed, high-strength concrete. The walls are 60 feet high and 16 feet thick. The base and lid of the cylindrical reactor are 22 feet thick.
Two computers are used in the control system. One computer monitors the many thousands of alarms and prints a record of every abnormal occurrence. It also displays on cathode-ray screens an analysis of a fault and the action needed to remedy it. A second computer scans signals from the burst cartridge detection equipment, and if signals are above a certain level an alarm warns the operator.
In the event of a reactor fault the safety system trips all 101 control rods into the core bringing about very rapid reduction in reactor power and temperatures.

Decanting—Harvey's 12th century cellars

Practical details: Write to the station manager or telephone the administrative officer. Individuals or groups of up to 40 people (aged over 14) can be accommodated Monday to Friday or, in exceptional cases, at weekends. Guides accompany visitors and there is no charge. Catering is provided in special cases only. Parking is available.

44   Wine Museum

Harveys (of Bristol) Wine Museum
12 Denmark Street, Bristol 1, Avon
Tel: Bristol 298011/27661

The Harveys wine museum is the only one of its kind in Britain. Here you can see how wines are made, and articles used in producing, serving and drinking wine. Harveys are makers of the world-famous Bristol Cream sherry, and Bristol Milk sherry.

The main gallery has a display of sherry butts. Illustrated panels tell the story of the main types of wine from the regions of Bordeaux, Burgundy, Champagne, Rhine, Moselle, Oporto and Jerez the home of Sherry, complete with maps and climate charts.

The bottle gallery shows how Bristol became Britain's most important glass-making centre, exporting all over the world; and explains the development of the bottle, including the mechanisation of bottle-making from 1900. The glass gallery has wine glasses with a variety of stems — baluster stems, engraved air twist stems and coloured glass.

The company's sherry can be bought, and gourmets can lunch or dine in the Harvey's restaurant, selecting complementary wines from the cellars seen on the tour.

A free booklet on the company is available.

There is a multi-storey car park 2 minutes away.

Practical details: Visits by appointment only. Write to the PR Office, 12 Denmark Street. Organised parties of 35 to 45 persons are welcomed at either 2.30pm or 6.30 pm, Monday to Friday (not at weekends nor on public holidays). There is a charge for the tour, and a guide takes the group around. Under 18's not admitted.

The museum is very popular. It is fully booked for group tours a year ahead. Individuals and small family parties can sometimes arrange to join one of the smaller groups, but even then notice is necessary.

45   One-man Pottery

Seckington Pottery
Winkleigh, Devon EX19 8EV
Tel: Winkleigh 478

At his North Devon pottery Michael Hatfield makes Devon cider mugs, animal and bird studies and figures, mice on cheese wedges, pendants, vases, miniatures etc, in red or white Devon Clay. Sheila Hatfield makes jewellery.

Practical details: Individuals and small groups welcome daily at this home pottery. Usually open on bank holidays, but phone on weekends or if more than 10 people

46   Costume Doll Factory

Peggy Nisbet Limited
Oldmixon Crescent
Oldmixon Industrial Estate
Weston-super-Mare, Avon BS24 9BD
Tel: Weston-super-Mare 21141

Peggy Nisbet started making dolls in Coronation Year when, with the permission of The Lord Chamberlain, she produced a limited edition of the Queen in her Coronation robes. Historical characters followed in quick succession, the Tudor period being one of the most popular, with King Henry VIII, his six wives and his

daughter Queen Elizabeth I stealing the limelight.

A tremendous amount of research into historical characters and costumes is involved and many of the patterns Peggy Nisbet uses are taken from reproductions of original drawings of clothes of the period, scaled down to fit the Nisbet 'little people'.

One hundred per cent wool tartans are woven for her in miniature in Scotland. The dolls' features are modelled mainly from paintings — often in the National Portrait Gallery.

Visitors are shown the various stages involved in producing the dolls — the art room, the cutting department, the machinists, the finishing section, the checkers, and the boxing and despatch departments. The factory tour takes about 45 minutes. There is no charge and visitors are usually able to obtain a cup of tea or coffee from the small canteen.

The dolls are not sold at the factory, but can be obtained from retail shops.

Practical details: The factory is open Monday to Friday from 8.30 am to 4.30 pm and visitors are welcomed, either individually or in parties of up to 12 people, providing 24 hours' notice is given by telephone or letter. Contact Mrs. D. Mantle.

SEE THE SOUTH AT WORK

THE SOUTH

**Essex, Kent, East Sussex
West Sussex, Surrey
Greater London, Hertfordshire
Bedfordshire,Buckinghamshire
Oxfordshire, Berkshire
Hampshire,Isle of Wight**

1   Farmhouse-style Furniture

Ridgewell Crafts
Ridgewell, Halstead, Essex
Tel: Ridgewell 272

Farmhouse-style furniture is hand made in
English Elm in a small workshop and sold
from a retail shop on the premises. They
specialise in Suffolk and Essex oyster stools
and tables, and spinning chairs. Visitors can
see the furniture being made by age old
methods. "We still use handmade type nails"
they say. A range of garden furniture is also
made.
Practical details: Telephone Mr. and Mrs.
Godsell or Mr. Crouch if you wish to visit the
workshop. The centre is open all year except
on Wednesdays. The workshop is on the A604,
six miles south of Haverhill.

2   Dairy and Livestock Farm

Hobbs Cross Farm
Theydon Garnon, Epping, Essex
Tel: Theydon Bois 2808

Hobbs Cross offers children a unique
opportunity to see round a farm. Normally
members of the National Farmers' Union are
obliged to keep to the rule that children
accepted on school visits to farms must be aged
eleven or older. However, Mr. W. A. Collins
has adapted his farm to deal with school
groups.

Between 7,000 and 8,000 children a year are
taken round the dairy, beef and pig units, and
receive an informal lesson in a heated
classroom which has wall charts and pictures.
Teachers are very enthusiastic, often turning
up a month in advance with cameras and tape
recorders to prepare.
At any time the farm has about 500 cattle, all
British Friesians. During the summer months,
April to September, the cows can be seen
grazing or being milked in the milking
parlour. The farm aims to produce one calf
from every cow each year, and 1,000 gallons of
milk.
The beef calves (150 of them) are fed mainly on
barley until they are ready for market, when
they are about a year old, and weigh about
8 cwt — as much as a small car or a dozen
children.
Sows, 450 of them plus 150 replacements, are
kept mainly for producing weaners (piglets).
When the piglets are three weeks old they go
into multi-suckling pens containing five sows
and their litters. The pigs are sold when they
are eight weeks old and weigh about 50 lbs
each, and every sow is expected to produce 20
piglets a year.
Some ewes are kept specially for the
entertainment of children, so that lambs can
be seen all year round.
The farm has 240 acres of land and the grass is
used for making hay and silage for the farm's
livestock. Children might see tractors, or
machinery for cutting, turning and bailing, in
operation.
Practical details: Hobbs Cross farm is suitable

for school parties of all ages and other organised groups. It is open in school term time and on some Saturdays, and up to fifty people can be taken on a guided tour. There is a small charge for each child, but adults accompanying children do not have to pay. A picnic area is available. For further information write to Mrs. R. C. Lynn or telephone between 9 and 10 am.

3   Car Manufacturers

Ford Motor Company Limited
Dagenham, Essex
Tel: 01-592 4591 Ext: 239/308

Visitors are received at the main entrance to the Ford Engine Plant at Dagenham. This plant is the largest single engine manufacturing operation in the world. The factory has its own blast furnace, power station and jetty, where raw materials are received at one end and finished vehicles are exported from the other end. Visitors will probably glimpse these areas from the coach. The tour of the engine plant enables visitors to see both machining and assembly operations for diesel and petrol power units. From the engine plant visitors are transported by coach to the body group. A walk through this section takes in the press shop, body framing, welding and assembly. Visitors cross from the body group into the final assembly building to inspect painting, trim manufacture and, of course, final assembly where the completed

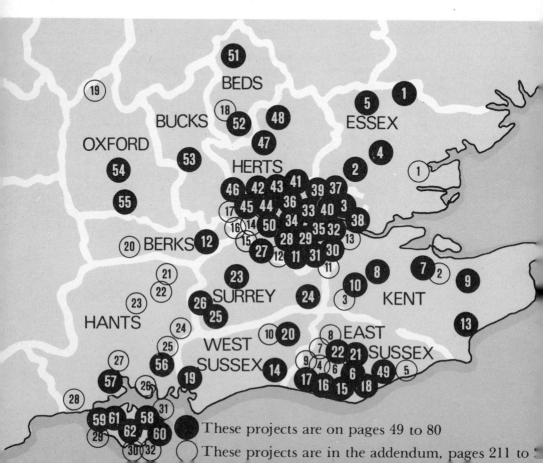

These projects are on pages 49 to 80
These projects are in the addendum, pages 211 to

cars are driven from the line.

Practical details: The factory is open all year Monday to Friday from 9.45 am to noon and from 1.30 pm to 4 pm. Telephone or write to the supervisor of factory visits, Mr. B. Smith, Room 4/311A in advance. Individuals or groups of up to forty people, aged ten and over, are welcome. There is no charge.

4   Agricultural College

Writtle Agricultural College
Near Chelmsford, Essex
Tel: Chelmsford 420705

Practical details: The college has open days a couple of times a year, usually in June, when the farm and glasshouse units can be seen. Entry is free. A programme and refreshments are on sale.

5   Hand-blown Glassware

Raymond G. Adnitt
Hand Blown Glassware
Parsonage Farm, Stansted, Essex
Tel: Harlow 39695

Visitors will see glassware made by two types of glassblowing. Most of the work shown is lamp or flame worked glassware, made from glass tubing or a rod which is melted in a flame. Other glassware is freeblown and the glass is melted in a furnace and taken by the glassblower on the end of a gathering iron, then shaped by blowing and by using traditional tools, usually made from apple or cherry wood. This type of working can be traced back more than 2,000 years.

Wine glasses on display are a sample of those made to customers' requirements, giving the customer a chance to play a part in designing drinking glasses. Arrangements can be made to have glasses engraved with initials or signs, using the diamond point engraving method. Chess sets are made by Ray Adnitt, each set being slightly different. Pieces are in plain and contrasting ground glass. Fitted boxes can be made to house the sets.

Vases, tankards, candlesticks and scientific and industrial glassware are made if there is a demand.

Practical details: Telephone well in advance to make an appointment. Up to eight people can be shown round at a time, including sixth form students accompanied by adults, but not small children.

Parsonage Farm is out in the wilds, with no public transport, but it is well worth the visit.

6   Vineyard

Drusillas
Alfriston, Sussex
Tel: Alfriston 870234

Drusillas has a vineyard with winetasting and tours, wine cellars and an exhibition of cider making methods. In autumn they make cider using a 120-year-old cider press. Then you will also find them harvesting grapes — and you can have a go yourself. There is also a working pottery, and on most days you will see a woodworker making country furniture, a leatherworker who produces bags, hats, belts, pouches etc. He dyes the cured leather and tools it himself. Sussex trug- (boat-shaped basket) making will probably start in 1978. Flamingoes and farm animals can be seen, and there is a miniature railway and adventure playground. Sussex mead, trugs, and bread and scones baked here are sold to take away. Phone first to avoid disappointment.

7   Brewing, Kegging and Bottling

Shepherd Neame
17 Court Street
Faversham, Kent ME13 7AX
Tel: Faversham 2206

The tour lasts about 1 to 1½ hours and covers the brewing, kegging and bottling plants. The visit ends with a sampling session in one of the brewery cellars. You can buy mementoes from the brewery, such as ties and beer mugs.

Practical details: The brewery is open all year round from 10.30 to 12 noon, and 2.30 pm to 4 pm — not including weekends or bank holidays. Applications must be made in writing to the head brewer, Mr. G. C. Ely. Advance notice of at least one month is needed as the tours are very popular. Individuals can join groups, but groups cannot be larger than forty people.

8   Carmelite Friary/Pottery

Carmelite Friary
Aylesford, Maidstone, Kent ME20 7BX
Tel: Maidstone 77272

This is a Friary of the Carmelite Order which was re-founded in 1949 and it is also a Shrine of the Virgin Mary. The site is impressive. Some of the original Cloisters date back to the 14th or 15th century and Samuel Pepys, the diarist, said, 'I was mightily pleased when I saw it'.
Pilgrimages are made to the shrine by Roman Catholics, Anglicans and members of free churches.
The pottery, run by the Carmelites, was started for them by David Leach and it produces typical Leach Japanese stoneware. The friars specialise in ecclesiastical pottery and all kinds of pottery for domestic use. These products have been sent all over the world. The Friary has a cafeteria, a car park, and a shop for postcards, souvenirs, religious articles, books and pottery.
Practical details: The Friary is open from 9 am until dusk throughout the year, including bank holidays. The guesthouse, tea room and shop are closed over Christmas. Admission is free. The pottery is open Monday to Friday. The friars like to have notice of visits by groups, and guided tours are by arrangement — contact the Friary at least a week beforehand. The tour takes an hour. All kinds of groups are welcome as long as they respect the religious character of the shrine. Contact the Pilgrimage Secretary.
Handicapped groups are welcome, including people in wheelchairs.

9   Traditional Weaving

The Old Weavers House Limited
1-3 Kings Bridge, Canterbury, Kent CT1 2AT
Tel: Canterbury 62329

The Old Weavers House in the centre of Canterbury has a riverside shop on the ground floor selling handwoven goods, leatherware, locally made pottery, candlemaking materials and stones and mounts for jewellery-making. Upstairs this striking Tudor building contains 150 year old looms, spinning wheels and weaving implements. A semi-retired weaver demonstrates weaving from 10.30 am to 2 pm.
During the reign of Elizabeth I the Walloons from the Spanish Netherlands came to England because they had faced religious persecution. Many of them were skilled weavers and they settled in Canterbury. The old Weaving House is believed to have been a centre for their work. The weavers' fortunes declined in the 18th century, because of competition from India, but the craft was revived at the beginning of the 20th century.
Practical details: Individuals are welcome to the house Monday to Friday from 9.30 am to 5.30 pm, and in the summer months the shop is open seven days a week. River tours on the Old Weavers Ferry leave from the house. Visitors in groups of twenty or more are given a discount on advance booking for the house or river tours. A tour of the house and weaving room lasts fifteen minutes, and there is a small charge. The river tour takes thirty minutes.

10   Wrought Ironwork

Hyders Limited
Plaxtol, Sevenoaks, Kent TN15 0QR
Tel: Plaxtol 215

Hyders' 14th century showrooms are of architectural interest and well worth a visit. The wrought ironwork displayed includes a museum of antique ironwork collected over many years. The display covers hand-forged wrought ironwork, gates, grilles,

weathervanes, lanterns and brackets, electrical
fittings of all kinds, fireplace fittings,
firescreens, dog grates, and there is also some
garden furniture.

Hyders specialise in restoring wrought
ironwork. Groups visiting the works will see
blacksmiths making scrollwork parts for gates
and railings. Canopies and lanterns are put
together in the sheet metal shop. Fitters put
together bigger items such as gates and
railings. Welders do smaller items such as
weathervanes, bootscrapers and chandeliers.
Finally, the wrought ironwork is painted.

Practical details: The showroom/museum is
open Monday to Friday from 10 am to 4.30 pm,
and on Saturday from 9.30 am to 1 pm. Not
open on bank holidays or works' annual
holiday. Individuals can only see the
showrooms and cannot be shown around the
works — groups of from ten to twenty people
are welcome by appointment.

11   Design Centre

Design Centre
28 Haymarket
London SW1Y 4SU
Tel: 01-839 8000

The Design Centre has displays of well-
designed British consumer goods and
thematic exhibitions. Also the Design Index

— information cards with photographs of
hundreds of British products.

The Design Council has its own magazine
'Design', and sells books on subjects such as
lighting, and bathroom and kitchen
planning.

Practical details: Open to the public Monday
to Saturday from 9.30 am to 5.30 pm, and until
9 pm Wednesday and Thursday. Groups
please phone first. A talk and design quiz are
given to school groups of 11-15 year olds.
Disabled visitors welcome.

12   Working Horses

Courage Shire Horse Centre
Maidenhead Thicket
Maidenhead, Berkshire SL6 3QD
Tel: Littlewick Green 3917

The Shire Horse is known for its great
strength and stamina, and has beautiful
'feathered' hair around the hooves. Some of
the horses work on farms in winter and
photographs show the history of Shire horses,
pulling anything from ploughs to coal carts,
railway or brewery delivery vans.

Harnesses are on display, plus photographs
of barrel-making and some coopers' tools. Free
dray rides are given in suitable weather.

Practical details: Open daily from March to
October except Monday, unless Monday is a
bank holiday. Hours are 11 am to 5 pm (last
admission 4 pm). Groups must pre-book for
guided tours. The entry charge is reduced for
children, pensioners, and booked groups of 20
or more. Pub, tea room, pets' corner and
playground. Handicapped welcome.

13   Nuclear Power Station

Dungeness Power Station
Dungeness, Romney Marsh, Kent TN29 9PP
Tel: Lydd 20461

Dungeness has steam plant using heat
supplied from nuclear reactors. Sea water
condenses the steam after it has been
exhausted from the turbine.

A refuelling machine at Dungeness

Visits last about one and a half hours and a short film on the principles of nuclear power is shown. Guides then take you on a conducted tour.

Practical details: The station is open to the public on Wednesday afternoons from June to September inclusive. Tours begin at 2 pm and 3 pm. Visitors must be fourteen years of age or over. Admission is by ticket only, available from the Seeboard shops at Bexhill, Rye, Hastings, Tenterden, Ashford, New Romney, Hythe and Folkestone. Details of electricity production are in this book.

14   Furniture Restoration

Aruncraft Workshops
Riffards, Burpham
Arundel, Sussex BN18 9RJ
Tel: Arundel 883143

'Ours is a country business, specialising in fine quality restoration. Our workshop is in one of the most attractive villages in Sussex and set in a landscaped garden with ample parking space. We are difficult to find but, in the end, people find their visit rewarding.'

Practical details: The workshop is open Monday to Friday from 9 am to 5 pm, and on Saturday mornings, also by appointment only on Saturday afternoons and Sunday. Individual visitors are welcome as long as they do not expect to be entertained. The few craftsmen are always working at full capacity.

15   Shellcraft and Jewellery

The Tropical Shells Company Limited
22 Preston Road, Brighton, Sussex BN1 4QF
Tel: Brighton 63178

The sea shell warehouse is a never-to-be-forgotten setting for all kinds of sea shells. It has a green floor, yellow walls and a brown ceiling. In the shop there are three palm trees and two stuffed crocodiles.

'I never thought there were so many shells,' is the usual exclamation when visitors come into the warehouse. There are more than three million shells here on open display on the shelves — that is if you count all the tiny rice shells, too! There are shells for craft work, jewellery making, flower arranging and for beautiful ornaments.

'In the middle of all the shells we clear a space for our visitors. They can sit down and hear a delightful talk given by a professional speaker who will tell them all they wish to know about any and every aspect of shells and shellcraft.

Visitors will also see jewellery designed by Millicent Rich, principal of the Millicent Rich School of Shellcraft, and she can give advice on shellcraft and jewellery design.

Practical details: Individuals may visit the shop only, on Mondays to Saturdays 9.30 am to 6.30 pm. They are free to wander into the warehouse if they wish. Groups of all ages are welcome to the warehouse seven days a week throughout the year. The minimum size of group is twenty-five people, the maximum sixty.

Unfortunately, you will have to make your arrangements far in advance, as they are now fully booked for about two years for the talk. However, you can still go to just look around.

16   Amateur Winemaking Supplies

Southern Vineyards Limited
Nizells Avenue, Hove, East Sussex BN3 1PS
Tel: Brighton 779971

Home winemaking in Britain has been increasing over the past twenty years and inflation and taxation are encouraging many more people to make their own wines. Southern Vineyards also export widely, though a few foreign visitors raise their eyebrows because it is neither legal nor profitable for them to make wines at home. Southern Vineyards import grape juices from all over Europe, blending them in England to produce a range of eighteen types of wines. They have just launched 'Ginora' which produces a gin-like drink by the winemaking method. Home distilling is illegal in the UK

and this drink contains less alcohol than gin. So the company recommends adding commercial gin to each gallon to improve alcoholic flavour and content. By serving a double 'Ginora' with less tonic than usual, a similar alcoholic effect is achieved at far less cost.

Wine enthusiasts will also be interested in the wine filter to remove cloudiness, the agitator to speed fermentation and reduce the risk of stuck fermentation, the hydrometer to measure sugar content as fermentation progresses, and the heater with patented holder to fit the traditional gallon jar without need for a special cork.

Practical details: The factory itself is not open to the public but their latest equipment is on display in the showroom, the receptionist answers questions about winemaking, and you can sample their wines. Open to individuals and groups without booking, Monday to Friday from 9 am to 12.30 pm and 1.30 pm to 5 pm.

17   Power Station

Brighton Power Station
Basin Road South, Portslade
Brighton BN4 1WG
Tel: Brighton 593131

The visit includes a short film on the generation of electricity followed by a conducted tour around the power station accompanied by a uniformed guide. Visitors see coal milling plant supplying pulverised fuel boilers, the steam driven turbo alternators generating electricity, and the central control room. The visit lasts about 1½ hours.

Practical details: The power station is open to the general public at dates and times advertised in the local press. These are usually Tuesday and Thursday afternoons during the months of July and August. Organised visits can be accepted by prior arrangement Monday to Friday at 10.30 am, 2.30 pm and 7.30 pm and four weeks' notice is requested.

The power station is at Southwick, three miles West of Brighton.

18   Theatre Complex

The Congress Theatre
Eastbourne, Sussex
Tel: Eastbourne 36363

A senior member of staff takes visitors on a
tour of the complex, giving them a
background history. Technical stations
throughout the building are visited and there
is opportunity for visitors to ask questions.
Practical details: Groups of ten to twenty
people are welcomed by prior arrangement.

19   Simulated Fur Manufacturers

Richesse Furs
Industrial Estate, Chichester, Sussex
Tel: Chichester 83748

Light refreshments are served when visitors
arrive and this is followed by an informal
fashion show and a tour of the factory to see
the manufacturing process involved in
making simulated fur. The visit lasts about 1¾
hours and no charge is made. There is no
pressure selling but any garment can be
purchased at wholesale prices.
Practical details: The factory is open Monday
to Friday and tours are held at 10.30 am, 2.30
pm and 7.30 pm, except on bank holidays.
Bookings need to be made about one month in
advance. Visitors are accepted in groups of
between twenty-five and forty-two people.
Children are not accepted.
The factory car park has space for coaches, and
anyone organising a day out for older people
will be interested to learn that no stairs are
involved.

20   Stoneground Flour Mill

Booker Health Foods Limited
Prewett's Mill, Horsham, Sussex
Tel: Horsham 3208

Prewett's have been milling flour here for
more than 100 years. The original William

Prewett bought the mill which he had been
renting when his landlord died in 1872.
Stoneground flour has been milled here ever
since, and the only change since William's day
is that driving belts which used to be driven by
a steam engine are now powered by electricity.
The wheat is ground by two circular granite
stones, each weighing up to 1½ tons. The
lower stone (bedstone) remains still.

The grinding surface is corrugated like the
spokes of a wheel. The grain is 100%
wholemeal, containing all parts of the wheat.
Heat is generated during milling and this
helps to spread wheat germ oil and other
flavouring through the meal and this cannot
be extracted by any later process.
The newer 'refined' flour we hear so much
about is ground in modern factories by steel
rollers. It is divided into piles of the various
parts of the wheat — bran, middlings,
wheatgerm, fibre and particles of semolina.
The semolinas are ground up by 'reduction'
rollers to make flour.
This flour does not have bran and wheatgerm
and it lacks vitamins and minerals. The law
requires that synthetic vitamins and minerals
are put in to compensate for those lost.
As germ oil is still present, stoneground flours
of 81% and over do not need to be fortified.
They have no potentially harmful additives,
they are darker in colour, and they have more
flavour. This, says Prewett's, is what
wholemeal flour is all about.
As well as flours, Prewett's make breakfast
foods including Scotch porridge oats and
meuslis — a muesli base, a semi-sweet muesli,
a honey muesli de luxe which has the highest
proportion of fruit and nuts. They also make
Golden Grains, a toasted granola (crunchy
grain-base breakfast cereal, very popular in
America). If you go into your local health food
shop you will probably spot their savoury
mixes for nut rissoles, their natural wheat
bran, sprinkled on cereals to to ensure that you
have enough fibre (roughage) in your diet, and
wheat embryo which is full of trace elements
and vitamins. Also bread mixes — three
varieties, brown, white and bran, with active
yeast in a sachet, plus five kinds of fruit bars!
Practical details: The mill is open to groups by
appointment. Write for further details.

21   Batik Artist

Mary Potter Studio
Laughton, Lewes, Sussex BN8 6DE
Tel: Halland 438

The Mary Potter Studio is set in the
countryside a few miles from Lewes. The
house is surrounded by fields with a backcloth
of woods. The studio is purpose-built for
making and displaying batik pictures.
Batik printing is a craft which originated in
Java and is now very popular, and Mary Potter
has adapted it to our own cultural needs. She
works mainly on silk, applying wax with a
brush or the tjanting or by hand, then dipping
the material into the dye bath or brushing dye
on to the design according to its requirements.
One of the attractions is the brilliant and
subtle colours possible in dyes.
At stages in the process the wax can be cracked
so that the dye penetrates the cracks, giving the
characteristic lined effect which a skilled artist
incorporates into the design. The English
countryside is the main source of inspiration
for Mary Potter's designs and pictures. She
sells batik pictures and wallhangings, batik
silk scarves, and she undertakes commissions.
You can also buy original silk screen prints —
cards with Sussex themes, handprinted scarves
and traditional prints of brasses and the
Bayeux Tapestry.
Practical details: The studio is open every day
including weekends and bank holidays, but as
Mrs. Potter is not always at home a phone
enquiry is advised. All visitors are welcome,
including small parties. Groups are accepted
by appointment only.

22   Hand Painted Porcelain

Sheila Southwell
'Farthings', The Ridings
Manor Road, Burgess Hill, Sussex
Tel: Burgess Hill 44307

The artist, Sheila Southwell, works from
home, decorating many differently shaped
pieces of porcelain and bone china. No two
pieces are the same. Each piece is designed,
decorated and fired, signed and dated by the
artist. The range of articles includes large wall
plates, vases, dishes, trinket boxes and
children's wall and door plaques. Pieces may
be commissioned to make a really personal
gift commemorating a special occasion. Most
of the designs have an 'olde worlde' effect.
Practical details: The workshop is open
Monday to Friday from 10 am to 5 pm and at
weekends. Individual visitors and groups
are welcome provided they telephone or write
in advance. Demonstrations and lectures can
be arranged for organisations. A small charge
is made, which includes tea and biscuits.

23   Unique Pottery

Wharf Pottery
55 St. John's Street, Farncombe, Godalming
Surrey GU7 3EH
Tel: Godalming 4097

Visitors have the opportunity of watching
potters at work — throwing on the wheel,
turning and decorating. In addition, Mary
Wondrausch writes, 'The work that we do here
is unique. I believe that I am the only potter
using the slip trail and sgraffito methods of
decoration on earthenware, in the seventeenth
century English tradition.
They specialise in making individual plates
to commemorate births, anniversaries
etc. These come in presentation boxes and are
sent all over the world. Most of the work they
do is for mail order.

Mary Potter — silk screen and batik work

Practical details: The pottery is open Monday to Saturday from 9 am to 5 pm. Visitors are most welcome but as it is a tiny workshop the maximum number of visitors at one time is eight, and a telephone call in advance is helpful.

24　Gatwick Airport

Gatwick Airport
Horley, Surrey RH6 0NP
Tel: Crawley 28822 or 01-668 4211

For security reasons there are no tours of the airport, but spectators are welcome to watch Britain's second busiest airport in operation from the special area on the roof of the international arrivals building.
Practical details: The airport is open every day from 8 am to dusk. There is a small admission charge. Refreshment facilities are available in the area and there is a car park, again with a charge.

25　Musical Instrument Makers

Arnold Dolmetsch Limited
Arnold Dolmetsch Workshops
Kings Road, Haslemere, Surrey
Tel: Haslemere 51432/3

Arnold Dolmetsch was a concert artist and a pioneer in the manufacture of musical instruments. His desire to play preclassical music on the proper instruments led him to make the first modern lutes, viols, harpsichords and recorders. His son, Dr Carl Dolmetsch, travels all over the world by air with his prototype little spinet which has become known as the 'jet spinet' or 'flying harpsichord', as it packs up like a suitcase. Arnold Dolmetsch was responsible for reviving recorder-playing, and his son developed the low cost plastic recorders which are now used by so many school children. The company makes and sells instruments, such as harpsichords, spinets, clavichords, viols, lutes, classical guitars and recorders.

It also restores and services harpsichords, square pianos and old stringed instruments.
Practical details: Individuals and groups of up to twelve people are accepted for tours on Thursday at 11 am or 2.30 pm by appointment. A conducted tour of the workshops is given and you can see the craftsmen making musical instruments — spinets, harpsichords and viols, all hand crafted. The woodworking is done by hand — wooden recorders are hand-turned and hand-cut.
Plastic recorders are injection-moulded elsewhere and assembled here.
As well as the workshops there is the Dolmetsch collection of Early Musical Instruments at Jesses, Grayswood Road, Haslemere. This is open to the public by appointment, Monday to Friday.

Viol-maker at Arnold Dolmetsch Ltd.

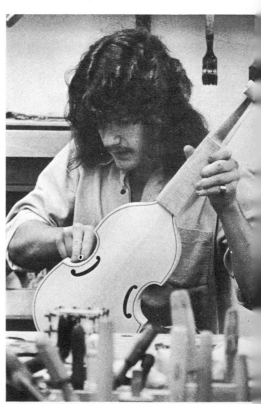

26   Grayshott Pottery

Surrey Ceramic Company Limited
Grayshott Pottery, School Road
Grayshott, Hindhead, Surrey GU26 6LR
Tel: Hindhead 4404

A wide selection of products is manufactured,
ranging from those made on the potter's
wheel, to more intricate shapes cast in moulds,
and other articles, particularly plates, which
are suited to machine manufacture. Visitors
can watch these processes at close quarters and
where a guide is not available the members of
staff are only too pleased to explain. Glazing
and decorating can also be seen.

The large pottery shop sells products at
reduced prices including seconds.

Practical details: The pottery shop and works
are open Monday to Friday from 9 am to 5 pm.
The pottery shop alone is open on Saturday
from 9 am to 5 pm. Both are closed on bank
holidays.

During opening hours (except lunch time 1 to
2 pm) visitors can go round the pottery. Small
groups of up to twelve people may do so
without notice, but no guide will be available.
These visits are free of charge. For groups of
twelve or more people the visit must be
arranged in advance and a guide will be
provided. These visits can be arranged
Monday to Friday. A charge is made for party
bookings. The numbers in a party can be up to
fifty-four and children may be included.
Morning visits can also be arranged for groups
of children up to the age of twelve and there is
no charge.

There is ample parking space.

27   Poppy Factory

The Royal British Legion Poppy Factory
20 Petersham Road
Richmond, Surrey TW10 6UR
Tel: 01-940 3305

Until 1975 the Factory of Remembrance
employed only ex-service men, with
preference being given to those who are
disabled. But now ex-service women, widows

Hand-thrown pots—Grayshott Pottery

of ex-service men and their disabled
dependents are also employed. Ninety-six per
cent of the employees are disabled in one or
several ways.

The making of poppies for remembrance was
inspired by the poem by Colonel John McCrae
who died in 1918.

'In Flanders fields the poppies blow
Between the crosses, row on row . . .'

'To you from failing hands we throw
The torch; be yours to hold it high,
If ye break faith with us who die
We shall not sleep, though poppies grow
In Flanders fields.'

In 1922 members of The Disabled Society
started making poppies for the British Legion,
and since then the factory has grown into 'a

human war memorial' employing about 150 full-time people and another sixty or so who are part-time or obliged to work in their own homes.

The factory now produces about 36 million poppies a year, 184 thousand remembrance crosses, and 70,000 wreaths. The disabled employees also make rosettes and show badges, and do printing work for the British Legion and for commercial organisations.
Practical details: Townswomen's Guilds, members of the Round Table and other groups, as well as royalty, frequently visit the factory, which has an average of 300 visitors each week. Individuals can join a group tour provided they arrange this beforehand. A tour of the factory takes 1½ to 2 hours and tea and biscuits are provided. There is no charge.

28   London Visits

The London Appreciation Society
17 Manson Mews, South Kensington
London SW7 5AE
Tel: 01-370 1100

Those who enjoy unusual visits, but would rather leave the organising to somebody else, may be interested in the London Appreciation Society. This society was started by Mr. Bryant Peers who, when he was a young teacher in 1932, used to take schoolboys out on Saturday afternoons around London. Many of the boys could not even afford the ½d. tram fare, but the outings were so popular that brothers and sisters, then mothers and fathers asked if they could join the groups. And so a society for the parents was started. Nowadays buildings and institutions are visited, with guide lecturers, and evening walks usually end in a friendly pub.
At the beginning of 1977 they visited the headquarters of the London Salvage Corps which salvages material from fires, toured the self-service Post House Hotel at Heathrow airport, the Reliance Security Services, which patrols factories and offices, the Greenwich District hospital, and Sanderson's fabric printing factory at Uxbridge.
Practical details: If you are interested in

joining the London Appreciation Society the subscription is £3.15 per year, payable on January 1st, but members joining in October to December pay only £2. The society's programme is published twice a year and covers the periods January to April and October to December.
Visits are limited in number, and places are allocated on a first booked first served basis, but often additional dates are arranged if there is heavy demand for a particular outing. Free copies of the programme can be obtained by sending an s.a.e. to the Hon. Sec. Mr. Bryant Peers. Most events take place on Saturdays and in the evenings. Anyone is welcome.

29   Science Museum

Science Museum, Exhibition Road
London SW7 2DD
Tel: 01-589 6371

While strictly speaking there is nobody 'at work' here, the Science Museum is full of interesting pieces of equipment, including working models. A visit to the science museum will quite probably teach you as much about how scientific principles have been applied to industry, as several visits to small firms which can show you only their own activities.
As the science museum is so vast, teachers should look around before bringing groups along, or if distance prevents this, they should write stating which galleries or exhibits they would like the children to see. There is a special application form for teachers. The science museum has a free lecture service, too. Some of the lectures are for the general public (adults only), others are for specialists. Lectures can be arranged on request to suit schoolchildren over the age of ten, or adults (including handicapped and blind people) depending on their ability and interests. Of special interest are their 'Joint Industrial Lectures' given by scientists and technologists working in industry. Details are given in the leaflet called 'Party Visits'. Public lectures are included in their quarterly programme.

A special lecture at the Science Museum

Practical details: The museum is open to casual visitors Monday to Saturday from 10 am to 6 pm, and on Sunday from 2.30 pm to 6 pm. It is closed on Christmas Eve and Christmas Day, New Year's Day and on Good Friday.

30   Dyes and Dye-craft Kits

Dylon International Limited
Worsley Bridge Road
Lower Sydenham, London SE26 5HD
Tel: 01-650 4801

In their theatre, Dylon demonstrate the art of home-dyeing, including tie-dyeing (creating patterns by sewing or knotting, pleating or folding the fabric and tying it with string before it is dyed to prevent the dye penetrating those areas) and batik (painting the fabric with hot wax to keep out the dye) and fabric painting.

Dyes can be used to change the colours of old (or new) clothes and accessories to make them match, or to give them the season's colours. Soft furnishings and wooden furniture can also be colour co-ordinated with dyes.

Dylon make dyes for fabrics, suede, leather and wood. There are also dye-craft kits, fabric paints, whiteners for sports equipment, rain and stain repellants, suede and leather cleaners and polyurethane wood seals.

Any member of the public can get individual advice and free leaflets on all aspects of home-dyeing by writing to Miss Annette Stevens. She will also send free leaflets and instruction sheets on dye-crafts to teachers. A set of four colour posters illustrating home-dyeing using multi-purpose dyes, cold dyes, tie-dye and batik, is available at £1.25 including VAT and postage. Educational establishments can obtain a special price list.

Practical details: Demonstrations are given during the day, Monday to Friday by prior arrangement. Schools, women's clubs, youth clubs and so on are welcome, and should contact Mrs. Anne Turner. Individuals who have a special interest can also come to these demonstrations, but may have to fit in with times and dates of other parties.

31   The County Hall

Greater London Council
The County Hall, Westminster Bridge Road, London SE1 7PB
Tel: 01-633 5000

Visitors are given a short talk. They then visit the Council Chamber if it is not in use. Literature and souvenirs can be bought from the Greater London Council Bookshop at County Hall.

Practical details: Meetings of the Council, when it is in session, are held on every alternate Tuesday afternoon at 2.30 pm and are open to the public.

Weekday visits can also be made for visitors to attend committee meetings. Weekday visits to The County Hall by parties, including school groups, can be arranged by the information officer. Applications should be made well in advance because this is a very popular visit.

32   Maritime Museum

National Maritime Museum
(including the Old Royal Observatory)
Romney Road, London SE10
Tel: 01-858 4422

You could easily spend the whole day at
Greenwich. The museum has more than a
mile of galleries showing British maritime
history using actual craft, paintings,
contemporary ship models, uniforms,
weapons, personal relics, photographs,
navigation and astronomy instruments, charts
and globes. More visitors come here than to
any other group of historic buildings in
Britain except the Tower of London.
The Half Deck (junior centre) can be booked
in advance by schools for practical work and
packed lunches can be eaten here. (The
museum threatens to throw children
overboard if they don't behave!) The boat
building plant can be booked for a series of
building sessions by senior classes, youth
groups and amateur builders who wish to use
traditional materials and methods.
Party visits can be arranged with the PR
officer, and school visits through the
education officer, both of whom require two
weeks' notice. The museum's three bookshops
stock souvenirs, posters, ship model kits and
books — and there is a licensed restaurant.
Admission is free and regular special
exhibitions are held.

One can approach Greenwich Park by
British Rail, by bus, or in summer by
passenger launch from Tower Pier. (Tel: 01-
858 3996 for details.)
Practical details: In winter, the museum is
open Monday to Friday from 10 am to 5 pm,
Saturday 10 am to 6 pm, and Sunday 2.30 pm
to 6 pm; in summer, Monday to Saturday from
10 am to 6 pm, and Sunday 2.30 pm to 6 pm. It
is open on bank holidays with the exception of
Christmas Eve, Christmas Day, New Year's
Day and Good Friday.

33   The Baltic Exchange

The Baltic Exchange
14-20 St. Mary Axe, London EC3A 8BU
Tel: 01-283 9300

The Baltic Exchange is the only International
Shipping Exchange in the world and handles,
at some stage, about seventy per cent of all the
world's shipping. It started in a seventeenth
century London coffee house and the basic
principle of business remains the same. It is a
meeting house where ship owners with
shipping spaces available look for shippers
with cargo to be carried all over the world.
The present building, with its splendid brown
and white marble pillars and domed ceiling,
was completed in 1903, and business is
conducted on the 'floor' of the exchange in
two daily sessions, one at mid-day and the
other for half an hour at 4 pm. Roughly 700
shipping companies in the world are members
of the exchange and they are represented by
about 2,400 members who conduct their
companies' business on the 'floor'.
Practical details: Visits of up to thirty students
and groups are accepted on two days a week. A
film is usually shown, followed by a
conducted tour of the 'floor' in action. This is
by appointment only and can be arranged
through Gordon Bradley Limited of 59 St.
James's Street, London SW1, Tel: 01-499 7870.
Individuals and small parties are welcome
provided they book well in advance.

The New Neptune Hall, Maritime Museum

34   The Stock Exchange

Offices of the Council
The Stock Exchange, London EC2N 1HP
Tel: 01-588 2355

Guides explain the activities on the busy
trading floor and colour films are shown in
the cinema to explain the work of the Stock
Exchange. This is where the fortunes of
companies, even the fortunes of countries, go
go up and down. It is an extremely popular
attraction with, sometimes, many thousands
of visitors in a week.
Practical details: The public viewing gallery is
open from 10 am to 3.15 pm Monday to Friday.
Individuals have no need to book. Groups of
up to a maximum of forty people should write
to the Public Relations Officer well in
advance. School parties are particularly
welcome and there is no charge.

Brokers at the London Stock Exchange

35   The Guildhall

The Guildhall
Gresham Street, London EC2

This has been the centre of the City's
government for more than 1,000 years and the
present Guildhall dates from 1411. In the
Great Hall the Court of Common Council, the
Local Council for the square mile of the City,
meets on a Thursday lunchtime every three
weeks, except during the Christmas and
summer recessions. The Lord Mayor presides
and arrives 'in state' with his officers.
Practical details: Apply to the City
Information Centre, St. Paul's Churchyard,
London EC4, Tel: 01-606 3030, for dates of the
Court of Common Council. School groups
and tourists often wish to see the Guildhall.

36   Vegetable and Flower Market

Spitalfields Market
65 Brushfield Street, London E1 6AA
Tel: 01-247 7331

Spitalfields is a wholesale fruit, vegetable and flower market just outside the City of London, serving not only London and the home counties, but all parts of Britain.
During the night, lorries bring in home grown produce for sale when the market opens at 4 am. Imported produce from all parts of the world arrives by lorry from the docks, or comes direct from Common Market.
Spitalfields Market includes the London Fruit Exchange which houses many firms distributing fruit nationally and internationally. About 1,600 people work there, including the 300 or so market porters. Trading takes place six days a week and lasts until 2.30 pm. It is here that your morning grapefruit arrives, long before you get up for breakfast.
The flower market houses wholesale flower distributors, many of whom have been in the flower business for generations. The building is specially designed to make sure that flowers are kept in the best possible condition. The lighting is arranged so that no direct sun rays wither the blooms. Beneath each stand are spacious cellars in which flowers can be stored at a cool, even temperature.
Practical details: Formal, conducted tours are restricted to people connected with horticultural or catering industries. Contact Mr. C. A. Lodemore, the superintendent, at the above address. There is no reason, however, why any early riser, or late night reveller, should not stroll through the market. There is no guarantee what you will see as a casual visitor, but at peak hours the comings and goings are very interesting.

37   Town Planning

The Barbican
London EC2

The Barbican is a residential and arts centre which is still under construction in the City of London. Built on a thirty-five acre site, it will

Acres of fruit and flowers—Spitalfields

have more than 2,000 flats and maisonettes, garaging for 2,000 vehicles, a theatre, cinema, concert hall, art gallery, library, restaurants and shops. The residential area is complete and the arts centre is due to open in 1979. Of course, the real test is, what is it like to live there? Some residents have reservations. They find it lonely at night and think it would be cheaper to shop in the East End.
Non-residents are usually full of praise. They bring children here on Sunday mornings to feed the fish in the ornamental lakes. They admire the tubs of unusual plants, and comment on the way that old-fashioned lamps and parts of old London Wall have been made part of modern surroundings.

Practical details: Individuals can walk through this development, and architects and planners will be particularly interested. Plans and models are on show in the Barbican Estate Office, Aldersgate Street, EC2Y 8AB, which is open Monday to Friday from 9.15 am to 5 pm. Conducted tours can be arranged for specialist groups of up to twenty-five people with particular interests; write to public relations

Children can touch animals at City Farm

office, Corporation of London, Guildhall, London EC2.

38   City Farm and Riding Stables

City Farm One
232 Grafton Road
Kentish Town, London NW5
Tel: 01-485 4585

The farm is run by Inter-Action, a non-profit organisation which specialises in youth and community activities. The farm contains an indoor riding school and children taking the guided school tour are shown one of the twelve horses, and the use of the bridle, harness and other equipment. In the farmyard, chickens run loose, and there are twelve ponies, a donkey, rabbits, guinea pigs, ducks, a cow, two goats, two sheep and two pigs. Children on pre-arranged tours are allowed into the pens in small groups to handle the animals. The eating habits of the animals are described and children can feed the animals if feeding time occurs during the visit.
Practical details: Adults and accompanied

children are invited to walk around on their own at any time until the stables close at about 8.30 pm. There is no charge. One-hour tours of the riding stables and farm can be arranged for school parties, Monday to Friday. Groups usually arrive at 10.30 am, 1.30 pm or 3 pm. There is a small charge for children (no fee for adults). Within ten days of the proposed date of an organised visit, the farm sends a map and confirmation.
After the tour children can eat sandwiches in a nearby picnic place.

39   National Newspaper

Daily Mail
Harmsworth Publishing
Carmelite House, London EC4Y 0JA
Tel: 01-353 6000 Ext: 872

The Daily Mail, founded in 1896 by Lord Northcliffe, has a circulation of more than 1½ million copies. An official guide takes visitors through the editorial offices and production areas, including the composing department, the foundry, the press room and, finally, the warehouse, where copies of the Daily Mail are loaded on to vans for delivery to stations and wholesalers.
The various departments are situated on many floors of the building and this entails walking up and down staircases.
Practical details: Tours start at 9 pm and finish about 11.15 pm on Tuesdays, Wednesdays and Fridays all year round, apart from public and religious holidays. Groups of up to twelve people, over fourteen years of age, are accepted. Contact the Daily Mail production manager, Mr. J. L. Cooper, at least twelve weeks in advance as the tours are very popular. There are no parking facilities.

40   Criminal Courts

Central Criminal Court
Old Bailey, London EC4

Proceedings rarely take place with the speed of the television court case with which we are all so familiar. A major court case may take days, even weeks. So, if you are visiting the courts for no more than a day, the shorter cases will be equally interesting as you will be more likely to see the conclusion.
Children often find visiting courts while they are in session rather boring. You have to sit still and keep dead silent in the gallery, and even then you may have to strain to hear a nervous mumbling witness. The people who find our courts most interesting are the foreign visitors. Commonwealth citizens are delighted to see this bit of British pageantry carrying on just as they had imagined it; Europeans find the mode of dress quite amazing, and, if they speak good English, are often impressed by British justice — au pairs love visiting the courts.
Practical details: The public are admitted to the courts during sessions from 10.15 am to 1 pm and from 1.45 pm to 4 pm. Visits can be arranged by writing to the Keeper.

41   Glassblowing Studio

The Glasshouse
65 Long Acre
London WC2
Tel: 01-836 9785

Five young artists make and sell glass at this groundfloor glassblowing studio and gallery. Glass objects on display include multi-coloured paperweights in numerous designs, goblets, bowls, perfume bottles, vases and plates. Prices range from £5 to £100. A weekend glassblowing introduction course is held here, and beginners can learn to blow glass and apply colour. Also evening courses.
Practical details: The Glasshouse is open Monday to Friday from 10 am to 5.30 pm and on Saturday from 11 am to 4 pm. Visitors are welcome to come here and watch glass being made. Groups of more than 5 people please telephone in advance. No seconds are produced they say, and no repairs undertaken. For further information contact Annette Meech at the above address.

42   Large Glassworks

Whitefriars Glass Limited
Tudor Road, Wealdstone
Middlesex HA3 5PF
Tel: 01-427 1527

Whitefriars glassworks is named after the
white robed Carmelite friars who lived near
the old glassworks. The original glassworks
was started in the 1600s and a symbolic white
friar is still used as the trademark today.
This fascinating tour starts upstairs in the
small museum area with a look at stained
glass. This was once produced by Whitefriars
for buildings as far apart as St. Paul's in
London, and a church in Fiji. Visitors learn
that bulls eye glass, often used in Georgian
windows, was blown as a bubble and then
flattened.
The guide explains how soda glass and crystal
glass is made and how impurities are removed.
The processes are explained before visitors
enter the furnace room, partly because of the
noise, and partly because you cannot walk
around much as red-hot blobs of glass are
being carried about.
Inside the works you see the teams of workers,
perhaps three men, waiting until a fourth
hurries over with a pole carrying a glowing
hot dollop of glass. Many of the workers are
school-leavers, who have taken over as a
generation of older people have retired. They
are wearing only coloured vests with their
jeans, because of the heat from the furnaces.

One of the most interesting processes is the
making of millefiore (meaning Italian for a
thousand flowers) paperweights. A flower
pattern is made and stretched out into a cane
like a child's stick of rock. Then disc-like
sections are cut off with a diamond drill and
put into a mould.
In another department glass-cutting takes
place. Guide lines are marked on the glass
with paint and rough horizontal and diagonal
cuts are made with a carborundum wheel. A
second cut with a natural stone wheel makes
the line more acutely angled and polishes it.

The tour ends in the shop where seconds and
discontinued lines are sold — gold, aqua, ruby

and glacier textured glassware is for sale, as
well as the friar-shaped jugs.
Practical details: Tours last about 1½ hours
and start at 10.15 am and 2.15 pm, Monday to
Friday, except for works holidays, throughout
the year. All individuals over fourteen, and
groups, are welcome although the tour is not
suitable for disabled people because of the
stairs. A small charge is made.

43   Photographic Film

Kodak Limited
Headstone Drive, Harrow
Middlesex HA1 4TY
Tel: 01-427 4380 Ext: 34

Kodak's Harrow factory, built in 1891,
originally housed all the company's British
manufacturing departments. Nowadays only
photographic film and paper are made in
Harrow — cameras are made at the Stevenage
factory, (which does not accept visitors),
and colour films are processed at Hemel
Hempstead.
Four thousand people are employed in the
Harrow complex alone, which has its own
medical centre, fire station, electricity
generator, and half a dozen canteens.

An hour is spent seeing a film which covers
aspects of the processes which you cannot see
on the tour. Then follows a visit to the
museum room, where, apart from the old
cameras and photographs, there are one or two
items to interest social historians.

The factory tour starts with a look at rolls of
white paper — viewed end on they are about
four feet six inches high. The ingredients for
light-sensitive coatings, paper and light-
sensitive films are mixed nearby — this
process is controlled by a sophisticated
computer. As well as more than 200 kinds of
paper for photocopying and photograph
printing, more than two hundred kinds of
film are produced.

In the next area non-specialists are taken to see
the paper-cutting and packing departments
and specialists — photographers, dental and
medical X-ray workers — go to see film-

Computerised control centre at Kodak

cutting and packing. As you enter this building you walk across a grille with vibrating brushes which wipe the dust off your feet. Then white coats are provided so that you can be seen when you enter the darkrooms. Corridors leading to the film cutting department are dark, with a white line down the centre, dim red lamps overhead, and green glow-worm lights on corners and obstructions.

On the way to tea a stop is made to see the finished boxes of film and cartridges being labelled, checked and packed. The familiar yellow Kodak boxes move on conveyor belts round the factory floor and overhead in the corridors.

Practical details: The supervisor, Mr. R. W. Pole, can arrange visits for individuals and groups of up to twenty-five people, Monday to Friday. Contact him a month in advance. Children must be fourteen years or over. Tours last about two hours and start at 2 pm except on Friday when they start at 10 am. Because there is a large amount of walking and some stair climbing the tours are not suitable for the disabled, although it is possible to modify tours. Morning visitors are served coffee and afternoon visits end with tea. Parking space is available.

44 Artists' Paints and Brushes

Winsor & Newton Limited
Wealdstone, Harrow HA3 5RH
Tel: 01-427 4343

Winsor & Newton's Wealdstone works is a vast site of several factories. Different workshops produce paints, inks, brushes, canvasses, not

A big paint vat at Winsor & Newton

to mention aluminium tubes and a host of artists' accessories.

The artists' materials industry is too small to be able to afford special machinery, so machines for making tubes and containers are adapted from the cosmetics and grocery industries. In some cases the tubes are filled by sausage-making machinery, and labelled with beer labelling machines!

To make brushes, sable tails are imported from Russia and China. It takes four years to learn how to make a brush. For sable brushes the fluff is combed out, the hairs are graded for size, and given a point. For hog brushes the bristles are bleached, put in a ferrule, and attached to the wooden handle.

Practical details: Unfortunately school children under fourteen years of age are not admitted for safety reasons. Groups of up to twenty, art teachers, practising artists and professionals are accepted. Tours are arranged by appointment Monday to Thursday, throughout the year. The usual starting times are 10.15 am and 2.15 pm and tours normally take two hours. A prompt start is appreciated as tours have to be carefully timed to avoid factory breaks.

For further information please telephone the publicity department.

45   Musical Instruments

Boosey & Hawkes
Deansbrook Road, Edgware
Middlesex HA8 9BB
Tel: 01-952 7711

Boosey and Hawkes are the largest musical instrument manufacturers in Europe. Five hundred people are employed at this factory, where brass and woodwind instruments are made. The tour includes seeing the press shop where tubing is pressed into shape, a look at brass being polished, and a visit to the tuning room. The instruments made are trumpets, cornets, trombones, flugel horns, tenor horns, clarinets, oboes and flutes.

The tour ends with a visit to the museum which has brass and woodwind instruments dating back to 1750.

Practical details: Guided tours are given on Wednesdays only, at any time of year except during works' holidays. Tours start at 10 am and 2 pm and last two hours. They are intended for people with musical connections such as schoolchildren (aged over eleven), orchestras and musicians. Individuals and couples can usually get on a tour within a fortnight. Full groups of forty people (maximum) need to book a year in advance, groups of up to ten people two months in advance. Telephone, and write to confirm dates.

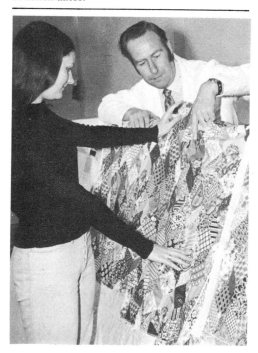

46   Fabric Printing

Sanderson Fabrics
100 Acres, Oxford Road
Uxbridge, Middlesex
Tel: Uxbridge 38244

Sanderson's print over 2,000 colourful material designs. Some of the fabric is expensive, 'But it doesn't wear out — you get tired of it first', jokes the guide. In fact, the same patterns continue to be popular for years. You may recognise a William Morris design from the late 1800s on furniture in a modern department store.

Customers often wish to re-order matching material for curtains and upholstery months or years after their first purchase. So Sanderson's keep a record of every colour used in a design. The squares of colour are printed on a piece of material the size of a traycloth, and it is locked away. Every time a new batch of colour is mixed, an experienced person compares the new squares with the old one before printing can begin.

As the fabric is printed it jerks along under a series of screens — one screen for each colour. The fabric moves. The screens come down. The screens go up. The fabric moves. Every piece of cloth now goes through several processes including rinsing, oxidising to fix the colour, soaping to make sure the colours are fast and a final rinsing. Overhead you can see the material running over steam filled cylinders.

Finally the material is checked against an illuminated screen. It is graded for colour, and weaving faults are marked with tags so that the cutter can cut up to the fault when despatching orders. Thousands of metres of bright, pretty material are despatched from here every day.

At the end of the tour, groups have tea and biscuits in the canteen and can ask the guide questions. The processes are quite complicated and as there is a certain amount of noise in the factory, visitors usually take this opportunity to discuss some of the processes.

Practical details: The factory tour is popular with groups such as school-leavers, home economics students, art colleges and women's clubs. Each tour is for up to twenty people, aged sixteen or over. Tours take place at 2.15 pm prompt, on Tuesday and Wednesday throughout the year except during holiday periods. Write to Mrs. B. Marshall, personnel and training officer, three months in advance. The nearest public transport is ten minutes away, so visitors come by coach or car. Allow extra time for finding the factory which covers a large area at the end of a long driveway.

47 Farm—Dairy, Pig and Arable

Oakridge Farms Limited
Blackbirds Farm
Aldenham, Near Watford, Hertfordshire
Tel: Radlett 6518

Cows and pigs are bred on the farm. Wheat, barley and oats are grown as fodder. Dairy products, yoghurt, pork, potatoes and vegetables are produced here, and sold through the Church Farm shop from 9 am to 5 pm, seven days a week.

Practical details: School parties are accepted on Mondays to Fridays. A farm trail will be arranged for children to follow. The public are welcome on the farm open day, on a Sunday in July, when a combine harvester is demonstrated and there are weaving and thatching displays. The open day attracts five to ten thousand visitors!

48 Jewellery Design and Engraving

Gosslow
Luton Road, Markyate, Hertfordshire
Tel: Luton 840378

Clare Street is a designer and craftsman in gold and silver jewellery. She makes wedding and engagement rings, and also does hand engraving, including the engraving of seals and miniature portraits. Some redesigning work is done for customers who want their gemstones in a new setting.

Practical details: Individuals and very small groups accepted by appointment.

49 Trug Making

Thomas Smith (Herstmonceux) Ltd
Herstmonceux
East Sussex
Tel: Herstmonceux 2137

A trug is a boat-shaped basket which gets its name from the old English word 'trog' meaning boat-like. Thomas Smith, the

Mrs Winnie Smith making a trug

founder of the firm, designed the original trug over 150 years ago, and Queen Victoria ordered several at the Hyde Park Exhibition in 1851. When they had been made, Mr Smith walked the 60 miles from Herstmonceux to London to deliver them to her personally. The modern-day trug has changed little. It is still hand-made from willow boards set in an ash or chestnut frame.It is a light strong basket and the open shape makes it particularly useful in the garden. In addition to garden trugs with supporting feet, the firm manufactures fireside log trugs, square trugs, bowls, and oval trugs decorated with pokerwork. A guide explains the processes, and you will see the pieces of wood used for the frame being shaved to the correct thickness, the bending of the frame around the shaping box, and the overlapping leaves of willow being hammered to the frame. Several of the staff of nine work only part-time, and there is more to be seen in the mornings. Perfect quality trugs are on sale to visitors at special prices.
Practical details: Individuals are welcome to call without notice. The shop is open Monday to Friday from 9 am until 5 pm, and the works keep the same hours but close for lunch at 1 pm. Groups (maximum 15 people) please book. School children over 14 years are accepted. The half-hour tour is free.

50   Public Records Office

Public Records Office
Ruskin Avenue
Kew, Surrey
Tel: 01-876 3444 Ext: 461

The most up-to-date archive building in the world, opened in 1977, has a computerised system for finding documents on the 80 miles of shelving, paging you and delivering them in 15 minutes by electric tricycle. Subjects include the wars, police, prisons, health and maps.
Practical details: Open Monday to Friday 9.30 to 5. Tours are arranged for schools, architects' groups etc.

51   Organ Building and Bread Baking

Robert Shaftoe
Woodlands Craft Centre
Thurleigh Road, Milton Ernest, Bedford
MK44 1RF
Tel: Oakley 2914

Woodlands craft centre is an old stone house which was once a vicarage. A converted barn in the grounds is a workshop for Robert Shaftoe who builds and restores organs, including barrel organs. He makes harpsichords on the premises. Although he is often away from Woodlands restoring church organs, he always likes talking to people who share his interest in the instruments.
Telephone in advance so that Robert can be there to meet you.
The old walled vegetable garden should prove of interest to those who like bees. It contains several hives, and talks and demonstrations can be arranged. Protection is provided for anyone who would like to see inside a hive!

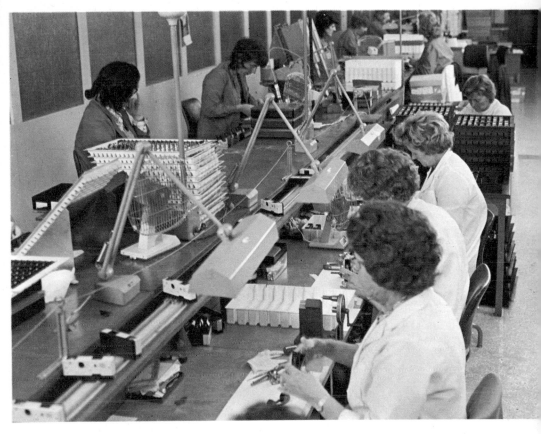

Assembly of Kodak Instamatics

Honey is for sale and home-made honey oatcakes, tea and coffee are available. Doreen Chetwood, who runs the Craft Centre, gives home-made bread demonstrations in her kitchen to a maximum of twenty people. There is no entry fee but a charge of 15p per head is made for demonstrations.

The recipes used for the home-made cakes and breads served for teas are on the Woodlands' English Country Recipe Cards. As their name Hastymake suggests they are easy to make and the cards are very attractive to hang in the kitchen.

Practical details: The craft centre is open Monday to Saturday from 10 am to 5.30 pm and on Sunday from 2 pm to 5 pm. Both individuals and groups are welcome but you must phone in advance.

Coach parties are welcome to the centre on Wednesday and Thursday and tea or coffee is available at Woodlands or in the nearby village hall, depending on numbers. Book well in advance.

The craft centre is opposite Milton Ernest Church, just off the A6, five miles north of Bedford.

52   Car Factory

Vauxhall Motors Limited
Kimpton Road, Luton, Bedfordshire
Tel: Luton 21122 Ext: 3321

There are three main types of visit — morning, afternoon and all-day tours — starting at 10

Visitors in Vauxhall's finish hall

am or 1.45 pm and finishing at 12.15 pm or 4.30 pm. Those visitors on the 'short tour' are shown a short film, then they see the complete car assembly procedure and finishing operations, including body panel pressing, body building, painting, trimming, final assembly and final finishing operations. All-day visitors also see the production of engines on ultra-modern transfer machines, and assembly and testing on flow-line principles. They have the choice of seeing Bedford van assembly or engine machining and assembly. Visits to the Bedford truck factory, five miles away, can also be made if requested in advance.

Visitors should wear comfortable shoes and be prepared for a lot of strenuous walking as the tour covers several levels of the factory. No wheel chairs are available. In short, the tour is only suitable for the fit and energetic. Children under 14 years are not accepted for safety reasons.

No souvenir cars are given away and you cannot buy 'seconds' (at least not from here), but as the tours, morning coffee and 4 pm tea are free, and all-day visitors get lunch in addition, it seems that visitors are treated quite generously and should have an interesting time.

A car park is situated behind the showrooms in Kimpton Road, where visitors are received. **Practical details:** Individuals and groups are welcome on guided tours. These must be pre-booked by contacting Mr. T. O'N. Crowley, the supervisor of factory visits, as guides and catering facilities deal with only thirty people a day and Vauxhalls cannot accept extra casual visitors who decide to 'pop in'. Tours are arranged Monday to Friday, except on bank holidays.

53   Small Weavers and Spinners

Joyce Coleman
Speen Weavers and Spinners
Speen, Aylesbury, Buckinghamshire
Tel: Hampden Row 303

'If you are enthusiastic about genuine handwoven fabrics, and would like to see some of the few remaining hand-looms still at work, you have only to come along to Speen and I will show you the whole operation,' says Joyce Coleman.

'Your interest may be in fine silks, curtains, or individual wall hangings; it may be in floor-mats; you may wish to indulge yourself in a once-in-a-lifetime luxury of a personal design which will be unique to yourself alone, and will never be repeated.

All goods are for sale.

A charge of 20p is made for parties of visitors who like to be shown the work in progress. No catering facilities are available but on occasion and with plenty of notice the W.I. are willing to do teas in the village hall not five minutes' walking distance.

Practical details: Joyce Coleman writes, 'In normal circumstances I am available any afternoon but if you find it more convenient to make your call in the morning, it would be as well to telephone in advance. I might also be out and everything shut up if people arrive out of the blue so a fortnight's notice is a great help. People come as individuals or in parties — only about eight to twelve people can actually come in at a time but others wait in their coaches or cars till there is room for another batch.'

Follow the 34 bus route out of High Wycombe, up the Hughenden Valley for about five miles, into Speen.

54 Milk Bottling

County Dairies Limited
Langford Lane, Kidlington
Oxford OX5 1JB
Tel: Kidlington 3833

Visitors see milk arriving, being processed and packed into bottles and cartons. Guided tours last forty-five to sixty minutes and there is no charge.

Practical details: The dairies are open during normal working hours, but not at weekends or bank holidays. Individuals and groups of up to twenty people are accepted, and children over eleven years. Contact Mr. P. J. Viggers or Mr. P. Vernon two weeks in advance.

55 Didcot Power Station

Central Electricity Generating Board
Didcot Power Station
Oxfordshire OX11 7HA
Tel: Didcot 813495

On arrival, visitors are shown a film about the power station. During the tour, which lasts for about 1½ hours, you see the boilers, steam turbines, generators, control room, gas turbines and coal unloading.

Power stations produce some staggering statistics. Didcot Power Station supplies 2,000 megawatts of electricity from 4x500 megawatt units — this is enough for ten cities the size of Oxford. Each of the boilers at full load burns 200 tons of coal and produces over 3¼ million pounds of steam per hour. There is a closed loop cooling water system which circulates a million gallons of water per minute. To re-cool this water there are six massive cooling towers, 375 feet high.

When you are standing outside you may be able to see the flue gases released from a 650 feet high chimney at 50 miles per hour.

Practical details: Tours of the power station are held Monday to Friday at 10.30 am and 2 pm, excluding bank holidays, and at 7 pm when lighter evenings make this possible. Requests for visits by individuals or groups should be made in writing to the station manager one month in advance. Up to thirty people can be accepted at one time. Restricted tours are given to children under fourteen years of age.

The power station is not very easy to reach by public transport — go by car or arrange a coach or minibus for your group if you can.

56 Wine-Making

Hambledon Vineyards Limited
Hambledon, Portsmouth
Hampshire PO7 6RY
Tel: Hambledon 475

This is an interesting visit for anyone who enjoys winemaking, wine drinking, or simply fresh air. Major-General Sir Guy and Lady Salisbury-Jones welcome visitors. They write, 'Visitors can see five acres of grapes growing on vines in the open. Notice boards explain the vineyard. Wine-making equipment can be seen in the press-house where a short tape-recorded talk explaining wine-making is given.

'We only make one wine and this is a dry white wine. It is not considered possible to make a good red wine in this northern climate, nor is it possible to make a natural sweet wine'. Most of the wine is sold to merchants and restaurants in the south of England but quite a lot is exported. All the wine is bottled here. It is drinkable after three months in the bottle, but it is at its best after about three years. You can buy wine at the vineyard (except when prohibited by Sunday licensing laws), and also from the local village grocers.

Light refreshments including a cup of tea, biscuits and cakes can be obtained at the vineyard. Afterwards you are welcome to relax in the gardens and enjoy the view over the Hampshire Downs. Also wine tasting.

Practical details: The vineyard is open to the general public every Sunday, including bank holidays, from 2.30 pm to 3.30 pm, from late July to early October. It is also open on certain Mondays, Wednesdays and Saturdays. Booked parties are accepted on several other dates.

Contact the secretary, Lady Salisbury-Jones. There is a small admission price and a free car and coach park adjoins the vineyard. The tour takes about an hour.

57   Oil-fuelled Power Station

Fawley Power Station
Fawley, Southampton, Hampshire
Tel: Fawley 551

Fawley power station is one of the largest in Europe, having an output of two million kilowatts. It is also the first station in this country to be under computer control. The station was built to meet the rising demand for electricity in the south. It is on the western shores of Southampton Water — this site is convenient for the supply of fuel oil from the nearby refinery and because sea water is available for cooling. There is no need for cooling towers.

About ten thousand tons of oil are consumed in a day when the full load is required. Each of the four main boilers has thirty-two burners and consumes about 110 tons an hour. For the cooling process, eleven and a half million gallons of sea water are needed every hour for each of the four turbine condensers.

Four extra gas turbine-driven generators cope with peak loads and emergencies. They produce enough electrical power to run all the electrical equipment associated with each main boiler and turbine. So, in the event of disconnection from the grid, or at times of very high load demand, the station has its own internal electricity power supplies.

Practical details: For permission to visit write to the station superintendent or telephone the training engineer or personnel office at Southampton 893051. Individuals or groups of up to fifty people (aged over fourteen) can be accommodated at any time. Younger children are given a restricted tour by special arrangement. A guide accompanies the tour, which is free. Catering can be provided in special cases only. Parking is available.

58   Cosmetics and Toiletries

Columbia Products Company Limited
Sherbourne Avenue, Binstead
Ryde, Isle of Wight PO33 3QA
Tel: Ryde 3761

A conducted tour is given of the modern factory where toiletries and some cosmetics are prepared, and toilet holdalls, cosmetic bags and beach bags are manufactured.

Visitors can buy items they have seen being made from the site shop at slightly preferential prices.

Practical details: Visitors are welcome Monday to Friday, except on bank holidays, and appointments should be made with the party receptionist. Organised parties of thirty to thirty-five people are preferred.

59   Small Glassmaking Studio

Michael Rayner
Island Glass, The Broadway
Totland Bay, Isle of Wight
Tel: Freshwater 2116

Michael Rayner claims that this is the smallest
full-time studio in the UK. You can see free
blown glass-making.
Practical details: The showroom is open
Monday to Saturday from 9 am to 6 pm (closed
1 pm to 2 pm). Visitors can only see the studio
by arrangement.

60   Ceramics and Paintings

Ventnor Pottery Studio
10 Victoria Street
Ventnor, Isle of Wight PO38 1ET
Tel: Ventnor 852871

'I am strictly a one-man potter-ceramic artist
and painter,' says John Reilly. 'The majority
of my time is spent on decorative painting

Aerial view of Didcot power station

with coloured glazes and, from Easter to
November, I do this in the studio-showroom.
Visitors can therefore watch me at work and I
am quite willing to explain the techniques
and answer questions.
My oil paintings are mostly done in the winter
months in a studio below the showroom and
visitors cannot watch me at work here.
However, I am willing to show people this
studio if they are sufficiently interested. My
paintings are modern semi-abstracts and are
on display in the small showroom.
'In ceramics I have over the past 20 years
developed my own unique technique of
painting decorative panels with coloured
glazes. A distinctive feature is that the design
motif is in colourful gloss glazes and the
background is in a matt grey finish of my own
invention.
Mr. Reilly also does single tiles, flat dishes,
lamp bases and vases decorated in the same
technique and style. Favourite themes are
story-book ships, fanciful fish and seahorses,

elephants with howdahs and friendly lions.
Practical details: The pottery is open Monday
to Saturday from 9 am to 1 pm and 2 pm to 6
pm. It is open on bank holidays but closed on
Sundays, Christmas week, and possibly for
one week at the end of October or early
November.
Individuals are welcome at any time but there
is only room for small groups of about ten
people at a time. No warning is required but it
is wise to telephone beforehand in winter in
case John Reilly is out for a short while.

61   Vineyard and Vine Nursery

Cranmore Vineyard
Yarmouth, Isle of Wight PO41 0XY

The vineyard was started as a part-time
venture in 1967 and is now a full-time business
run by Bob Gibbons and Nick Poulter —
enthusiasts who point out that southern
England has similar temperatures to some of
the German winegrowing regions and
sometimes better sunshine. Winegrapes are
sweet and as good to eat as dessert grapes, but
only the winegrapes will produce a really
good wine.
The vineyard produces high quality Estate
Bottled Wine and vines from its own nursery.
In 1976 36,000 plants were produced. Visitors
are shown round the vineyard and see vines,
from first year plants to those bearing mature
crops. The cellar is included in the tour and
the process of making wine is described. The
grapemill, press, fermentation tanks and
bottling equipment can be seen. A tasting of
the wine is given after the tour and questions
are welcomed. Wine, potted vines and books
on vinegrowing and winemaking are on sale.
Practical details: Guided tours of the vineyard
and cellar are given on Sunday afternoons at 3
pm from the last Sunday in July to the first
Sunday in October inclusive, and on Saturday
afternoons from the last Saturday in
September to the first in October, at the same
time.
Visitors cannot be seen at other times because
of a heavy work load and lack of free staff.
Parties of more than six should book in

writing to avoid overcrowding. Up to sixty
people can be accepted in a group. The
admission charge is 50p for adults and 35p for
children.
Approach the vineyard from Cranmore
Avenue, an unmetalled road leading north
from the A3054, 2½ miles out of Yarmouth.

62   Restored Water Mill

Yafford Mill
Shorwell, Newport, Isle of Wight
PO30 3LH
Tel: Brightstone 740610

This beautifully restored eighteenth century
water mill is in full working order and has a
unique collection of carefully restored antique
farm machinery and tools. The mill is
surrounded by ponds and streams stocked
with trout and teeming with wildlife.
Features include natural displays of waterfowl,
rare cattle, sheep and pigs, and the Yafford
seals.
Tours are not guided but all exhibits are
clearly marked and staff are readily available
to answer questions. Children in school
groups are given a free brochure and
worksheet.
There is a beautiful riverbank nature walk, a
children's play area, refreshment bar, and
well-stocked gift shop.
Practical details: The mill is open Easter to
October from 10 am to 6 pm and on Sunday
from 2 pm to 6 pm. There is no limit to the size
of groups but as reception for coaches is
limited, it is advisable to give advance notice.
There is an admission charge, with reductions
for children, o.a.ps and parties.

SEE THE MIDLANDS AT WORK

including East Anglia

Suffolk, Norfolk, Lincolnshire
Cambridgeshire, Northamptonshire
Leicestershire, Nottinghamshire
Derbyshire, Staffordshire
West Midlands, Warwickshire
Gloucestershire
Hereford and Worcester, Salop

1   Pottery—Oven-to-table Ware

Henry Watson's Potteries Limited
Wattisfield
Diss, Suffolk IP22 1NH
Tel: Walsham-le-Willows 239

In front of this factory the remains of an old
Roman kiln are displayed. Pottery-making
has been carried out in Wattisfield since before
the age of recorded history.

By the factory door is a large beehive-shaped
kiln, last used in 1961. It was fired by seven
coal furnaces. Now the factory uses electric
kilns. Inside you will see oblongs of mixed
clay which have had air bubbles squeezed out
of them, and these are then made into the rows
of moulded teapots and crockery. One woman
shows you how she sponges the lines where
two halves of a pot are joined together, while
another presses handles onto mugs.
Coloured glaze is then sprayed on by a group
of girls in another area, and across the way, in
the warehouse, finished articles are stacked

high. Here you will find the seconds shop
where you may buy a souvenir of your visit.
Practical details: Tours of the factory can be
arranged by appointment Monday to Friday
except for a fortnight in the July-August
period when the annual holiday is taken.
Times of arrival are 10.45 am, 2.15 or 3.15 pm
and the visit takes about three-quarters of an
hour. Groups may also visit the factory in the
evening although there is no production in
progress.
The shop, selling seconds, is normally open
Monday to Saturday from 9.30 am to 5 pm,
and remains open if there is a special
evening tour.
No conducted tours can be arranged for
individuals.

2   Jigsaw Puzzles

The Jigsaw Puzzle Centre
Mill Green, Stonham Aspal
Near Stowmarket, Suffolk IP14 6DA
Tel: Stonham 263

The puzzles are all for children up to about ten
years of age, starting with the Baby Jigsaws in
ten designs which are a silk-screened tray type
of jigsaw where the pieces fit into a
background. This type of puzzle is repeated in
the Junior Jigsaw, Nursery Jigsaw, Double
Inset Jigsaw and the Caroline Ford Puzzles.
There is a Lift-Out Puzzle of similar design —

the pieces lift out to reveal a coloured print underneath.

Practical details: The factory is open in the summer on Tuesday or Wednesday afternoons to individuals. Parties should book in advance. Schools and playgroups are very welcome and the visit is suitable for any age group. Evening visits can be arranged for a minimum of twenty-five people. There is no charge for visiting the factory or showroom. Factory seconds are available in the showroom which is open daily from 9 am to 4 pm closing for lunch between 12 noon and 1.30 pm and usually at weekends, too — but as they do a number of shows and exhibitions it is best to phone first.

3   Food Manufacturers

Colman Foods
Carrow, Norwich NR1 2DD
Tel: Norwich 60166

The factory buildings are spread over a vast complex of sixty acres and you will see

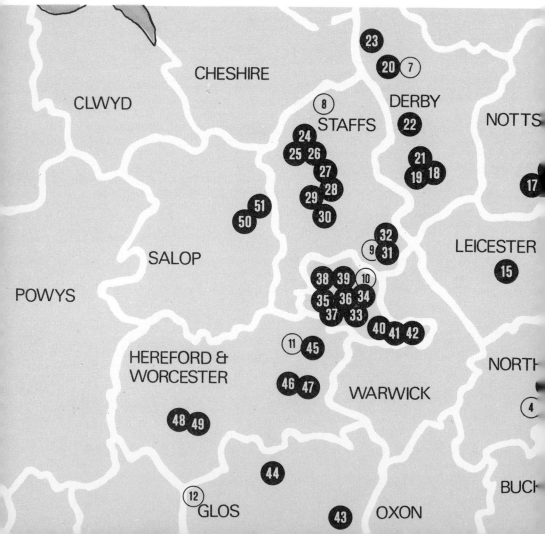

mustard flour being milled and packed: also many other products which are produced and packed here, such as barley waters, whole-fruit drinks, baby foods and honey.

Practical details: Conducted tours of some of the manufacturing departments of the factory are held from April to October, except during holiday periods at Easter, Whitsun and August when most of the factory is closed. Tours take place on Tuesday, Wednesday and Thursday afternoons starting at 2 pm prompt and lasting until 4 pm. Tea is then served and visits usually finish about 4.30 pm.

The number of people in any party is limited to thirty-five. Children over the age of twelve are accepted provided they are accompanied by an adult. School groups are welcomed if the students are fourteen years old or over. As the tour involves a good deal of stair climbing it is not recommended for elderly people or those with heart troubles. Party visits are heavily booked but five places are reserved each visiting day for people who wish to make a visit on that day or within that week. Bookings can be made at The Mustard Shop, 3 Bridewell Alley, Norwich.

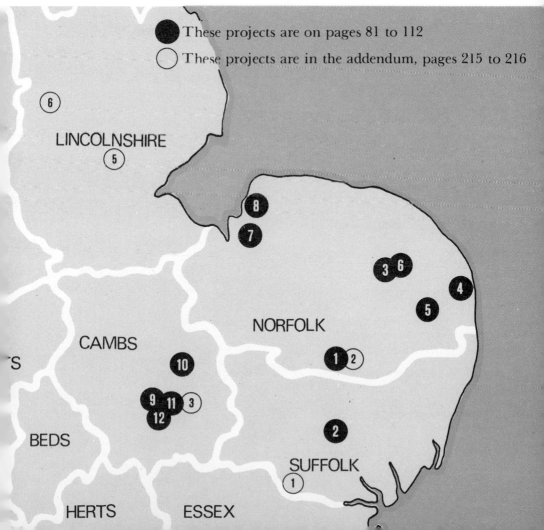

These projects are on pages 81 to 112

These projects are in the addendum, pages 215 to 216

LINCOLNSHIRE

NORFOLK

CAMBS

BEDS

SUFFOLK

HERTS   ESSEX

4   Power Station

South Denes Power Station
South Denes Road
Great Yarmouth, Norfolk
Tel: Great Yarmouth 4983

The visit consists of a short film show
followed by a guided tour of the plant lasting
in all about fifty minutes.
Practical details: Tours are organised Monday
to Friday from June to September each year at
10 am and 11 am and at 2 pm, 3 pm and 4 pm.
Admission is free by ticket obtainable from the
power station gatehouse or Great Yarmouth
Information Bureau.
Visits outside these times can be arranged by
writing to the station manager. Individuals
are welcome and the station prefers groups of
less than forty.

5   Feathercraft and Taxidermy

Pettitts Rural Industries Limited
Reedham, Norwich
Norfolk NR13 3UA
Tel: Freethorpe 243/4

Pettitts Rural Industries include feathercraft
and taxidermy. The products, which are on
sale to visitors, include feather flowers,
foliage, posies, quill pens, coffee tables,
plaques with feather designs and many other
feather products unobtainable elsewhere.
The feathers come from the main business of
the company, which is table poultry and
game.
Apart from making wedding bouquets to
order (two months' notice needed) Pettitts hire
out their stuffed animals. So if you want to
hire a baby sea-lion for an exhibition, or
perhaps a crocodile or python (coiled with
head raised), this is where to get it. Some of the
creatures are unnervingly realistic.
After you have seen the taxidermy you may
also like to look at the collection of natural
history specimens. Then, flocks of live
peacocks and many ornamental birds,
including waterfowl and black swans, can be

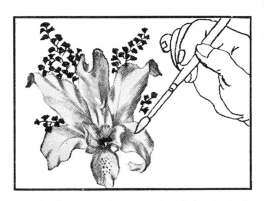

seen in the attractive grounds, which include
pools, bridges and summer-houses.
Pettitts were pioneers of the oven-ready
chicken, and poultry is sold from the freezer in
their showroom. Take a freezer bag along if
you are likely to want to buy something.
Practical details: Pettitts Rural Industries are
open throughout the year, Monday to Friday
from 9 am to 5 pm, and on Saturday from 9 am
to 12 noon; also on bank holidays, except for
Good Friday, Christmas Day and Boxing Day.
Individuals and groups are welcomed
including children and school parties. Large
groups should get in touch with the company
a week in advance. There is an admission
charge.
Pettitts is near Reedham's fine thatched
church. Approaching Reedham from the
South you must cross the river Yare by chain
ferry, which cannot carry coaches. Allow
about 20 minutes extra for travelling.

6   Large Shoe Factory

Norvic Shoe Company Limited
St. George's Plain, Norwich
Norfolk NR3 1DB
Tel: Norwich 23171

Norvic employs 2,000 people in Britain, with
factories in Northampton and Mansfield.
There are two factories in Norwich, both open
for factory visits. The Kiltie factory at St.
George's Plain specialises in children's
footwear. Ladies' shoes are made at the

Heathside Factory, Vulcan Road North, Norwich.

The Heathside factory has been described as a football pitch with a roof, because it has an area of 26,000 square feet under a single span roof. The 400 or so employees mostly work on a piece work basis and they produce 18,000 to 20,000 pairs of shoes a week. The building incorporates as much automation as possible — given that the fashion industry demands changes of styles every season.

During the tour you will visit the leather room and learn about different types of leather. Leather is tanned to make it soft and flexible and less smelly. The top or hair side produces grain leather. Thick skins can be divided so that the underside can be used as suede. The split side, not the flesh side, is buffed to make suede. Leather may also be plated (pressed smooth and flat with a hydraulic press), printed (embossed with a pattern such as the crocodile look), or made into patent (covered with PVC).

In the pattern clicking room the leather pieces are stamped out — this is rather like cutting biscuits out of pastry. To ensure that the leather will stretch, clicking must be done diagonally from the centre or backbone. The front of both shoes of a pair must have a similar shade of colour and must be cut from the best part of the skin. The patterns are in many styles, made in several sizes, so clicking is a real skill.

Uppers are passed to a cyclic muller which conditions leather in four minutes — a job which once took a whole day. The ends of the flat leather uppers are then joined at the heel seam using the natural stretch of the material to make the curved top part of the shoe. Parts are glued together and sewn. Machinists also do fancy stitching at high speed to decorate the uppers. On the making tracks the uppers are pulled tightly on to the wooden lasts for the appropriate style of shoe and the upper takes on the shape of the last. The insole is placed under the last and the toe of the upper is pulled down over the insole.

The next operation is that of attaching soles and heels. Finally, the shoes are given linings, straps, tabs, buckles and bows — and toe puffs

are stuck inside. Any traces of glue are removed and shoes are given their final inspection before being packed into boxes. At intervals along the assembly lines there are inspection points. Shoes which show faults early on must be discarded, but shoes which are rejected at the last stage — polishing — may have only a small scratch in the leather, and can be sold as rejects. You can buy them at roughly half normal retail prices in the cobbler's shop near the children's shoe factory entrance. The shop sells men's, ladies' and children's shoes to employees and it is also open to the public (even if they are not on the tour) Tuesday to Friday in the afternoon.

Practical details: The guides are retired members of staff who are called in specially to take parties around, so small parties or families will be asked to fit in with dates chosen by larger groups. Tours are arranged during factory working hours, Tuesday to Thursday. No tours are held on bank holidays nor for a few days at Christmas, Easter and Whitsun as well as for a fortnight at the end of July or the beginning of August. All kinds of groups, including school parties, are accepted, but children touring the factory must be at least thirteen years of age. Telephone or write to Mrs. D. J. Hazell in personnel.

7 Hand-blown Glass Ware

Wedgwood Glass
Oldmeadow Road, King's Lynn, Norfolk
Tel: King's Lynn 3899

King's Lynn was a glass-making centre from the seventeenth to the nineteenth centuries. But when the Wedgwood glass factory was opened in 1967 glass-blowers had to be brought from abroad — mainly Sweden — before local people could be trained. Now about one hundred are employed here making hand-blown glass-ware, including full lead cut crystal.

Glasses, decanters and candlesticks are made, and paperweights in apple, pear and mushroom shapes. There are also glass animals — seals, whales, snails, polar bears,

mice, birds, ducks, penguins and owls.
Practical details: Guided tours of the factory
are given Monday to Friday from 10 am to
2 pm. Write for an appointment, giving at
least two dates, and as much advance
notice as possible. All are welcome. The
factory is closed on bank holidays.
There is a small admission charge. The
souvenir shop is open Monday to Saturday.

8   Lavender Harvesting

Norfolk Lavender Limited
Caley Mill, Heacham
King's Lynn, Norfolk PE31-7JE
Tel: Heacham 70384

Norfolk Lavender are the largest growers and
distillers of lavender in Britain. Linn Chilvers,
whose name appears on all Norfolk Lavender
products, started growing Norfolk Lavender
for distillation in 1932 with two acres of fields.
Now nearly one hundred acres of lavender are
harvested each summer and six varieties are
distilled. Lavender used to be cut by hand, but
today the flowers are harvested by the
company's specially designed cutters.
The perfumer's art lies in blending the
different oils. The formulae are based on an
eighteenth-century recipe, when lavender was
a favourite with both sexes. Until recently,
flower perfumes have been more popular
amongst the older generation, but nowadays
flower fragrances are back in fashion.
If you wish to take home a little of 'the scent of
English summer' you may buy lavender
perfume, talcum powder, bath cubes, travel
soap, mini soap tablets for guests, hand-made
sachets containing dried lavender flowers,
after-shave or talc for men — all dried by the
company's new drying plant which you may
see in operation. You may also purchase
lavender seedlings in pots for your garden.
Practical details: Visitors are welcome during
the period when the lavender is in full bloom
and being harvested and distilled. This takes
place every year from early July to mid-
August. Individual cars may call at Caley Mill

to obtain directions to the fields and distillery.
Visits for coach parties may be booked in
advance and a guided tour will be arranged for
them, if they write for a list of suitable dates.
These start at 10.30 am, 12 noon, 2 pm and 3.30
pm when the company's representative will
join your coach for the drive to the field where
harvesting is in progress, then to the distillery
and back. The round trip involves about
fifteen miles and takes about 1½ to 2 hours.
Visitors are not accepted on Sundays.
There is no charge but naturally the company
hopes that you will stop at Heacham after you
have enjoyed the lavender's colour and scent
out in the fields, so that you may look at the
company's products and perhaps buy
something. There is a tea room in the
mill grounds. Caley Mill is on the A149
two miles south of Hunstanton.

9   Doll Houses and Furniture

Den Young
63 Earith Road
Willingham, Cambridgeshire CB4 5LS
Tel: Willingham 60015

Den Young specialises in doll-house
construction, including small sixteenth and
seventeenth century Tudor houses. He models
individual period rooms complete with such
details as panelling and miniature chairs.
Practical details: Visits by telephone-
appointment only, for individual collectors
and really interested people. Sorry, no large
parties.

Norfolk Lavender—harvesting in July

10   Rural Weaving Workshop

Fenweave
37 Main Street
Witchford, Ely, Cambridgeshire
Tel: Ely 2150

All-wool tweeds, linens and many other kinds
of woven goods are made in this rural
workshop. Interested visitors will be shown
power looms at work and the processes will be
explained to them. There is a shop where
goods may be bought, and groups are
entertained with coffee and tea.
Practical details: Individuals are welcome
from 9 am to 5.30 pm, and in the evenings by
appointment. Closed on Sunday, Monday and
all bank holidays. Telephone Mrs. I. F. Allen
about an hour in advance. Parties of ten or

more should give two or three days' notice and
are accepted only in the evenings. No small
children.
The workshop is at the east end of the village.

11   Sculptor and Lettering Designer

Keith Bailey, FSDC
63 Eden Street, Cambridge
Tel: Cambridge 311870

Visitors will see various sculptures standing
around, together with any lettering work in
progress. He designs and carves individual
headstones and memorial tablets in stone,
slate or wood. Some of his work is restoration
carving but he prefers his own designs for
architectural, garden and domestic sculpture.
Practical details: It is advisable to telephone
Keith Bailey prior to a visit. He welcomes
small parties and individuals only.

12   Newspaper Production and Journalism

Cambridge Evening News
Cambridge Newspapers Limited
51 Newmarket Road, Cambridge CB5 8EJ
Tel: Cambridge 58877

Visitors are given a slide presentation and a tour, and a local school reports that they had a most enjoyable visit. The Cambridge Evening News is a large and well-known provincial paper, and the printing and production processes make this a worthwhile and exciting outing.
Practical details: The newspaper welcomes groups of up to fourteen people. Bookings are handled by the circulation department.

13   Large Modern Brewery

Carlsberg Brewery Limited
140 Bridge Street
Northampton NN1 1PZ
Tel: Northampton 21621

'You wouldn't necessarily expect a brewery to be a beautiful building,' say the company, 'but with our Scandinavian background we felt we had a certain design reputation to maintain. So Knud Munk, an award-winning Danish architect, was commissioned to design the brewery. The result, we like to think, demonstrates quite clearly that industrial design can be beautiful as well as functional.' Carlsberg Brewery spent over £20 million on designing and building this brewery and claim that it is one of the most beautiful lager breweries in the world.

The brewery has all the latest equipment, including a computer, and the control panel in the brewhouse controls the brewing process from the silo to the fermenting vessels. The process begins with the steeping vats and mills, then during the mashing process the crushed malt is mixed with water and heated in giant coppers.

Eventually the high-speed bottling section automatically fills, caps and labels every

High-speed bottling line at Carlsberg

bottle. This is one of the most fascinating sights, just like one of those films where bottles on an assembly line go jerking away to jangly modern music.

The output is about 54 million gallons a year. They make sure that the 'Carlsberg taste' is maintained by bringing over the strain of yeast developed way back in 1883. Samples of the brew are periodically sent across to Denmark where they are matched with the original brews.

Practical details: The brewery welcomes everyone except small children throughout the whole year, from Monday to Friday at 9.30 am and 2.30 pm. Contact Mr. Jorgen Kjeldback for an appointment.

14   Glass Modelling

The Glass Workshop
(The Rear of) 1 Bridge Street
Rothwell, Kettering, Northants.
Tel: Kettering 760165

Mr. Martin makes glass animals, birds, flowers and trees from glass rods and strips in thirty different colours. The figures take from five minutes to half an hour to make, depending on their size. He uses an oxy-butane lamp, which mixes one jet of oxygen and eight of gas. The oxygen makes the flame hotter. Most of the shaping is done with glass rods but he sometimes squeezes an ear or wing into shape with 'flappers'. These are strips of metal with U or V shaped or flat ends. Mr. Martin makes a range of about seventy items, from galloping horses carrying miniature jockeys, to cartoon-like elephants. All items are on sale. There are no seconds. 'Anything with a crack in it would eventually fall to pieces,' he explains.

Practical details: The workshop is open most times but phone to fix a definite time as Bob

Glass-modelling with an oxy-butane lamp

Martin does many shows and demonstrations to clubs. Individuals and small groups are most welcome to visit, though groups over ten in number would make viewing difficult.

15   Milk Bottling

Kirby & West Limited
Dairymen, Western Boulevard
Leicester LE2 7BS
Tel: Leicester 20131

Don't take your daily pinta for granted. As you may have noticed on holiday abroad, in countries where milk is not treated to make it safe you have to boil it, and this alters the taste — ruining your cup of coffee or tea. Here at the Western Boulevard dairy you can see milk being sterilised and pasteurised, then bottled. Twenty thousand gallons arrive every day in bulk tankers, also cream is separated from the milk and sold in cartons.

Practical details: Tours are arranged on Tuesday, Wednesday and Thursday. The guided tour, which is free, lasts about an hour and up to thirty people may be shown around at a time. Individuals and groups should contact Mrs Moore four to five weeks in advance. Tea and coffee are provided. You can also visit the company's herd of pedigree Guernsey cows at New Ingarsby Farm, Houghton on the Hill, Leicester.

16   Power Stations

Staythorpe 'A & B' Power Stations
Near Newark, Nottinghamshire
Tel: Newark 3371

The tour lasts approximately two hours. It begins with a short film about how electricity is made, followed by a tour of the plant, which is steam plant using pulverised (coal) fuel. The tour also includes a visit to the coal and ash plant, the boiler house and the turbine hall.

The Central Electricity Generating Board produces helpful booklets explaining how

power stations work. An electric current is made when you turn a loop of wire in a magnetic field. You can try this yourself in a small way using a small horseshoe magnet and a paperclip. The dynamo of a bicycle or car makes power in the same way. So does the power station, but on a very large scale. Here you will see the people and the machinery who make it possible for you to turn on the lights and use electrical appliances every day of your life.
Practical details: The power station is open from 10 am to 5 pm Monday to Friday. Applications should be made in writing to the station manager, giving at least three weeks' notice. Children under thirteen years are not eligible. Parties up to twenty-five in number can be accommodated. Sensible footwear should be worn at the station as it is an industrial site.
There are several other power stations in the Nottingham district which may be visited, so choose whichever one is the most convenient for you. All have similar facilities for visitors, and all provide a tour. We suggest that perhaps you select one of these three: West Burton power station near Retford; Ratcliffe-on-Soar power station; or High Marnham power station near Newark.
Write to individual station manager for appointments.

17   Bicycle Manufacturers

Raleigh Industries Limited
Lenton Boulevard
Lenton, Nottingham NG7 2DD
Tel: Nottingham 77761

This company is the largest cycle manufacturer in the world and the largest wheeled-toy manufacturer in Europe. They make more than 2,000 specifications of bicycles which are exported to more than 130 different countries. Raleighs are based on a 64-acre site in Nottingham, and have a total of eight factories.
Other products are car-seat slides, seats for commercial vehicles and many products

which are supplied to the motor industry.
Practical details: Individuals and groups should contact Bob Williams, the public relations officer, to make an appointment for a visit. The minimum age for visitors is sixteen years.

18   Airport

East Midlands Airport
Castle Donington, Derby DE7 2SA
Tel: Derby 810621

This international airport deals with a variety of types of aircraft from the most modern jet to the smallest private aircraft. Services include scheduled flights to the Continent and holiday flights to the majority of popular resorts. The airport has a spectators' area which provides a picnic place and a children's playground. You will also find a restaurant, buffet and car parks.
Practical details: The airport is conveniently near to the M1 motorway — take turn-off 24. For further details write to, or telephone, the Airport Director.

19   Industrial Museum

The Silk Mill
Silk Mill Lane, Off Full Street
Derby DE1 3AR
Tel: Derby 31111 Ext: 740

The first-floor gallery has the theme 'An Introduction to Derbyshire Industries'. Displays show how the county's geology has determined its industries including lead mining, coal mining, iron founding, limestone quarrying, ceramics and brick making. The textile industries are introduced with displays of handframe and machine knitting and narrow tape weaving. More sections are planned to show the rapid growth of railways and other engineering in the nineteenth and twentieth centuries.
The Rolls Royce aero engine collection shows the development of aero engines over the past

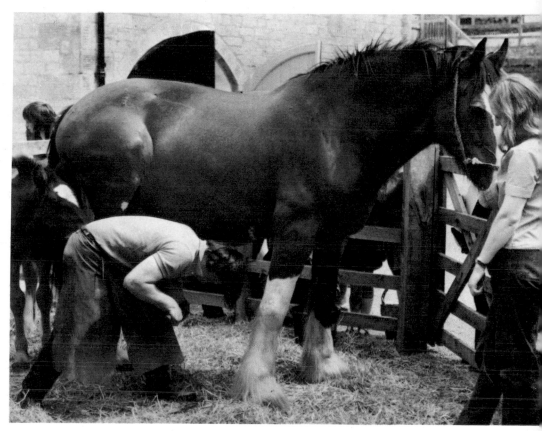

sixty years, plus the history of flying and aircraft, from the brilliant successes of the Wright brothers in 1903 with 'Flyer No 1' to the VTOL (vertical take-off and landing) aircraft of today.

Practical details: The museum is open for all members of the public on Tuesday to Friday from 10 am to 5.45 pm, and on Saturday from 10 am to 4.45 pm. It is closed on Sundays, Mondays, Good Friday, Christmas Day, Boxing Day and New Year's Day. There is a shop where goods may be purchased but no catering facilities are offered.

Admission is free and the nearest car park is in Full Street. Lessons offered in term-time include subjects like 'How aircraft fly' and 'Coal mining'. Teachers should contact the museum's education officer on extension 793.

20 Farming Demonstrations

The Farmyard at Chatsworth
Chatsworth, Bakewell
Derbyshire DE4 1PJ
Tel: Baslow 2242

The live farming and forestry exhibitions show visitors how the farms and woods on the Chatsworth Estate are managed. A milking demonstration takes place in a modern milking parlour every afternoon. Other demonstrations of farming and forestry activities are shown from time to time in summer.

The livestock on view include beef and dairy cattle and their calves, sheep of several different breeds, pigs (both sows with litters and fattening pigs), poultry of old-fashioned breeds and modern egg-producing birds. A number of working horses including a Shire, Haflinger, and Shetland ponies are also on view. The life-cycles of the animals are described and an explanation is given of their use on a farm.

There is plenty to see and do, even on wet days, as there are several undercover exhibitions on farming and forestry. You can also take lovely walks through the woods or visit Chatsworth House, with its palatial apartments and frescoed ceilings. The house is closed only on those Mondays and Tuesdays which do not fall on bank holidays.

Practical details: The farmyard is open to the public every day from the beginning of April to mid-October, Monday to Friday from 10.30 am to 4.30 pm. It is also open Saturdays and Sundays from 1.30 pm to 5.30 pm, and bank holiday Mondays and Tuesdays from 10.30 am to 5.30 pm. There is no guided tour of the farmyard, but school parties are catered for, and two-thirds of the visitors are children. School parties should write to the manager. Tea, coffee and biscuits are available in the Stables Tea Room (no need to book) and good catering facilities are available in Bakewell — famous for its tarts .

21   Porcelain Factory

Royal Crown Derby Porcelain Co. Limited
Osmaston Road, Derby DE3 8JZ
Tel: Derby 47051

Visitors are taken round the factory, where they may see fine bone-china tableware, figurines, china-handled cutlery, china brooches and ear-rings being made, and the final stage of the whole process, which is painting the china by hand.

The factory has a museum and visitors learn something of the factory's history. China has been made in Derby since 1752. The owner of the factory, William Duesbury, later bought the Chelsea works and moved some of its artists and workmen up to Derby. King George III gave his permission for the crown

to be incorporated into the backstamp in 1775, and in 1890 Queen Victoria agreed that the word 'Royal' could be added to the title.

A museum open day is held on the first Tuesday of every month (except on bank holidays) when members of the public may bring pieces of old Derby ware to be identified. If you have a well-cluttered attic, it might be worth checking to see if you have any old china.

Practical details: Morning tours are mainly reserved for overseas visitors. They start at 11 am on Monday, Wednesday and Thursday, and at 10.30 am on Friday. Up to fifteen people can be accepted on a tour. Afternoon tours are held Monday to Friday at 2 pm for up to thirty people. Individuals and groups should contact Miss E. Gore in advance. The admission charge covers the cost of a booklet on the history of the Derby factory.

Refreshments are available for organised parties if requested in advance.

22   Engine House of Inclined Railway

Middleton Top Engine House
High Peak Trail
Middleton-by-Wirksworth, Derbyshire
Tel: Matlock 3411 Ext: 7165 (Derbyshire County Council)

The engine house contains steam-winding equipment which was built in 1829 and hauled wagons up the Middleton slope. The incline is one in eight feet, and 708 yards long. The Derbyshire Industrial Archaeological Society has restored the engine house and a member of this society, or the countryside ranger, will explain the history of the railway and how the machinery works. There is a small entrance charge.

The Middleton incline is part of the Cromford and High Peak Railway which linked the Cromford and Peak Forest canals. It ran for thirty-three miles, carrying coal, iron, lime, corn and minerals to the main towns surrounding Derbyshire.

Practical details: The engine house is open on Sunday from 10.30 am to 5 pm. Everyone is welcome and groups may take mid-week visits by arrangement with the countryside ranger. He is Mr. K. Harwood, Rangers House, Middleton Top Picnic Area, Middleton-by Wirksworth, Derbyshire. Tel: Wirksworth 3204. Motorists may leave cars in the car parks at Middleton Top Engine House or Black Rocks picnic site. Both have picnic areas and toilets.

Testing blue Stilton cheeses

23   Stilton Cheese

J. M. Nuttall & Company
Dove Dairy, Hartington
Buxton, Derbyshire
Tel: Hartington 231/273

Here you can see Stilton cheese being made and stored in a modern factory — and rounds of cheese are on sale. The tour is free and, if the sight of all that food makes you hungry, there are several places where you may eat afterwards in Hartington village. These are open mainly in the summer months.

Practical details: Contact the manager of the dairy, Mr. I. C. Millward, to make an appointment. Factory tours are arranged from January to September, but are booked up well in advance. Groups of up to twenty-five or thirty people are welcome, though the tour is not suitable for small children or the elderly. Individuals and small family groups are welcome as long as they book ahead.

Painting a Royal Doulton figurine

24   Traditional Fine Bone China

Doulton Fine China
Nile Street, Burslem, Stoke-on-Trent
West Midlands ST6 2AJ
Tel: Stoke-on-Trent 84271

This is the largest factory in the Royal
Doulton Group, and it produces fine bone
china tableware, oven-to-tableware,
decorative wall plates and figurines.
Visitors see all the processes from the mixing
of raw materials, through firing clay in a kiln,
to decorating. The figurines are painted by
hand. Tableware is decorated with transfers —
the technical term is slide lithography.
In addition to making traditional bone china,
the company won the Queen's Award to
Industry for developing and producing ETC
— English Translucent China, which is
cheaper to produce yet approaches the beauty
and translucency of bone china. During the
tour you visit the factory shop.

Practical details: Tours are held all year round
— except on bank holidays — on Tuesday,
Wednesday and Thursday afternoons. Contact
the personnel department to make an
appointment. Children under fourteen are not
accepted in the factory, because of the
Factories Act, although they are allowed in the
showroom and shop. Up to ten people can be
accepted in a group and, though group visits
are booked a year ahead, individuals can join
one of the smaller parties if sufficient notice is
given. The shop is open to the public and you
may be interested in seeing the shop, if you are
in the area, but have not been able to get on a
tour. The factory is a modern, four-storey
building and the staircases might prove tiring
to the elderly or infirm. There is no charge.

25   Spode Bone China

Spode Limited
Stoke-on-Trent, Staffordshire ST4 1BX
Tel: Stoke-on-Trent 46011

The first Josiah Spode founded the Spode
factory in 1770. He perfected the method of
printing in blue underglaze and left his son a
thriving factory. The son, Josiah Spode II,
discovered the correct formula for bone china,
fifty per cent of which consists of calcined
cattle bone. Calcining is heating a substance
to a temperature at which it can be crushed or
refined. Spode issue a booklet which tells you
a great deal about the history and manufacture
of Spode wares. This information is very
useful if you are interested in pottery making
in general, as, for example, they list the main
ceramic colour groups.
The factory stands on its original site and
some of the first buildings are still standing.
Several of the manufacturing processes which
you will see on the tour have changed little
since the earliest times.
Practical details: Guided tours of the Spode
factory are arranged from Monday to Friday
each working week, and start at 10.15 am and
2.15 pm. The maximum number of people
acceptable is forty and because of factory
regulations children are only accepted if they

A printed transfer for a Spode plate

are aged twelve or over. Individuals and groups must write in advance — people who 'pop in' are not catered for. Groups should try to arrive promptly so that there is time to visit all the processes which are normally seen on the tour, which lasts 1¼ hours. There is a small charge but you may redeem some of this charge on a minimum purchase in the Spode gift shop, where ware is sold at greatly reduced prices.

26   Fine Bone China Factory

The Minton Factory, London Road
Stoke-on-Trent, Staffordshire
Tel: Stoke-on-Trent 47771

The Minton Factory is a modern two-storey building and it produces fine bone china tableware and fancy items such as vases, jugs and boxes. Downstairs you will see the raw materials and the making departments. Cups and plates are cast in moulds and handles are put on by hand. The china is fired in the biscuit kiln, dipped into glaze and fired a second time ready for decorating.

Upstairs you will see painting, decorating, lithography and gilding. One of the most interesting processes is gold acid work. This produces a design that is in relief by acid etching. Before immersion in the acid the areas of the plate where a relief design is not wanted are protected by a resistive material applied by a print and hand painting. After etching the resistive material is washed off and then gold in liquid form is applied to the etched areas and then fired. After firing the gold must be burnished.

On the ground floor is the works museum and people who cannot manage stairs, or antique collectors with a particular interest in old china can opt to spend their time in the museum instead of following the tour upstairs.

The shop has a stock of gift ware. Articles on sale include ashtrays, coasters, marmalade pots, cruet sets, cachepots for plants, oblong

A skilled engraver cuts the pattern for gold decoration of a Minton plate

sandwich trays and pairs of candlesticks.
Practical details: Morning tours are held on Tuesday, Wednesday and Thursday starting at 10.30 am and lasting one to one-and-a-half hours. These are for up to ten people. Afternoon tours for up to twenty people are held on Tuesday, Wednesday and Thursday starting at 2 pm. Individuals can sometimes join small groups which do not reach these numbers. Contact Mrs. E. Charlton. Tours take place all year except on bank holidays. Children aged thirteen or over are accepted. Five of the factories in the Royal Doulton Group have been described in the Midlands. The group covers twenty-two factories and there are plans to start factory visits to several more of them in 1977. For details, contact Mr. J. C. L. Sparre at the Royal Doulton Tableware Company's headquarters here at the Minton Factory.

27 Earthenware Factory

Royal Doulton Tableware Ltd (Beswick)
Gold Street, Longton
Stoke-on-Trent, Staffordshire
Tel: Stoke-on-Trent 313041

Seven hundred people are employed here and this is only the third largest of the Royal Doulton factories. (The largest is the factory at Nile Street, Burslem.) This factory specialises in animal and character studies.

On the tour you see the clay department, where the figures are made, sponging to remove the seams on moulded items, the decorating department where hand painting takes place, aerographing (colour spraying) before glazing, the kilns, and decorating on the glaze.

The shop sells seconds only. You will not find items from the connoisseur range here but there are many tempting and attractive items which would make ideal gifts for children and animal lovers. There are Beatrix Potter figurines, Winnie-the-Pooh, Kittie McBride characters such as the Family Mouse, Alice in Wonderland, foals, cattle, cats and dogs.

Practical details: Tours are held from March to October excepting bank holidays on Tuesday, Wednesday and Thursday afternoons for groups of up to twenty-four people. The minimum party booking is twelve, but individuals or couples could probably manage to join a group which was slightly smaller than the maximum accepted number. Children aged 14 and over are accepted. People who cannot climb stairs would not find this visit suitable. No charge is made for the tour. Contact Mrs. I. Underwood well in advance to make arrangements.

Royal Doulton—modelling a dog study

28   Pottery Museum

Gladstone Pottery Museum
Uttoxeter Road, Longton
Stoke-on-Trent, Staffordshire ST3 1PQ
Tel: Stoke-on-Trent 319232

A living and working museum of the British
pottery industry, which won the museum of
the year award in 1976. Named after Gladstone
in the late 19th century, it is an original and
typical early Victorian 'potbank', with four
spectacular bottle ovens, cobbled yard, engine
house (steam power once drove clay mixing
machinery) and workshops. Craftsmen and
women are working and demonstrating
pottery skills. Also historical, tile, colour and
sanitaryware galleries, and a museum shop.
Practical details: From April to September the
museum is open Monday to Friday from 10.30
am to 5.30 pm and on Sundays and bank
holidays 2 to 6 pm. Also Wednesday evenings
6.30 to 9 pm for booked parties only. From
October to March the times are as above but it
is closed on Monday and Wednesday evenings.
All visitors are welcome but groups of 10 or
more should book in advance. Guides are
available (maximum 20 persons per guide) at a
fixed cost for a 1½ hour session. Admission
charges for individuals are reduced for
children, students and senior citizens, with
half price for all on Saturday mornings. Write

enclosing an sae for party booking forms,
publications lists etc. There is a teashop.

29   Gardens/Horticultural Centre

Trentham Gardens Limited
The Estate Office, Trentham Estate
Staffordshire ST4 8AX
Tel: Stoke-on-Trent 657341

Trentham Gardens covers a huge area of seven
hundred acres around Trentham Lake. In
addition to the demonstration gardens, there
are shrub beds, a garden for the blind, a rose
garden, a peat garden and rockery, a sculpture
garden, a flower arrangers' garden and two
garden shops.
Plenty of entertainment is provided for all
ages. Throughout the summer season there
are special outdoor horticultural shows.
There are also such recreations as ski-ing,
scrambles, a swimming pool, boats, crazy golf,
miniature railway, pony rides, jungle
playground, ballroom, conference centre and
short-stay caravan site.
Practical details: Trentham Gardens estate is
open seven days a week. The Italian Gardens,
created by Capability Brown, are best seen in
the July to September period.
Campers and caravanners will find this a very
good place to stop on a touring holiday. The
location is most convenient, with the M6, exit
15 on one side, and the A34 Stafford-Stoke
trunk road on the other.

30   Wedgwood China

Josiah Wedgwood and Sons Limited
Barlaston, Stoke-on-Trent
Staffordshire ST12 9ES
Tel: Barlaston 3218

In 1759 Josiah Wedgwood — the 'Father of
English Potters' — founded his company.
Now in its third century, Wedgwood
manufactures a wide range of traditional and
modern ornamental and tableware in fine
bone china, Queen's Ware (fine earthenware),

Gathering molten glass at Webb Corbett

early 19th century. Examples of almost all the ceramic wares made by the first Josiah and his successors are displayed, with trials, early moulds, original wax models and documents. Full-length cases re-create parts of an 18th century pottery factory, such as a mouldmaker's workshop and a modelling studio. In the demonstration hall visitors see the traditional hand processes, many unchanged since Josiah's time, used to make Wedgwood today. For Jasper ware — throwing on the wheel, turning, figure-making and ornamenting. Also the casting of busts, figures and other ornamental items — mainly in Black Basalt, Josiah's first ornamental ware. Traditional and modern techniques for decorating fine bone china are usually also shown, including hand-lining, raised enamelling or colour transfer applications.

Practical details: The Wedgwood museum and visitor centre is open Monday to Friday 9 am to 4 pm except in certain holiday periods. An appointment is advisable. Parties up to 250 can be accommodated in a single visit. Children under 10 are not admitted and 10 to 15 years olds must be accompanied. Special arrangements can be made for schools.

31   Glass Blowing and Cutting

Webb Corbett Limited
Tutbury Glassworks, Tutbury
Near Burton-on-Trent
Staffordshire DE13 9NG
Tel: Burton-on-Trent 813281

On the tour you will see the jars of ingredients used in glassmaking, then glass making, hand blowing and hand cutting with diamond impregnated wheels. No intaglio work is done.
The factory shop sells first quality glassware at normal retail prices and seconds at reduced prices. Ware from the factory is sold in the shop — mainly 'fancies' — stemmed ware such as wine glasses — plus bowls, vases, jugs and tumblers. Useful advice is offered on how to look after glassware.

oven-to-tableware, Jasper and Black Basalt at this extensive modern factory near Stoke. Recently Wedgwood has expanded more than at any time in its 218-year history, acquiring famous, long-established and large tableware manufacturers. Wedgwood employed 2,400 people in 1966 and grew to a group of companies with over 9,000 employees in the UK by 1977. Its 20 factories produce a fifth of the British ceramic industry's output and a quarter of its exports.
Visitors see an award-winning film and tour the museum and craft demonstration area.
You will learn about Wedgwood's invention of Queen's Ware, Jasper and Black Basalt, and the development of fine bone china in the

Visitors touring the Wedgwood factory

Practical details: A small charge is made for tours which are held in the afternoons on Monday and Tuesday. Groups (up to 36 people) are accepted on Monday, and members of the public in twos and threes (up to 12 people on the tour) on Tuesday. In January 1978 Monday afternoon tours were already booked in advance until 1982! Tuesday afternoon visits were booked until July 1978. So get on the waiting list as soon as you can, by contacting Mr. W. M. Byatt. Secondary school parties are accepted and children, aged at least twelve, accompanied by parents. Please note that the tour involves quite a few stairs.

The factory shop is also open to members of the public who are not taking the tour, Monday to Friday from 9.45 to 11.45 am and 2 pm to 4 pm. As the shop is crowded on Monday afternoons because of party visits, casual callers are asked to choose another day of the week if possible.

32   Coal-fired Power Stations

Drakelow 'A', 'B' and 'C' Power Stations
Near Burton-on-Trent, Staffordshire
Tel: Burton-on-Trent 3341

The tour lasts approximately two hours. It begins with a short film about how electricity is made, followed by a tour of the plant, which is steam plant using pulverised (coal) fuel.

The tour also includes a visit to the coal and ash plant, the boiler house and the turbine hall. There are also the Rugeley 'A' and 'B' power stations at Armitage Road, Rugeley, which may be visited. Write to the individual station managers for details.

Practical details: The power station is open from 10 am to 5 pm Monday to Friday. Applications should be made in writing to the station manager, stating the time and dates preferred and the number in the party, giving at least three weeks' notice. Children under thirteen years are not eligible. Parties up to twenty-five in number can be accommodated. Individuals can arrange to visit on days when a small party is booked.

Sensible footwear should be worn at the station as it is an industrial site.

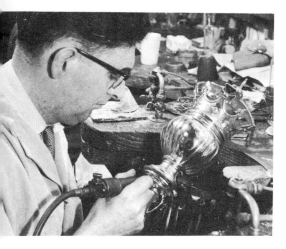

33   Silverware Factory

Thomas Fattorini Limited
Regent Street, Birmingham B1 3HQ
Tel: 021-236 1307

Seventy people work here making articles from silver and gold. Thomas Fattorini Limited produce silverware such as coffee pots, jewellery, insignia and badges of all kinds. The awards and medallions are ordered by schools, clubs, universities, hospitals, local authorities and foreign governments. On the tour you see several processes — items are designed, pressed, silversmithed, engraved, enamelled and plated. Among their well-known products are the CBE and MBE. 'Seconds' are not sold!

Practical details: A limited number of tours can be given every year, mainly to school leavers, but also to women's clubs and similar groups. They prefer groups of between eight and fifteen people. You will need to book about six months in advance. Tours are held in working hours, usually on a Thursday afternoon, but sometimes Monday, Tuesday or Friday. Visits last about two hours. Contact the general manager, Mr. M. J. Smith. There is no charge. Individuals are not catered for — but several interested people could join together to make up a group.

34   Newspaper Production

Birmingham Post and Mail Limited
28 Colmore Circus
Birmingham BA 6AX
Tel: 021-236 3366

The tour of the Post and Mail building covers various stages in the production of a newspaper and culminates in the excitement of watching the paper being printed and then despatched to newsagents.

Practical details: Tours take place at 2 pm Monday to Friday and at 10 am on Saturday mornings.

Groups of up to twelve people can be given a one and a half hour tour, and the minimum age limit is twelve years. Parties should apply in writing well in advance.

35   Hand-made Crystal Glassware

Thomas Webb & Sons
Dennis Glassworks
Stourbridge, West Midlands DY8 4EZ
Tel: Stourbridge 2521

The Dennis Glassworks produces crystal glassware including stemware such as

Engraving of a sixteenth century glasshouse

and they will learn something about the company's history.

Glassmaking has been carried out in the Stourbridge area since 1691. Huguenot refugees, skilled in glassmaking, settled in this area at a time when timber for burning in the furnaces was becoming scarce, because Stourbridge had a good supply of coal. And here the industry has stayed.

Practical details: Guided tours take place all year round. Individuals and groups of up to thirty people (children aged eight years and over only) should contact Mrs. P. Venables in advance. The small admission charge is waived in the case of school parties. The tour is not suitable for the elderly or infirm. Seconds are sold in the works shop.

36 Large Brewery

Ansells Limited
Aston Brewery, Aston Cross
Birmingham B6 5PP
Tel: 021-327 4747

Five thousand years before Christ, beer was popular in the harems of Babylon and the Druids were brewing beer in England before the Roman invasion. In the thirteenth century children drank beer because it was less likely to harbour infection than milk or water. At the time when Anne Boleyn was a maid of honour, Henry VIII allowed her and her companions a gallon of ale a day, and men-at-arms received double that quantity!

Beer is made from germinated barley (called malt), mashed and brewed like tea with hot water. Brewing sugars and yeast are added to ferment it and to produce that creamy head. Hops, introduced to Britain from the Low Countries in the fifteenth century, are used to give that distinctive bitter flavour.

Ansells, the Midlands and Wales

wineglasses and salad bowls, decanters, vases and reproduction Bristol Blue ware. The Bristol ware is in blue, green or amethyst and consists of about seven pieces — a cream jug, a covered jar, candlestick, decanter, a cider mug and an open bowl.

On the tour visitors see various aspects of producing crystal and other glassware — the raw materials, glassmaking, cracking off, marking, cutting, washing and acid polishing plus the warehouse and packing room. The factory also manufactures industrial glassware, which visitors will see on the tour,

appointment. There are no tours on public holidays. Individuals and small parties can join larger groups as long as they write in advance.

This is the only Midlands brewery belonging to the Allied Breweries group which accepts other than trade visits. Admission is free and refreshments are served with the company's compliments.

37 Traditional Cut Crystal

Webb Corbett Limited
Coalbournhill Glassworks, Amblecote
Stourbridge, West Midlands DY8 4HF
Tel: Stourbridge 5281

Their range covers stemware (wine glasses with stems), bowls, vases and dishes.
The factory specialises in cased glass — crystal glass dipped in glowing colours. Stunning effects are created when the decorator cuts through the colour — perhaps ruby or cobalt blue — so that patterned gleams of crystal show through. The technique is used mainly for vases. It was originally pioneered at this factory for decorating paperweights, which you will see here, but it is now also used on hock glasses which are made in ruby, amethyst, cobalt blue and yellow.
The person who runs the shop, says that sherry glasses sell more than anything else. She also tries to make sure that there are also some inexpensive small items available for children and students to buy as a souvenir of their visit. Favourites for children are the glass animals in varying sizes — a swan, penguin, horse, duck, owl, or a family of three bears. On the tour you learn how all these popular objects are made.
Crystal occurs naturally in the form of quartz or silica. The basic ingredient is sand, so it is not surprising that the secret of making glass came to the Mediterranean countries from the Middle East. The Egyptians were making pressed or cast glass objects as long ago as 1500 years BC. The technique of blowing was not

marketing company of Allied Breweries (UK) Limited, was founded in 1857 by Joseph Ansell and became part of Allied Breweries, the largest drinks group in Europe, in 1961. Beers brewed at the Birmingham brewery are Ansells Mild and Ansells Bitter, which are distributed throughout a network covering a population in excess of eleven million people.
Practical details: Organised groups of fifteen to thirty people, including school parties over fifteen years, are accepted by arrangement, for Tuesday, Wednesday and Thursday at 2.15 pm and 7.30 pm. Contact Dennis Litchfield, in the commercial department, for an

Brewing beer the modern way at Ansells

Copper-wheel engraving at Stuart & Sons

discovered until the first century BC.
On the tour you will see the traditional
English techniques of glass blowing and hand
cutting, together with the more sophisticated
methods of decoration such as intaglio
cutting, copper wheel engraving and diamond
point etching.
Practical details: The factory is open Monday
to Friday throughout the working year. Tours
are held in the mornings on Monday,
Wednesday and Friday for up to twenty
people. Individuals and groups are welcome
and should telephone or write to the tour
organiser in advance. The factory shop is open
Monday to Friday from 10 am to 5 pm and it
sells first quality goods at normal retail prices
and seconds and discontinued lines at reduced
prices. The small admission charge is waived
in the case of students and schoolchildren.

38 Lead Crystal Glassworks

Stuart and Sons Limited
Redhouse Glassworks, Wordsley
Stourbridge, West Midlands DY8 4AA
Tel: Brierley Hill 77391

Visitors are met by guides and parties·are
divided into groups of eight to ten people.
During the one-and-a-half-hour tour visitors
learn a great deal of interesting information
about Stuart and Sons as well as glassmaking
in general.
The glass is made by heating it in pots which
are placed inside the furnace. Pots take about
two months to build and three months to dry
— but once in the furnace they last a mere six
months. The pots are heated up to about
1000°C before being transferred to the furnace.
Each pot holds about fifteen cwt of glass, the
same weight as a small car. It takes about

thirty hours for the glass to melt or 'found'. A furnace remains lit year after year. It is never put out.

Glass cracks if it is cooled too quickly so the glass is cooled or 'annealed' very slowly by passing it through electrically heated lehrs on a conveyor belt. The longest lehr here is seventy feet and a glass takes between three and four hours to pass through.

The fact that glass cracks at a point of strain can be turned to the glassmaker's advantage. In order to cut off surplus glass, a line is marked round the article with a hard tungsten carbide point. The glass is heated along the line with a propane gas air flame, and it cracks. The cut edge is rubbed smooth and then reglazed by melting in a flame.

Now the glass is ready to be decorated. Patterns are cut using carborundum wheels (containing carbon again), and stone wheels. Cutting brings out the full beauty of the lead crystal. The glass is engraved by using copper wheels. Finally, the name Stuart is stamped on with a rubber stamp using an acid etch solution instead of ink.

Five hundred and ten people are employed by the company. The firm's designers have included Graham Sutherland and Dame Laura Knight. The old Redhouse works is now used as a showroom, and at the end of your tour you can buy reject glassware in the factory shop.

Practical details: The glassworks is open all year except for bank holidays, spring bank holiday week, the last week in July and the first week in August. An appointment must be made to join factory tours which take place Monday to Friday at 10 am and 2 pm.

The morning tour is for small groups of up to thirty-five people. The afternoon tour, intended for group bookings, is often booked a year ahead.

But individuals could possibly join one of the afternoon groups by arrangement. School parties are accepted only if the children are aged fourteen years and over, but children accompanied by parents are accepted if they are eight years of age or older.

Contact Mrs. V. Hayward to make arrangements. There is no charge for the tour.

39 Full Lead Crystal Glass

Royal Brierley Crystal
Stevens and Williams Limited
North Street, Brierley Hill
West Midlands DY5 3JS
Tel: Brierley Hill 77054

Royal Brierley Crystal is full lead crystal — which has to contain at least thirty per cent lead oxide. The company makes utilitarian glassware, meaning that it is useful as well as beautiful. Their range includes decanters and wine suites. Each suite has a range of seven or eight shapes — liqueur glass, sherry glass, tumbler and so on. Suites are made in about twenty different patterns. They also make holloware, such as salad bowls and rose bowls — with flower arranging wire added in the packing department. Their vases range from three and a half inches to twelve inches high. On the tour you see the raw materials being mixed, the craftsmen forming molten glass into beautiful shapes and the skilled cutters creating designs on the glass by hand.

Though the actual making of glass is the thing which impresses most first-time visitors to a glassworks, the decorating is just as fascinating. In addition to the straight cuts made with carborundum and stone wheels, you will see intaglio work. The glass is held and manoeuvred under a small stone wheel, as water drips on to it. This enables more elaborate patterns to be made — floral shapes, and freely curving designs.

There are bargains in the Brierley shop which offers visitors good export rejects and discontinued lines at about a third under recommended retail prices.

Practical details: Individuals and groups of up to fifty-five are welcome — to book a place on a tour contact the visits organiser well in advance. Morning tours are held at 10.30 am Monday to Friday and afternoon tours at 2 pm from Monday to Thursday. Allow about two hours for the tour. It is not suitable for the elderly or infirm and no children under sixteen are admitted.

Small charges are made for the tour and for afternoon tea and biscuits.

40   Newspaper Printers

Coventry Newspapers Limited
Corporation Street, Coventry CV1 1FP
Tel: Coventry 25588

The Coventry Evening Telegraph sells about 120,000 copies a day, and as two or more people read each copy, the estimated readership is 350,000. The newspaper was founded by the late W. I. Iliffe in 1891 as the Midland Daily Telegraph, a four-page broadsheet newspaper selling for a halfpenny. The first editions of the Evening Telegraph appear on the streets before lunch. By tea-time, when visitors leave, the presses have printed the last edition of the day, and work has already begun on the next day's issue. This award-winning newspaper was the first one in the country to print a full-colour news picture of a man on the moon.

Practical details: Visits are arranged on Monday and Tuesday afternoons by prior appointment, starting at 2 pm and continuing until about 4 pm. The visits are very popular with local schools so it is advisable to book as far as possible in advance. Individuals are welcome if they are prepared to join groups — so they should book in advance. Numbers are restricted to a maximum of fifteen, and children under ten years of age are not allowed for safety reasons.

There is no charge for the tour and free light refreshments are provided.

41   Specialised Weaving

J. & J. Cash Limited
Kingfield Road, Coventry CV1 4DU
Tel: Coventry 23001

Cash's most famous product is their woven name-tapes, used to identify the owners of items of school uniforms and other such clothing. The firm was started by the brothers

Specialist at J. & J. Cash

John and Joseph Cash in 1846, at which time the weaving of small items was one of the main industries of the Midlands.

In the 1860s the lifting of restrictions on imported silk goods caused many of the Coventry weaving firms to go out of business. J. and J. Cash, however, widened their activities and started making woven pictures and bookmarks — still one of their lines — then cotton frilling which was popular with the Victorians. After this came labels, and then the famous name-tapes.

In the weaving department you will see the Jacquard weaving machines (invented in 1790 by Jacquard), which use punched cards to direct the loom to intersect threads, producing intricate patterns and woven pictures. In the printing department three types of printing processes are to be seen. Cash's factory, sole survivor of the old Coventry weaving firms, is now up to date with computer and electronic controls, making iron-on patches and promotional items, badges for scouts, guides, clubs and schools.

Practical details: Individuals and groups can make an appointment with Mr. L. Pounder, the personnel manager, to tour this fascinating factory on Tuesday, Wednesday or Thursday at 10 am or 2 pm. There are no tours during the third week of September. The showroom is open on weekdays from 9 am to 4.30 pm Monday to Thursday. It closes at 3.30 pm on Friday, and also closes every day for lunch from 12.30 to 1 pm.

Organised groups of up to eighteen people are accepted for factory tours, and there are special arrangements which can be made for coach and travel agents' parties. These include a visit to sights of historical interest in Coventry itself. There is a long waiting list for tours but groups of overseas visitors and individuals (up to three in number) can usually be accommodated at short notice. School parties and children under twelve years old are not accepted. Admission is free, and the tour, which lasts about 2½ hours, starts with an introductory talk.

The tour ends with refreshments in the showroom where the factory's products are on sale.

42　Fork-Lift Trucks

Coventry Climax Limited
Widdrington Road
Coventry CV1 4DX
Tel: Coventry 24100

Coventry Climax manufactures a wide range of industrial fork-lift trucks which can lift loads from 2,000 to 18,000 lbs. They are powered by electricity, diesel, petrol or liquefied propane gas. Visitors can be shown various stages in the manufacture of these trucks, including the basic machining of metal components, the assembly of electronic control systems, the assembly of the trucks themselves, the painting and finishing operations.

Practical details: The normal working hours of the company are 8.30 am to 4.30 pm Monday to Friday, excluding public holidays. As there are no full-time guides, individuals and groups are accepted by prior appointment only. Give at least two weeks' notice of your intention to visit. Educational or industrially-oriented groups are preferred.

43　Trout Farm

Bibury Trout Farm
Bibury, Cirencester
Gloucestershire
GL7 5ND
Tel: Bibury 215

The farm was founded in 1902 by the famous naturalist Arthur Severn and its main purpose is breeding and rearing brown and rainbow trout to restock angling waters throughout the country. In the farm's five acres there are forty ponds of different sizes containing trout in their various stages of development.

The farm is a great attraction for young and old alike and a visit offers a peaceful, relaxing interlude. You can buy food and watch the fish feeding on it. Anyone who has ever kept an aquarium will be interested to learn that the fish here are fed on floating pellets of food, which helps prevent under- and overfeeding.

Practical details: The farm is opened to visitors from the end of March and closes at the end of October each year. During the visitors' season, the farm is open on every day of the week from 2 pm to 6 pm. The small entrance charge is halved for organised parties, for which prior bookings can be made. Advance bookings are not necessary, although they are helpful. Although guided tours are not given, many school parties ask for a talk on the aims of the farm, and a brief introduction to its work is often given.

Fresh trout are on sale to visitors at the entrance kiosk.

44   Falconry

The Falconry Centre
Newent
Gloucestershire
GL18 1JJ
Tel: Newent 820286

Most people are surprised to hear that falconry has a commercial use. Trained falcons can disperse birds from airfields, and the centre trained the first successful attempt for the Royal Navy at Lossiemouth.

Nowadays falconry is not used by farmers except as a means of catching the odd rabbit. At the centre talks are given on the subject of eagles, hawks and owls, and are illustrated by slides if you request a lecture in advance. A trained falconer will give demonstrations, perhaps of a falcon flying for a lure.

The centre has many live birds; falcons, golden eagles and beautiful snowy owls, and it is of great interest to natural-history students, photographers and animal lovers in general.

Practical details: The centre is open every day except Tuesday, from 10.30 am to 5.30 pm (or dusk if earlier) all the year round except December 1st to January 31st inclusive. There is an admission charge, with reductions for children and o.a.ps. Parties of twenty-five or more on midweek visits get a ten per cent reduction except on bank holidays. Parties should book in advance.

A guided tour lasts one to one and a half hours.

45   Artists and Craftsmen

Worcestershire Guild of Artist-Craftsmen
12 Finstall Road
Bromsgrove, Worcestershire
Tel: Bromsgrove 72123

The guild is an association of independent professional craftsmen formed over twenty-five years ago to link together people who by the nature of their craft tend to be isolated. The crafts include glass and slate engraving, miniature painting, batik painting, silversmithing, jewellery-making, wood carving and turning, rush weaving, potting and so on.

Practical details: Contact Robert Pancheri at the above address for a list of craftsmen, most of whom will show their work by appointment.

46   Worcester Royal Porcelain

The Worcester Royal Porcelain Co. Limited
Severn Street, Worcester WR1 2NE
Tel: Worcester 23221 Ext: 741

The Worcester Royal Porcelain has been in continuous production since 1751 — a record that cannot be matched by any other British china factory. Today it manufactures top-quality tableware and decorative china which is exported all over the world.

Visitors gather in the Dyson Perrins Museum which houses the finest collection of Royal Worcester porcelain in the world. Among the items on display are pieces of famous Blue and White, First Period, or Dr. Wall Period porcelain, manufactured when the factory first started.

Practical details: Factory tours take place Monday to Friday from 10 am to 1 pm and 2 pm to 5 pm; they last about $1\frac{1}{4}$ hours, and to avoid disappointment you are advised to book in advance. Individuals and groups of up to forty people will be accepted. A charge of 40p is made, with half price for school children. Children under eight are not admitted on factory tours. No tours take place during the

company's holiday period. For details of these dates and to make a booking contact Mr. Henry Sandon at the above address.

The museum, which is next to the factory, is open during the same hours and in addition on Saturday through April to the end of September.

In addition to the factory tour and the museum there are a superb retail shop and showroom with a complete range of contemporary Royal Worcester items, and two 'seconds' shops where the visitor may pick up a worthwhile bargain.

The factory tour includes a number of staircases so it is not possible to accommodate visitors in wheelchairs.

47   Newspaper Printing

Berrow's Newspapers Limited
Berrow's House, Hylton Road
Worcester WR2 5JX
Tel: Worcester 423434

Visitors see how the Worcester Evening News is printed by the web-offset process, and a first visit to a newspaper press is always an exciting and worthwhile experience.

Practical details: Tours take place on Wednesday and Thursday evenings between 5.30 pm and 7 pm by arrangement, and last about one hour. Groups of between four and sixteen people are acceptable (children aged eight and over). Contact them at least two months in advance.

48   Cider-making

H. P. Bulmer Limited
Ryelands Street, Hereford
Tel: Hereford 6411

Visitors see a film about cider-making, tour the cider-processing and bottling factory, and the vat-house. The tour includes cider-tasting and a variety of ciders may be purchased.

Massive cider vats at Bulmers

Bulmers use 50,000 tons of apples per year. These are unloaded into concrete silos at the factory and carried by water to the pressing mill. The pressing season lasts from October until December. Bulmer's underground vat-house at Hereford has 236 vats varying in size from 60,000 to 100,000 gallons. One vat named Strongbow holds 1.6 million gallons and is the largest container of alcoholic drink in the world.

Practical details: Groups of up to forty people may visit the factory from April to December, by making arrangements with the public relations manager twelve months in advance. Children over fourteen years are accepted. The tour is not suitable for the elderly or infirm. There is no charge.

Individuals and small parties are welcome provided notice is given. They are normally attached to groups.

Hand-throwing by the Ironbridge potter

normal open days. Write to the Herefordshire Waterworks Museum Trust — the secretary is Mr. H. R. Penhale, Reay House, 49 Bodenham Road, Hereford HR1 2TR (telephone number as above).

There is a small entrance charge which may be higher on Steam Days to meet the cost of fuel.

49 Waterworks Museum

Herefordshire Waterworks Museum
Broomy Hill, Hereford
Tel: Hereford 2487

This unique museum is intended to show not only the complete Victorian waterworks but also a large collection of pumping engines and other fascinating items connected with the history of water supply.

Practical details: The museum is open to individuals and small groups on the first Sunday in each month, from April to September inclusive, and on the Easter, spring and late summer bank holidays, from 11 am to 5 pm. It is helpful if parties can give notice when they intend visiting. Parties may be accommodated at other times on special request. It is essential that six weeks' notice is given for visits which do not take place on

50 Open Air Industrial Museum

Ironbridge Gorge Museum
Ironbridge, Telford
Shropshire TF8 7AW
Tel: Ironbridge 3522 (at weekends call Blists Hill Open Air Museum, Tel: Telford 586309)

The museum is spread over a number of sites within Ironbridge Gorge. In the Severn Warehouse a slide and tape show, and exhibitions, outline the industrial developments in the Gorge between 1700 and 1900. The Coalbrookdale Museum contains the furnace where iron was first smelted using coke as a fuel. Walk on around Coalbrookdale to the Coalbrookdale Forge Workshop at Rose Cottage where wrought iron is sold.

Next see the Iron Bridge, cast here in 1779 — the first iron bridge in the world. It has an information centre in the old tollhouse at one end.

Compositors pasting up pages at the Worcester Evening News

The Blists Hill Open Air Museum is a forty-two acre woodland site where local industries are re-created. There are working exhibits, and iron, coal, clay and early transport scenes. The museum also has a completely furnished cottage in the Shelton Toll House, which has a pig sty complete with pigs. Two blast furnace beam blowing engines called David and Sampson stand at the museum entrance. The Coalport China Works Museum contains exhibitions on the crafts of the Coalport Works and a magnificent display of porcelain. **Practical details:** The museum is open to the public every day of the year from 10 am, closing at 5 pm November to March and 6 pm April to October. Special arrangements, including a guide, are made for booked parties. Organisers write for party booking form. Free car parking. Admission charge covers the four major museum sites and the free exhibition centre. Small extra charge to enter the 100 metre long 18th century mining tunnel (Tar Tunnel) under Blists Hill.

51   Brickmaking

Blockleys Limited
Hadley, Telford, Salop TF1 4RY
Tel: Telford 51611

The company's buildings have all been built since 1965 and are the most modern of their type in Europe. Bricks are no longer set by hand, but by setting machine, and the company plans buying machinery to draw the bricks from the kiln when they are fired, so that the number of people who are employed to carry out arduous duties may be halved. The bricks are made from marl (dry clay) and shale. The processes you see can be roughly divided into grinding and making, cutting, drying and firing. **Practical details:** All are welcome at Blockleys but obviously it will be students of architecture or building who are most interested in this subject. Those who wish to see the factory should contact the assistant managing director, Mr. A. H. Jones, to establish when a visit may be arranged.

**Gwent, South Glamorgan
Mid Glamorgan, West Glamorgan
Dyfed, Powys, Clwyd, Gwynedd**

1 Rumney Pottery

Rumney Pottery
Rumney, Cardiff
South Glamorgan CF3 7AE
Tel: Cardiff 78096

The pottery was started in the late 1400's, using the local red terracotta clay, but now imports white clay for making earthenware and other pottery. Most of the pottery is made to order for commemorative items. It specialises in large plates with golf and yachting club symbols, and dinner services with special designs. So, if you wanted to order a christening plate with your child's name or godchild's name, or if you'd always hankered after a coffee set carrying your coat of arms, this would be a good place to visit.

Practical details: The pottery is open to visitors all year Monday to Saturday from 9 am to 12 noon and 1 pm to 5 pm, and on Sunday from 9 am to noon. For further details contact Robert Giles.

2 Newspaper Production

Western Mail and Echo Limited
Thomson House, Cardiff CF1 1WR
Tel: Cardiff 33022 Ext: 290

Thomson House is the home of two newspapers, the Western Mail, the national morning newspaper of Wales, and the South Wales Echo, the largest circulation evening newspaper in Wales — both are part of Thomson Regional Newspapers Limited. Visitors are shown editorial and production departments and see the processes involved in planning and producing a newspaper. By the end of the tour visitors have a good idea of how the news and pictures are received, and how type is set and blocks are made before the papers are actually printed.

Practical details: Tours are conducted by prior arrangement only, Monday to Friday at 2.15 pm and 8 pm, with the exception of Thursday afternoon and bank holidays. The minimum number for groups is six, the maximum is twenty-four and the minimum age limit is eleven years. Because there is a heavy demand for tours the promotions department requires two to three weeks' notice.

Tours are free, and last about one and a half hours, including time for tea or coffee and biscuits.

3 Television Studio

HTV
Television Centre, Pontcanna
Cardiff CF1 9XL
Tel: Cardiff 21021

The IBA (Independent Broadcasting Authority) publishes a handbook which includes a chapter on each of its fifteen television companies (and independent radio companies). This gives addresses which you

TV stations like Harlech often take local visitors. (Pic: Teddington Studio)

should contact for studio tickets. Members of the public from the HTV Wales area, are invited to see behind the scenes, usually in the evening. They are given a guided tour during which they learn how the company fits into the independent broadcasting network. HTV broadcasts between six and six and a half hours of Welsh language programmes each week, and three and a half hours in English — these are locally produced programmes. On the tour visitors see the cameras, the studios and the props store which houses furniture and sets. Viewers from the HTV Wales area can also appear on television in one of the programmes requiring an audience. There are entertainment programmes and discussion programmes. **Practical details:** Write to the above address to request a tour or programme tickets. Try to give a choice of dates and also mention the kind of programme you'd like to see. Groups are welcome to take the tour; individuals are also welcome, provided they write in advance.

4   Photographic Products

Gnome Photographic Products Limited
Gnome Corner, Caerphilly Road
Cardiff, South Glamorgan
Tel: Cardiff 63201

Visitors see lens grinding, press work, capstan and lathe work, painting, electro-plating and final assembly work. The firm makes slide projectors, enlargers and visual aids. There is very careful quality control, which perhaps explains why Gnome products sell well throughout the United Kingdom and in many overseas countries. **Practical details:** Visits to the works take place on Wednesdays at 2.45 pm and last about one and a half hours. A written request is required at least three weeks in advance. Write to Mr. J. Hallsworth, joint managing director. Groups

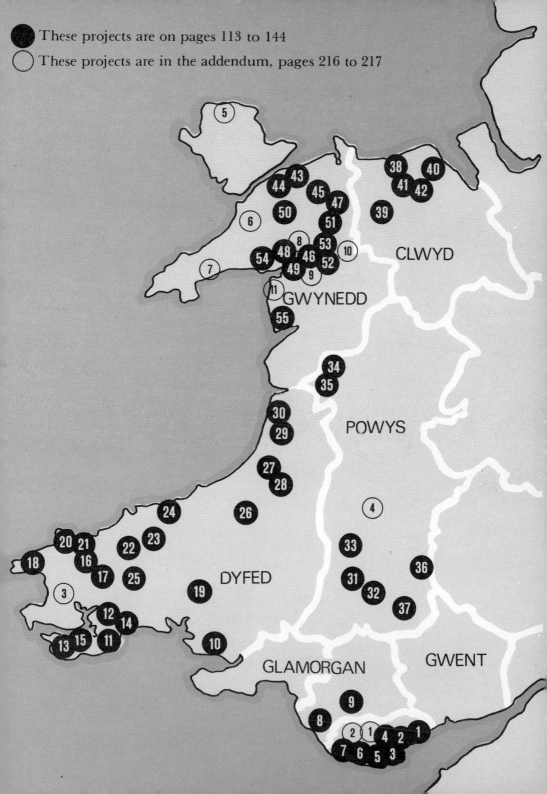

These projects are on pages 113 to 144

These projects are in the addendum, pages 216 to 217

of twenty to twenty-five persons can be shown around the factory. Interested individuals may also make an appointment to join a group.

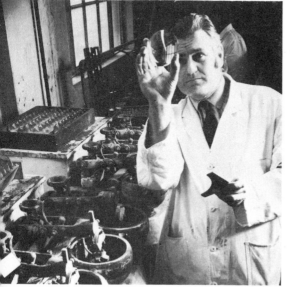

Lens grinding shop at Gnome Photographic

5   Mixed Light Industry

The Spastics Society
Sully Work Centre
Hayes Road, Sully CF6 2SE
Tel: Barry 3418

Sully Work Centre is one of six similar national units, built by the Spastics Society. Spastics have disordered movement, usually due to damage to a small part of the brain which controls movement. They may have other problems, such as hearing and speech defects. The factory employs seventy physically handicapped people.

At the start of the tour you see the making of a spirit level. Aluminium extrusion is squirted out like toothpaste from a tube, cut to a critical length and milled (cut) ten times. Nearby is the area where expanded polystyrene is sculpted and hand shaped with hot wire and iron. Other workers put together the insides of fruit machines.

The printing department was set up to help with publicity for the Spastics Society, but also undertakes jobbing-printing for all kinds of customers — letter headings, dance tickets or invoices. Wall lanterns are made and assembled in another department. Punched metal sheets pass along a line of bright red presses, emerge as shaped parts and are welded. After being painted black in the spray room they come back for glazing, wiring and testing, to ensure that they are well insulated. The centre's own products are cast antique-pattern house signs made to customers' requirements, plus impressive weathervanes, both topped by the national emblem of Wales — the dragon.

In the sales area the centre's products are on display, as well as the spirit levels by A. B. Salmen's (Successors) Ltd and Emess Lighting lanterns for which Sully Centre is the sub-contractor. Seconds are sold.

Practical details: Visiting hours are 9.30 am to 12.30 pm and 1.30 pm to 3.30 pm Monday to Friday. They are not open in the evenings, nor on bank holidays. Individuals are welcome to pop in and look around the workshop and shop — in fact, the workers are very pleased to talk to them and explain all the processes. Three conducted tours per week can be arranged for visiting the workshops. The maximum number per party is twelve. Children under sixteen must be accompanied by an adult. Pets are not admitted. Groups should book at least three weeks in advance for these tours. Individuals can join group tours as long as they write in advance.

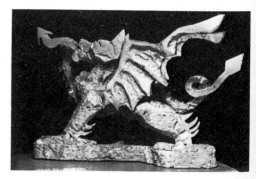

6 Royal Air Force

Royal Air Force St. Athan
Barry, South Glamorgan
Tel: Llantwit Major 3131 Ext: 3356

This is the largest multi-role engineering
station in the RAF. It covers an area of about
two thousand acres in the Vale of Glamorgan
and employs more than three thousand people.
The station opened in 1938 and was originally
a large wartime training school. Nowadays,
though training still goes on here, the main
role of the station is effecting major servicing
and reconditioning of front-line aircraft for
operational squadrons throughout the RAF.
During a two to three hour tour visitors can see
inside the service hangars, where aircraft such
as the Vulcan or Victor are being stripped
down and reconditioned.
Visitors also see the workshop facilities and
the aircraft museum, which has a unique
collection of aircraft from the first and second
world wars.
Practical details: Visits can be arranged for
groups of up to twenty people. Interested
individuals are also accepted. You must apply
in writing to the community relations officer.

7 Glamorgan Airport

Glamorgan (Rhoose) Airport
Maes Awyr Morgannwg (Y Rhws)
Near Cardiff, South Glamorgan CF6 9BD
Tel: Rhoose 710296

The airport is in the Vale of Glamorgan near
Cardiff. From the spectators' terrace you can
watch the planes arriving and taking off. The
terrace is in the passenger terminal building,
where you'll also find a restaurant, snack bar
and licensed bar.
Five million pounds was spent on developing
the airport, and a new passenger building, a
cargo building, a major runway extension and
control tower were completed in 1972.
Practical details: All visitors are welcome to
see the airport's activities and use its
amenities. There is a large car park.

A World War Two Junkers at RAF St. Athan

8 Ewenny Pottery

Ewenny Pottery
Ewenny, Near Bridgend, Mid Glamorgan
Tel: Bridgend 3020

The local rich brown glacial clay has been
used for making clay for several centuries and
Ewenny pottery was started in 1610. In those
days clay was prepared by treading it with bare
feet, in much the same way that grapes are
trodden by winemakers. The feet of the person
who was 'puddling' would become so
sensitive that they could feel the tiniest stone
in the mixture.
In our antiseptic twentieth century, the idea of
treading wet clay seems rather strange,
although the idea of getting one's hands
covered in clay is still quite appealing.
Anyway, this old-fashioned method was
replaced by using a roller pulled by two men,
then the roller was pulled by donkeys, then by
horsepower, and today modern machinery is
used.
The earliest potters would have made bread
pans, water pitchers, drinking mugs and crock
jugs. Nowadays you can see ashtrays, tankards
and decorative mugs being made.
Practical details: The pottery is open all year
Monday to Saturday, 9.30 am to 5.30 pm,
except for Saturdays in winter, when it closes
at 12.30 pm.
The potters here say they are only too happy to
show their methods to children, so families
will be sure of a welcome.

9 Welcome Characters

John Hughes Gallery
Broadway
Pontypridd
Glamorgan
Tel: Pontypridd 405001

'Visitors from all over the world call here,' says John Hughes, 'mainly because we are Welsh, working in Wales, making identifiably Welsh objects in a personal, slightly "primitive" style, probably also thought of as being Welsh'.
The shelves of the gallery are filled with Welsh miners (as befits Pontypridd on the South Wales coalfield), plus hill farmers and coracle men as well as mythological figures.
Visitors see sculptured figures from Welsh folk lore (the Mabinogion), Rugby rogues, and amusing animals (Groggs) made in unglazed, highly textured stoneware clay.
John Hughes' amusing Welsh rugby characters include such figures as Push-over Pugh, Blind Side Bevan — a freelance Dutch Elm Disease Carrier, Davie the Dash — who got his blue at the open university, and Lewis

the Leap — who has been asked to go North many times — by the Welsh Rugby Union! The Celtic creatures, individually handmade in light buff stoneware, have their texture emphasised in black. They rejoice in such names as Happy Hedgehogs and Welsh Love Birds. Cast and hand finished dogs are described as 'very friendly to burglars and no use at all as guard dogs'. Some of them resemble Welsh mountain cow terriers. Others are foreign, such as the Irish Bogghound, and they keep company with Scruffy pups, Lolloping Lion and Welsh Patchwork cows whose tails are the nesting place of the lesser fluffy lovebird.
For some reason lions sell well to Scandinavians and dogs are the firm favourites among the Japanese.
Visitors wander in informally to watch the team of five — John Hughes, daughter Kim, son Richard, plus Susan Liveridge, a friend of Kim, and Robert Osborne, a caster-modeller-salesman. There is always a variety of figures being made, some as small as three inches high and others weighing up to a hundredweight.
Practical details: The workshop is open 9 am to 6 pm including bank holidays and all visitors are welcome. You will receive a cordial and if necessary informed welcome. It is difficult for them to deal with large numbers (more than twenty) but an informal conducted explanatory tour can be given to groups, and evening visits can be made by appointment. By telephoning in advance, groups can ensure that members of the team are working on things of visual interest.

10 Coal-fired Power Station

Carmarthen Bay Power Station
Burry Port, Dyfed
Tel: Burry Port 3491

Carmarthen Bay, known locally as CarBay, is not as modern as other power stations we have described in south Wales. CarBay station's capacity, for example, is 345 megawatts while

John Hughes making one of his characters

Pembroke power station's is 2,000 megawatts. Electricity is generated when a loop of wire is rotated in the magnetic field created by a magnet. In a power station it is the wire loop which is kept stationary and the magnet which is rotated, but the principle is the same. Tremendous force is needed to turn the shaft against the resistance of the magnetic field but this energy is converted into an electric current in the coils. The source of the original energy is steam, which can be created by burning coal or oil to raise the temperature of water. The Central Electricity Generating Board issues booklets which explain the general principles fully, as well as booklets and leaflets on many individual power stations. For South Wales, contact the Public Relations Officer, CEGB South Western Region, 15-23 Oakfield Grove, Clifton, Bristol BS8 2AS. **Practical details:** To arrange a visit to CarBay power station contact the station manager. Individuals and groups of up to thirty people can visit the station at mutually agreed times. Larger groups are accepted by special arrangement. Children under eleven years old cannot be admitted.

11   Hand-made Pottery

Tenby Pottery
Upper Frog Street, Tenby, Dyfed
Tel: Tenby 2890

Anthony and Mary Markes make hand-made pottery here in Tenby. The showroom is in front of the workshop and all processes are visible to visitors from there — throwing, firing, decorating, glazing and kiln-packing. There is always something to watch except at coffee break!
They make black-and-white, wax-resist, decorated pots and also slip decorated dishes. All pots are hand-thrown.
Practical details: The pottery is open all year, Monday to Friday from 10.15 am to 1 pm and 2.15 pm to 5.30 pm. In summer they are open in the evening 7.45 pm to 9 pm on weekdays, except Wednesday. On Saturday they open until 1 pm all year. All visitors are welcome.

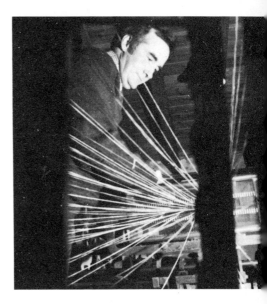

12   Small Hand-loom Weavers

Stoney Park Weavers
Stepaside, Narbeth, Dyfed SA67 8JJ
Tel: Saundersfoot 813868

The weavers' loft is a small stone converted grain store, on a lonely country lane. The weavers work on domestic hand looms converted from foot pedal to power. They produce ties and rugs. The looms are normally working, but not always, because of pattern changes. Similarly the warping process can usually be seen, though there is no guarantee. The raw material is, of course, wool, which is bought in from all over the country. As a hobby, Linda and David Noon also hand-spin the fleece of their two tame sheep 'Lamb Chop' and 'Midge'.
The Noons have one and a half acres of land. When they came here five years ago from the industrial Midlands, wanting to get out of the rat race and work for themselves, Stoney Park was a small farm which had been empty for twelve years. Their dream home and workplace had no water or electricity, and the privy was in the garden. However, they got to work, and two years later had managed to

convert the farm cottage, grain loft and outbuildings.

Practical details: Individuals are welcome without notice Monday to Friday from 10 am to 5 pm between April and October, including bank holidays. They do open in winter but telephone first to avoid disappointment. The approach roads to Stoney Park are very narrow and therefore they cannot take coaches.

13   Cabinet and Furniture Maker

J. Owen Hughes Workshop
Building 69, Llanion Park
Pembroke Dock, Dyfed
Tel: Pembroke 4360

Mr. John Owen Hughes makes traditional and contemporary furniture and woodcraft products, such as tables, chairs, Welsh dressers, settles, coffee tables and corner cabinets. The woods he works with are chestnut, ash, elm, mahogany and pine. He also makes turned woodware and cabinets to customers' own specifications. A small showroom is next to the workshop, to which visitors are welcome, by arrangement.

Practical details: The workshop is open on normal working days, by prior arrangement. There is no charge. Up to five people can be 'entertained' by Mr. Hughes, and he will allow children in provided they are supervised by an adult. The workshop is not very easy to find. It is within the area of the 'Old Barracks' close to the Borough Offices.

If you wish to write to Mr. Hughes, his postal address is 1 Beach Road, Llanreath, Pembroke Dock, Dyfed SA72 6TP. Tel: Pembroke 4360.

14   Popular Pottery

Saundersfoot Pottery
Wogan Terrace, Saundersfoot, Dyfed
Tel: Saundersfoot 812406

The hand-made earthenware pottery made in Saundersfoot by Carol Brinton has been designed for both modern and traditional settings. Care has been taken to preserve the warmth and texture of the natural clay. The glazes have been carefully chosen to offer a range of colours which blend with the red earthenware clay itself — an important part of the decorated pots.

Visitors to this studio may see all the stages in the making of the ware and there are frequent demonstrations of all processes. It is visited by thousands of holidaymakers every summer. As well as a wide range of table and domestic ware the pottery produces a number of limited edition and individual pieces from time to time — these may be seen here at the studio.

Practical details: Saundersfoot Pottery is open from April to September, Tuesday to Saturday, from 10 am to 6 pm. Viewing is by appointment in winter. On some summer evenings the studio is re-opened from 7.30 pm until 9 pm for demonstrations. All visitors are welcome.

Control room at Pembroke Power Station

15   Oil-fired Power Station

Pembroke Power Station
West Pennar, Pembroke, Dyfed
Tel: Angle 321

Pembroke is one of the largest oil-fired power stations in Europe. It is comparatively new, having opened in 1974. Nearby Milford Haven was a naval base until after the last war, and its deep waters are ideal for oil tankers.

Visitors see most areas including the computer control room. A surprisingly small number of staff control this large industrial complex with the aid of automatic processes. If the computer breaks down, the station continues working as safety devices are independent and engineers do the computer's work.

Practical details: From June to September tours are held on Tuesday, Wednesday and Thursday afternoons. Individuals and small groups are welcome and may telephone the administrative officer to make arrangements. Children under the age of twelve are not admitted. Larger groups should write to the station manager. Arrive early, as the guides leave the Visitors' Reception Centre promptly at 2 pm and 3 pm. In winter there are no regular tours but guides can be called in specially to take round large groups. Individuals can sometimes join one of these tours.

16   Textile Manufacturers

Wallis Woollen Mill
Ambleston, Haverfordwest, Pembrokeshire
Tel: Clarbeston 297

Wallis Woollen Mill is in a quiet rural valley beside a stream which runs down from Wallis moor. It was established in 1812 and the water drove a waterwheel until the 1930s.

In earlier times the mill supplied yarns for hand weaving, but nowadays it specialises in weaving cloth from pure new wool, specially dyed to the mill's chosen colours. Traditional Welsh tapestry is a heavy material, ideal for bedspreads. In the early 1970s Wallis Woollen mill introduced a lightweight tapestry suitable for clothes — the first mill in Wales to do so. In 1976 they added a new superfine flannel which handles like silk.

During the day when the mill is working visitors are free to walk around. Some of the looms are sixty or seventy years old. In the evening visitors are given a talk about the history of the Welsh woollen industry and a loom is switched on to demonstrate the principles of weaving.

You will see the sewing room and the fabric room. David and Margaret Redpath, who run the mill, aim at quality garments, not mass production.

Each girl in the sewing room makes up a completed garment. The clothes are hand-finished — fully lined, with the buttons sewn on by hand. Garments are designed here at the mill and can be made to measure.

You can also buy made-up garments direct from the mill shop. It sells woollen fabric, bedspreads, jackets, coats, waistcoats, skirts, capes, tunics, tops, evening wear, handbags,

two-ply is roughly equivalent to English three-ply in thickness. Welsh wool softens with washing and does not shrink, they tell us.
Practical details: Tregwynt Mill can be seen in operation Monday to Friday from 9 am to 5 pm. The shop is open at the same times and also on Saturday. Coach parties, supervised school parties and all visitors are welcome. There are no conducted tours because of the noise of the mill working. There is plenty of car-parking space.
The mill is five miles south of Fishguard, approached by turning west off the Goodwick-St. Davids A487.

children's clothes, hats and Arran knitwear.
Practical details: Individual visitors are welcome between 10 am and 5 pm on normal working days. Guided tours are occasionally run in the evening for groups, according to demand. Individuals can join a group if they write in advance. The mill is small and coach parties must make previous appointments. A small tea room is open during the height of the season.

17   Woollen Mill

Tregwynt Woollen Mill
(Henry Griffiths & Son)
Letterston, Haverfordwest, Dyfed
Tel: St. Nicholas 225

The mill building dates back to the mid-eighteenth century and woollen yarns have been made here since that time. The site was chosen because water power was available. For many years Welsh mills such as Tregwynt have been famous for flannel and blankets woven by hand. The arrival of the power loom, and changes in fashion, have resulted in a greater variety of goods being produced. Tapestry bed covers are woven in various designs, including one based on the coat of arms Cross of St. David. The mill shop sells tweed clothes, tweed and flannel, skirt and dress lengths, blankets, travelling rugs, scarves, stoles, and ties. Their speciality is knitting wools in two, three and four-ply; the

18   Cottage-style Furniture

Hugh and Betty Loughborough
The Craftsman, Solva
Haverfordwest, Pembrokeshire, Dyfed
Tel: Solva 294

Hugh Loughborough is a countryman who worked for the Forestry Commission and on a dairy farm for many years. He made furniture as a hobby, before taking it up full-time. The workshop is a small concern, making cottage furniture from homegrown hardwoods. Visitors will see small furniture and old-fashioned kitchen utensils being made in the workshop. Dining tables and dressers are usually made to customers' orders. They also specialise in rush-seated ladderback and rocking chairs.
Visitors can buy at ex-workshop prices — paying no more than they would for mass-produced items. Corn dollies are also sold in the shop. Betty Loughborough makes them from winter wheat.
Practical details: The workshop is open to individuals from April to September 10 am to 5 pm Monday to Friday, and from October to March, Monday to Saturday. Groups of up to twenty people are accepted by arrangement and should give two weeks' notice. Young people are welcome so long as they are under supervision. The shop stays open on Easter Monday, Spring bank holiday, and Autumn bank holiday.

19   Mixed Crafts

Celtic Crafts Limited
Cwmduad Woollen Mill, Dyfed
Tel: Cynwyl Elfed 337

Cwmduad Mill is no longer a working
woollen mill, but is now a retail craft shop and
picturesque country workshop.
Visitors can watch Keith Durrant painting
and restoring heavy gilt picture frames. The
workshop also features handloom weaving
and spinning, illustrated inn and shop
signs and the work of a landscape and marine
artist. The craft shop carries a wide range of
local products.
If you are a self-caterer, you can take
advantage of the picnic area in the mill
field, skirted on either side by two well-
stocked trout streams. The atmosphere is one
of peace and tranquillity.
A natural history display features some of
the local animal and plant life, and there is
a short nature walk along the watercourse.
Although it is no longer a working mill,
Cwmduad has a great tradition of handmade
woollen goods behind it. It was in
operation until the 1960's producing flannel,
tweed and blankets.
Today, a growing collection of items
associated with the district is on view in the
mill — old shuttles, an old spinning wheel, a
sock knitting machine: also a vintage radio,
a vintage motorbike, butter churns, a
handloom and large photographs of the
village and the Lampeter Horse Fair.
The mill has one of the few turning waterwheels left in Wales today.
Practical details: The centre is open May to
September from 9 am to 9 pm and October to
April from 10 am to 5.30 pm. The tea rooms
are open during the summer season only and
the shop is closed on Sunday in the winter
months.
All members of the public, including coach
and organised parties are welcome to visit
Cwmduad.
Situated on the A484, nine miles north of
Carmarthen, the centre is well signposted and
has a large parking area.

20   Suede and Leatherwork

Inskin
West Street, Fishguard
Pembrokeshire, Dyfed
Tel: Fishguard 2510

Ben and Elizabeth Morris use finished leather
to manufacture clothing, bags, belts, hats and
so on. Elizabeth Morris obtained a Diploma of
Art and Design from Manchester College of
Art, and when she experimented with suede
and leather goods she found people very
willing to buy her products. She gave up the
teaching she had been doing, and, as business
flourished, her husband gave up his job as a
qualified mechanical engineer to set up in
partnership with his wife.
Inskin designs include suede appliqué with a
strong Celtic influence and bags in
Welsh tapestry and flannel as well as in leather
and suede. They have developed a range of
embossed wine mats recently which are
proving very popular. These are embossed
with Celtic designs on natural hide.
Practical details: The *shop* is open Monday to
Saturday from 9 am to 5.30 pm. It is closed on
Sundays and most bank holidays. The
workshop is very small and can only
accommodate two or three visitors at a time.
Visits are restricted to times when pressure of
work permits.

21   Craft Workshop Complex

Just one of the crafts at Workshop Wales

Workshop Wales
Lower Town, Fishguard
Dyfed SA65 9LY
Tel: Fishguard 2261

Workshop Wales is on the edge of Lower
Town fishing village. The six-acre site
includes the outbuildings of a mansion estate
used as small individual workshops. The ten
main craft activities are silversmithing, woodturning, screen-printing, bellows-making,
wood-carving, pottery, toy-making, clothes-
making, leatherwork, and harness-work.
The complex is not a commune. Each person
is responsible for making his or her own
workshop pay its way. The retail craft shop
also operates independently, ordering only
those goods which it believes it can sell — but
it does help the workshops by paying for
goods on delivery, not on a sale or return basis.
Craftsmen have to prove the quality and
saleability of their work by selling it through
the shop for a year before joining the complex.
Products include gold and silver jewellery,
leather clocks with Celtic patterns on the faces,

bags and belts with Celtic patterns, and
passport pouches, again decorated with Celtic
patterns. Traditional wooden cawl (broth)
bowls and bara (bread) boards are made.
Clothes sold here include Dai-bach caps (full-
crowned baker boy caps), fishermen's
jumpers, fishermen's smocks in denim with
matching caps and jeans, and ties and scarves
with Celtic patterns such as Celtic knots.
Practical details: The shop and workshop
complex are open seven days a week from two
weeks before Easter until the middle of
October. In winter, hours are sporadic, but
there is always someone on hand to help
visitors, and workshops will open on request.

22   Woodturning (and Fruit Picking)

Peter Bossom
Glyn-y-fran, Crymmych, Dyfed
Tel: Crymmych 347

Visitors can see woodturning of all kinds here.
Mr. Bossom makes a great deal of kitchenware

and nearly all the articles are functional.
Visitors can watch the work in progress.
The workshop is on a small holding in the
Welsh hills. Soft fruits — gooseberries,
raspberries and blackcurrants — are grown
commercially and are sold on a 'pick it
yourself' basis in the season.
Practical details: Mr. Bossom's workshop is
open from Monday to Saturday at any time of
day from Easter to the end of September. From
October to Easter inclusive it closes at 5.30 pm.

23   Tweed Manufacturers

Cambrian Mills (Velindre) Limited
Drefach, Velindre
Near Newcastle Emlyn, Dyfed
Tel: Velindre 209

Visitors can see the weavers at work and buy
tweed, flannel cloth, tapestry, flannel shirts,
rugs and blankets. A textile museum has been
opened next door with the help of the
National Museum of Wales.
Practical details: The mill is open to the
public all year round on Monday to Friday
from 9 am to 4.30 pm, and in summer on bank
holidays from 10 am to 4.30 pm.

24   Mixed Crafts

The Studio Craft-Workshop
Tresaith, Near Cardigan, Dyfed
Tel: Aberporth 810512

The workshop produces most of its crafts
during the winter months. During the
summer season there is barely enough time to
sell goods. Occasionally, however, there is a
demonstration of enamelling or painting on
tiles and other work.
Trevor and Valerie Green, who run the
workshop, also make hand-built pottery,
furniture and clothes. The clothes are
made from natural materials, batik dyed, or in
peasant styles with embroidery.
Practical details: The Greens have a studio
cum workshop which is open all day.

25   Honey Farm

Preseli Honey Farm
Hebron, Whitland, Dyfed
Tel: Hebron 443

Visitors will see the apiaries, demonstrations
of queen rearing and general bee work,
depending on the season. A small pottery
produces honey crocks.
Practical details: Open to individuals and
small groups 9.30 am to 5.30 pm Tuesday to
Friday, and 9.30 am to 1 pm on Saturdays.

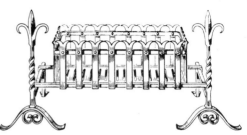

26   Wrought Ironwork

John M. Price & Son
Forge Works, Talsarn
Near Lampeter, Dyfed SA48 8QB
Tel: Aeron 565

The title John M. Price & Son should really be
John M. Price, Son & Daughter. Gwyneth
Price, aged twenty-one, is serving a five years'
apprenticeship to her father. She is the only
girl in the country taking a full
apprenticeship. In the old smithy she practises
firework, forging, and welding, acquiring the
ancient skills from her father, a master smith.
She works on a hundred year old iron anvil
and her father insists that she must make all
her own tools. In the forge, old bellows made
in 1851 are used to heat coal, so that the iron is
at just the right, malleable temperature. You
might see Gwyneth at work in the modern
workshop. Here and at Hereford Technical
College she learns the latest techniques.
At one time smiths would do all the ironwork

J. Price's daughter—apprentice smithy

and repairs for a village community, shoeing
horses, re-rimming wagonwheels, and fixing
machinery. Nowadays they make ornamental
work such as house names, fire irons, bed-
heads, balconies and gates. Mr. Price still does
some farriery — making horse-shoes, and
some industrial work (profile cutting) but
most of the work is on articles for the home
which are designed and forged on the premises
Practical details: The workshop is open
Monday to Friday from 8.30 am to 5.30 pm
and at weekends by appointment.

27   Blacksmith and Welder

The Smithy
Penpompren, Ystrad Meurig, Dyfed
Tel: Pontrhydfendigaid 248

Mr. T. D. Davies does agricultural repairs and
wrought-iron work to order in this village
smithy. This is a one-man business and as
such is a fascinating place to visit. Mr. Davies
is a member of the Guild of Wrought
Ironwork in Wales.
Practical details: As this is very much an
individual operation, visitors are welcomed at
any time.

28   Hand-thrown Pottery

Abaty Pottery
Pontrhydfendigaid
Ystrad Meurig, Dyfed
Tel: Pontrhydfendigaid 667

The pottery produces hand-thrown stoneware
tableware including mugs, jugs, casseroles,
coffee sets, plates, plant pots and salt kits.
Practical details: The pottery is open all year
round Monday to Friday, from 7.30 am to
1 pm and 2 pm to 4 pm, and at other times by
appointment with D. R. and E. M. Lacey.
Individuals and parties of not more than
twelve may visit the pottery and see the
processes. Parties should advise them
beforehand. No charge is made — 'We prefer
to sell you a pot'.

29   Silver-lead Mine Museum

Llywernog Silver-lead Mine Museum
Ponterwyd, Near Aberystwyth, Dyfed
Tel: Ponterwyd 620

In the restored buildings of this Victorian
silver-lead mine, you can discover the
fascinating history of metal mining in Wales.
An audio-visual programme introduces a
series of authentic exhibits displayed in a
traditional underground setting, re-created in
the large museum building. This shows how
the ores of silver and lead were mined, and
explains the techniques of gold and slate
mining.

Practical details: The mine is open to all
visitors every day, Easter to September, from
10 am to 5.30 pm and at other times by
arrangement. Please write or telephone for
bookings and information on special
facilities.

The mine has a bookshop, a craft centre —
with a large selection of silver jewellery,
lapidary and other local craft items — a tourist
information centre, picnic site and a large free
car park. There is a small admission charge.

30   Hydro-electric Power Stations

Rheidol Power Station
Cwm Rheidol, Capel Bangor
Aberystwyth SY23 3NF
Tel: Capel Bangor 667

At Rheidol you can see a picturesque and
award-winning hydro-electric scheme.
Hydro-electric power can only be produced in
areas where there is sufficient rainfall and
suitable, normally hilly land. The classic
hydro-electric power station is built by
collecting water behind a dam and allowing it
to flow through turbines (electric power
generators) on its way downhill.
Rheidol power station is situated in the valley
of the river Rheidol. The scheme was
completed in 1963 and has a generating

capacity of fifty-six megawatts. The dams and
lakes are open to the public and a nature trail
has been established along the river bank.

At Ffestiniog in North Wales you can see
another interesting development of the hydro-
electric use of waterpower. This is an example
of a pumped storage scheme — currently one
of the largest daily pumped storage schemes in
Europe. Using low-cost electricity during the
night, water is pumped uphill from a lower
reservoir to fill the higher reservoir so that it
can be used during peak demand the next day.
Trees and shrubs have been planted at
Ffestiniog which will, it is hoped, survive
being submerged daily with rising water.
From the power station you can go to Stwlan
Dam, 1,000 feet up in the mountains.

The very latest scheme, also in Snowdonia, is
Dinorwic, the only underground power
station in England and Wales, the largest
power scheme of its kind in Europe. It is due
for completion in 1981 and visitors will be
taken by mini-bus through a tunnel,
previously used for construction, to the
turbine hall one kilometre down inside the old
slate quarry.

Practical details: At Rheidol guided tours
leave the reception area, a mile from the

Hand-shaping the clay at Abaty Pottery   *Rheidol Power Station control room*

station, at intervals from 11 am to 4.30 pm each day from the Easter holiday to the end of September. Individuals and small groups may come along without notice. There is a small charge. School parties free.

At Ffestiniog guided tours leave the reception centre at intervals from 9 am to 6 pm every day during the Easter holiday, and from spring bank holiday until the end of October. Small parties and individuals need not give notice. Small charge, but school parties free.

During the summer a coach service runs from the reception centre to Stwlan Dam at half-hourly intervals from 10.30 am to 4.30 pm. The address is Ffestiniog Power Station, Tan y Grisiau, Blaenau Ffestiniog, Gwynedd LL41 3TP. Tel: Blaenau Ffestiniog 465.

31 Salmon Hatchery

Cynrig Salmon Hatchery
Near Brecon, Powys
Tel: Llanfrynach 212

Cynrig Salmon Hatchery is on the Cynrig, a tributary of the river Usk. The hatchery is run by the Central Electricity Generating Board which is very concerned with protecting the environment around its power stations. It takes care that as few fish as possible are harmed when they accidentally get into the water cooling systems, by using special screening chambers. What is more, positive action is taken to breed fish at this hatchery. In the salmon hatchery adult female salmon are milked of their eggs. The salmon hatchery can cope with 250,000 eggs, which are incubated until they hatch. When the fish are ready to start feeding they are transferred outside to a series of tanks and ponds where they are kept in fresh, running, unheated water — just as in their natural conditions. The smolt are usually about two years old when they are ready to be set free — up to ten thousand smolt are released every year. Every third year the entire stock is anaesthetised and numbered tags are attached so that they can later be traced. The young salmon make their way to sea and two years later they find their

way back to their home river — nobody quite knows how. Fishermen have co-operated in the experiment by sending salmon tags back to the hatchery from as far away as Greenland. An illustrated booklet about the hatchery is available from the Public Relations Office, CEGB, 15-23 Oakfield Grove, Clifton, Bristol BS8 2AS. Tel: Bristol 32251.

Practical details: Casual visitors can usually call at the hatchery between 10 am and 12 noon and from 2 pm to 4 pm without notice. One of the staff will take visitors round. As there are only two people working at the hatchery at present, it is advisable to telephone first. Groups should definitely make an appointment. A film is shown to school parties and other groups visiting by prior arrangement.

32 Welsh Whisky

Bryn Teg
Alexandra Road, Brecon, Powys
Tel: Brecon 2821/3479

You have heard of Scotch whisky and Irish whisky — why not Welsh whisky? Swn y don (sound of the wave) is a malt whisky blended with seven secret herbs, all grown in Wales. Since 1971 Mr. Dafydd Gittens and his partner have been making it here, employing about ten people. Production is ten thousand gallons a month — which is small compared to the world renowned whiskies. However, business is expanding and a new modern distillery is being built.

If you want to buy Swn y don, it is sold in miniatures (for the tourist trade), in a one and a half-pint size. A giant two-litre size goes to pubs.

Practical details: The modern distillery with its visitors' centre is being built two miles away from the above address. It will be open for Easter 1979. When it is ready you will be able to see the mashing of barley, worting, distillation and bottling. Meanwhile, if two or three people were particularly interested, they could have a quick look at the vats in the

Young parr at Cynrig Salmon Hatchery

cellars of the present business, by appointment with Mr. Dafydd Gittens, the managing director. As the cellars are rather small, larger groups should wait until the new centre is open.

33   Sheltered Weaving Workshop

Cambrian Factory Limited
Llanwrtyd Wells
Powys LD5 4SD
Tel: Llanwrtyd Wells 211

The main purpose of this factory is to act as a sheltered workshop employing disabled people.

All the processes carried out here can be seen in logical sequence: wool sorting, dyeing, blending, willeying, carding, spinning, warping, winding and weaving. Knitting, doubling the yarn, hanking, rug fringing and other activities can also be seen.

All the products are made to Woolmark and Welsh Woolmark standard from wool grown, spun, woven or knitted in Wales. Much of the tweed is now turned into garments by outside workers for sale in the factory shop. Bed covers are made as well as clothing — including made-to-measure suits and sports jackets, tweed caps, trilby and deerstalker hats, capes, car coats, socks, ties, scarves, purses, handbags and spectacle cases.

Practical details: The factory is open Monday to Friday, summer and winter, from 8.15 am to 5.30 pm; on Saturday in summer from 9 am to 4.30 pm, and in winter from 9 am to 12 noon. It is open on bank holidays with the exception of Christmas.

Individuals are welcome to arrive without prior notice and walk round the works. Groups of more than fifteen should make an appointment, as much in advance as possible, but sometimes a day's notice will be adequate. The factory sells by mail order as well as through its shop on the premises. The tea room serves refreshments from May to September and there is a picnic area on the factory site. The mill is on the main A483, a half mile east of Llanwrtyd Wells.

34   Weavers

Meirion Mill
Dinas Mawddwy
Machynlleth
Powys SY20 9LS
Tel: Dinas
   Mawddwy 311

The Meirion Mill nestles in a valley at the southern tip of the Snowdonia National Park, dominated by Foel Dinas and Foel Benddin. Fleece from local sheep is woven into a cloth that is renowned for its quality, design and texture.

The power-driven looms are carefully supervised by craftsmen who mechanically and mathematically steer the process. Double-woven tapestry cloth, flannel cloth and blankets are woven. The cloth is traditional in every way and carries the Welsh Woolmark — the guarantee that it is pure new wool.

Practical details: The weaving shed is open to visitors all year Monday to Friday from 9 am to 4.30 pm.

The coffee shop is open Easter to October plus the Christmas period.

The retail shop is open all year Monday to Saturday 10 am to 4.30 pm. Admission is free and children are able to amuse themselves in a well-equipped playground surrounded by a scenic picnic area and car parking space. You will find Meirion Mill by the River Dyfi on the A470.

35   Self-Sufficiency Centre

National Centre for Alternative Technology
Llwyngwern Quarry, Machynlleth, Powys
Tel: Machynlleth 2400

A disused slate quarry overlooking Snowdonia National Park has been turned into a demonstration of 'how to live happily on limited resources, causing a minimum of pollution and waste without returning to the hardships of the past'. Here they practice what they preach. Not only are there exhibitions of machinery and systems, but the exhibition hall itself is heated by a solar roof and the guide booklets are printed on one hundred per cent re-cycled paper. They have installed their own energy systems, housing and horticulture. They re-cycle their rubbish, and have an electric truck and other transport powered by electricity produced on site from natural resources. Exhibits show how you can produce your own energy from sun, wind and water and grow your own food.

As you walk around you pass cottages built for and by the staff, using re-cycled materials, incorporating solar panels and heat conserving techniques. You see vegetable plots showing the results of different methods of organic cultivation, and learn how domestic sewage can be used to provide compost and bio-gas for cooking in the home. If all these new ideas make you want to learn more, you'll be pleased to find the bookshop at the end of the tour. It stocks DIY plans and information sheets, magazines and books.

Practical details: The centre is open to all every day of the year except over the Christmas holiday, from 10 am to 5 pm (dusk in winter). Parties and coaches are welcome but they must make arrangements with the centre in advance. Children must be accompanied by an adult as some of the exhibits could be dangerous. There is a three hundred yard walk up a seventy foot hill from the free car park to the centre. Invalids may drive up. There is an admission charge. No pets are allowed as this is a nature reserve. Most of the exhibits are out of doors so take rainproof clothing just in case. The centre is three miles north of Machynlleth, just off the A487.

36   Distinctive Pottery

Wye Pottery
Clyro, Near Hay-on-Wye
Via Hereford, Powys HR3 5LB
Tel: Hay-on-Wye 510

In 1956 Adam Dworski, an ex-lawyer from Yugoslavia, came to Clyro with his wife and family and started the Clyro Pottery. He makes a distinctive type of earthenware pottery using majolica glazes and brushwork decoration. He also produces figures, plaques and pots in oxidised stoneware and has recently started to work in porcelain.

Although Mr. Dworski does work on commission and exports to Europe and America, he prefers to work on his own and most of his work is sold direct to people visiting his studio, where he can be seen working on most days.

Practical details: The pottery is open to the public daily from 9 am to 1 and 2.30 to 6 pm, all year. Also on Sunday by appointment. Mrs Dworski also has a studio nearby, where blanket chests, stools, spoonboxes and egg-cups are painted in traditional designs. Visitors by appointment — telephone number as above.

Clyro is on the A438 between Hereford and Brecon — a mile from Hay-on-Wye.

37   Furniture Craftsmen

Grahame Amey Limited
The Granary, Standard Street
Crickhowell, Powys
Tel: Crickhowell 810540

A tour of the works includes brief details about the manufacture of furniture, its history and the processes involved. Visitors are shown the whole sequence from rough sawn timber to assembly and polishing. There are five people employed.

They say, 'Come and see craftsmen making beautiful furniture in the heart of the Brecon Beacons National Park. We work in solid hardwoods — mainly ash or oak. If oak is the king of British hardwoods, then ash is the queen. It is a light and beautifully grained wood, not unlike pine in colour, but with all the strength, durability and resistance to bruising of oak.'

They take as much care with what is normally out of sight as with what is on show. For example, cupboard units are backed in solid timber, not cheap plywood, and are fixed by means of brass screws. Their standard finish is a matt, heat and stain-resistant polish which is then hand-waxed to perfection.

By buying direct from the workshops you can save as much as seventy per cent, which is the usual mark-up when furniture is sold in retail shops. Solid, hand-made dining tables cost from around £75 and coffee tables start at about £45, which represents good value for money. You are paying only for the high quality of materials and craftsmanship. Lord Snowdon, honorary adviser to the Design Council, apparently visited the workshop and said, 'It is perfection in craftsmanship and woodwork'.

Practical details: The showroom and workshop are open Monday to Friday from 8 am to 5.30 pm and on Saturday from 9 am to 5 pm.

Skilled craftsmen at Grahame Amey Ltd.

Individuals are welcome to arrive without prior notice and walk around the works. Groups of up to ten people should telephone for an appointment.

The workshops are in a thirteenth century granary, forty yards from the centre of town.

38 Life-boat Station

The Life-boat Station
East Parade, Rhyl, Clwyd

The life-boat in use here at Rhyl is a self-righting life-boat called Har-Lil after Harry and Lilly, parents of the donor. You will probably not see the life-boat going out unless there is an emergency, though the crew of seven sometimes do exercises. Every six weeks they go out on a practice run. Every six months they have bad weather practice, and

every six months they have a 'black-out' practice on a moonless, starless night.

The life-boat most likely to be called out to rescue holiday makers — children floating out to sea on airbeds, picnickers cut off by the tide, and capsized boats—is the inshore life-boat. The full size life-boats are more often launched in bad weather. When you hear your radio programme interrupted by the announcement, 'Attention all shipping . . .' you can be sure that small fishing boats and pleasure craft in stormy areas will head straight for the nearest harbour. But it is just then that the life-boat crew are likely to be called out. They must be ready to put to sea at a moment's notice, day or night, summer or winter.

The people who man these life-boats are not full time crews. An RNLI life-boat station normally has only one full-time paid employee. The coxswain at St. David's in

South Wales is a verger at the cathedral and other life-boat crew members have included a farmer, a power station worker, the manager of a building firm and a printer.

You can't miss the life-boat station at Rhyl because it is on the Parade with the Coastguard's look-out on top and a slipway running down from it. The life-boat house contains a display of life-boat pictures and a range of model life-boats.

Practical details: The Rhyl life-boat station is open in summer (Easter to the end of September) seven days a week, from 9 am to 9 pm and in winter a mechanic is on duty from 10 am to lunch time (12.30 pm). There is no charge and individual members of the public can walk in. School parties, rotary clubs and other groups who wish to receive a talk and guided tour should write to Mr W M Smith-Jones, the Honorary Secretary, RNLI Rhyl Branch, Timber Works, Voryd, Rhyl.

Clwyd (Tel: Rhyl 50394).
There are about 250 RNLI stations around the
coasts of Great Britain and Ireland. If you
would like to visit another one, write,
enclosing a stamped addressed envelope, to
Mrs Heather Deane, RNLI, West Quay Road,
Poole, Dorset (Tel: Poole 71133). Mrs Deane
will send you the address of your nearest life-
boat station. No charge is made but donations
are always welcome as the RNLI rescues
people without charge.

39   Candle Making

Candles in the Rain
The Old Smithy, Nantglyn
Near Denbigh, Clwyd
Tel: Nantglyn 389

This eighteenth century smithy is both
workshop and showroom for Val and Bill
Norrington. They specialise in hand-made
leather goods, shoulder bags, saddle stools,
boxes, belts, chessboards, watch straps and, of
course, candles. They have won awards at
several exhibitions for their craft work.
All the goods are made by hand on the
premises and leatherwork is always in
progress. The candle workshop is closed to the
public when pouring is taking place, but
carving and finishing can sometimes be seen.
Goods are for sale and orders can be taken.
Practical details: The workshop and
showroom are open Monday to Saturday from
10 am to 5 pm, and closed on Sunday. Up to
ten people can be accommodated, and no
advance notice is necessary.

40   Textile Mill

Holywell Textile Mills Limited
Holywell, Clwyd CH8 7NU
Tel: Holywell 2022

Spinning and weaving have been carried out
in this valley since the late eighteenth century
and Holywell Mills became an established
limited company in 1874. The mill specialises
in making tweeds from the wool of Jacob
sheep. These sheep are named after the ones
mentioned in the Bible, in the story of Jacob's
courtship of Rebecca.
Visitors to the mill are taken on a conducted
tour and the processes of spinning and
weaving are explained. Besides Jacob tweeds,
visitors see the making of Welsh tapestry
tweeds, Welsh tapestry bed covers, blankets,
travel rugs and Welsh flannels. 'Welsh
tapestry' does not only mean 'made in Wales':

Leathercraft at Candles in the Rain

it is also a cloth which had been traditionally made in Wales from Welsh wool.
Practical details: The mill is open for previously arranged visits Monday to Friday all year, including some bank holidays. Tours take place at 10.30 am and 3.15 pm. Evening visits can also be arranged, and for these a small fee is charged to cover the cost of reopening the mill. Individuals and parties welcomed.
The mill is next to St. Winifred's Well on the B5121.

41 Ladies' and Children's Clothing

Pandy Garments
Pandy Lane, Dyserth, Rhyl
Clwyd LL18 6AL
Tel: Dyserth 570240

'Pandy' is a Welsh word meaning 'cloth mill', and garments for ladies and children are made here in traditional Welsh Woolmark fabrics at the sixteenth century Pandy and twelfth century Old Mill. Neighbours from Dyserth village are enlisted to help.
Visitors can see modern garments being cut from the traditional cloths, made up and hand-finished. They can purchase craft items and garments from stock or made-to-measure. They may also see the making of smaller items such as purses, mats and dolls.
Practical details: The cottage workshop is open Monday to Friday from 10 am to 5 pm, and at weekends by appointment with John and Heather Dracup. Individuals and small parties are welcome. Advance notice is necessary on public holidays.

42 Hand Weavers

Dyserth Hand Weavers
Netherton, Elwy Avenue, Dyserth, Rhyl
Clwyd LL18 6HW
Tel: Dyserth 570256

Three foot looms are in daily use here, and, as weaving classes are held, there are usually

Learning about hand-weaving at Dyserth

various sizes of table looms set up for teaching purposes. Visitors can watch hand weaving. Hand-woven materials such as dress lengths are on sale, and there are finished goods such as skirts, stoles, neck-ties, aprons, table mats, tray cloths, cushion covers and antimacassars. Articles are available for sale and others can be ordered.
Practical details: Mr. Cecil Rhodes and his nephew, Mr. Donald Lander, welcome individuals and small groups of interested people to their workshop at all reasonable times throughout the year. No advance notice is necessary.

43 Boat Builders

Denis Ferranti Laminations Ltd
Caernarvon Road, Bangor, Gwynedd
Tel: Bangor 53232 Ext 59

Makers of plastic moulded products, including a range of boats. Also electro-mechanical equipment made, including telephones, coin boxes and aircraft headgear.
Practical details: Individuals may visit the boatbuilding department during working hours. Groups write well in advance.

44 Plastics Manufacturers

Hi-Speed Holdings Limited (Plastics)
Llandegai, Bangor, Gwynedd
Tel: Bangor 4281

On one side of this modern factory you can see
men making watering cans, washing machine
components, wheels for trundle toys, screen
wash bottles for motorcars, and other hollow
components. There is a long line of blow-
moulding machines, each of which produces a
continuous tube of hot plastic which is
clamped into a mould and then automatically
inflated.
The women work on the other side of the
factory making articles which go into motor
cars — sun visors and parcel shelves — what
is known as soft trim components.
Practical details: Visits are arranged by the
personnel officer and educational and other
restricted groups are accepted. Individuals are
welcome provided they write for an
appointment.

45 Woollen Mill

'Y DdRAIG GOCH'

Trefriw Woollen Mills
Vale of Conway Mills
Trefriw, Gwynedd
Tel: Llanrwst 640462

Trefriw Woollen Mill was built on the banks
of the River Crafnant in order to use the river
water to drive the water wheels, and for
washing wool and cloth.
For more than one hundred years wool has
been spun here and tapestry quilts, blankets
and tweeds have been woven.
Visitors can still see these goods being made,
together with travelling rugs, honeycomb
quilts, and tapestry cloth produced by the
yard.
Practical details: The mill is open to all
visitors Monday to Friday from 8 am to
12 noon and 1 pm to 4.45 pm. The mill shop is
open Monday to Friday from 8 am to 4.45 pm
on Saturday from 10 am to 4 pm; in July and
August it is also on Sunday from 2 pm to 5 pm.

46 Slate Mine

Gloddfa Ganol
Ffestiniog Mountain Tourist Centre
Blaenau Ffestiniog, Gwynedd LL41 3NB
Tel: Blaenau Ffestiniog 664

At one time this was the world's largest slate
mine. In the museum you can learn about the
history of slate extraction, transport (from
pack mules to steam locomotives), and a miner
will describe mining of the past, comparing it
with today's methods. Then visitors go to the
picture windows to look down at the quarry
hole 350 feet below.
At the beginning of this century the industry
employed over three thousand men but
nowadays only one hundred and twenty men
work in the four local quarries and, over the
past ten years, underground mines have been
replaced by open-cast quarries.
In the Slab Mill you can see slabs of slate being
sawn by diamond saws before being split,
planed, drilled, cored, sanded and polished.
The final products are roofing slates,
monumental slabs, ornamental fireplaces and
other craft goods which are on sale.
Quarrymen's cottages nearby have been
furnished in styles covering a period of more
than a century. You should also walk across to
the viewpoints to see the panoramic view of
the town of Blaenau Ffestiniog below.
You can take children to see the Grotto, a
tunnel decorated with fairytale characters, or
leave them in the supervised play area while
you take a Land-Rover safari or a specialised
tour of the old mine workings wearing a
miner's lamp and helmet.
Practical details: The mountain centre is open
daily Easter to October from 10 am to 5.30 pm.
The charges are 60p for adults and 30p for
children under fourteen. There are special
admission rates for booked parties and
reductions are made for block bookings in the
restaurant. Teachers and party organisers can
obtain an educational questionnaire or guide
book in advance.
Ffestiniog Mountain Tourist Centre is on the
A470 between Blaenau Ffestiniog and Betws-
y-Coed.

Slate-splitting at Gloddfa Ganol

47 Taxidermy

Snowdonia Taxidermy Studios
Fron Ganol, Llanwrst
Gwynedd LL26 0HU
Tel: Llanwrst 640664

The taxidermists make models and
reproductions of animals and birds for
museums, schools and home decoration. The
models are hired for window displays,
exhibitions, photographic work and
theatricals.

The skins are prepared and tanned so that they
can be made to fit accurately reproduced
models of the anatomy of the subject being
prepared. A small exhibit shows photographs
of the various stages of the work and moulds,
casts and so on.

The taxidermy workshop is within
Encounter! The North Wales Museum of
Wild Life, so visitors would normally visit
both. Encounter! has a wildlife museum and
nature walk. Guided tours last an hour and
there is a small admission charge. Light
refreshments and souvenirs are sold in
summer.

Practical details: The studios are open all the
year round and visitors are accepted by
appointment between 9 am and 6 pm.

48 Stoneware Pottery

Trefor Glyn Owen and Gillian Morgan
Crochendy Twrog
Maentwrog
Near Porthmadog, Gwynedd

The pottery produced is wheel-thrown
domestic stoneware. Many individual pieces

are made by resident and visiting craftsmen. All are fired in the wood kiln. Many local materials are used in the glazes, such as pine ash from the kiln and Criccieth clay. Although the work follows the Chinese tradition, many Celtic forms are used.

There is a showroom where pots and books can be bought.

Practical details: The pottery, showroom and shop are open to visitors seven days a week from 10 am to 7 pm. A pottery demonstration and talk is given on Saturday morning at 10 am, 11 am and 12 noon to a maximum of twenty people. The charge is 50p per person. You will find the pottery one mile from Maentwrog on the A487.

49   Beddgelert Pottery

Beddgelert Pottery
Cae Ddafydd
Penrhyndeudraeth, Gwynedd
Tel: Beddgelert 213

The pottery was originally made in Beddgelert, hence the name. The pottery's main product is pomanders, which contain home-grown and blended pot pourri. In fact the making of the pottery containers came about as a means of marketing the pot pourri. Attractive domestic ware, including coffee sets, jugs, mugs and butter dishes are also made in a variety of beautiful glazes, and all items are replaceable if they get broken.

On a sunny day you can wander round the garden among the sweet-smelling plants, the rhododendrons and the flowering trees, which the owners have planted in the past fourteen years. The valley is very sheltered and sub-tropical plants flourish.

Ornamental poultry is kept, including pheasants, and there are peacocks which wander about among the visitors. Children enjoy the rabbits, guinea pigs, siamese cats, the dalmatian, the sheep dog, sheep, goats, ponies and donkeys. The aviaries house doves, finches and cockatiels, and a Mynah bird and an African Grey Parrot which talk back at you.

Practical details: The pottery is open daily

between 10 am and 6 pm from Easter to the end of August, after which time the coffee bar is closed. From September visitors can still watch the potters working and see their animals, but the place is occasionally closed completely during the winter. There is no guided tour. Visitors are welcome to wander about so long as they keep an eye on their children. No admission price is charged but collecting boxes for the World Wildlife Fund and North Wales Naturalist Trust are on display. The coffee bar sells simple snacks like hot scones. There is plenty to see and do, and if your day is not complete unless you have spent money, you can always buy a pomander.

Beddgelert pottery is off the main road between Llanfrothen and the famous Aberglaslyn bridge. Do not go through Nantmor village — it is a very hair-raising road.

50   Slate Quarrying Museum

Dinorwic Quarry Museum
Llanberis, Caernarvon, Gwynedd
Tel: Llanberis 630

Slate quarrying has been described as the most Welsh of Welsh industries, but for a number of years the slate quarries of North Wales have been closing down. Among the most recent of these is the Dinorwic Quarry, near Llanberis, which closed in 1969 after nearly two hundred years of working.

It was once the biggest slate quarry in the world. Three thousand men were employed in the great quarry, which rises in steplike terraces for 1,400 feet above the waters of Llyn Peris.

The workshops and their contents have been developed into a slate industry museum, and a new Museum Bookshop has also been opened recently.

Four of the original ten blacksmiths' hearths have been retained to make up one smithy, which contains many tongs and shaping tools. In the fitting shops machine tools are displayed, including different kinds of lathes, slotting machines, and drilling machines.

Slate dressing is featured in a section containing slate-sawing tables, slate-dressing machines and hand tools.
One of the museum's chief attractions is the waterwheel — over fifty feet in diameter, eighty horse-power and installed in 1870.
A film called 'Craftsmen of Dinorwic' is shown at regular intervals throughout the day.
Practical details: The museum is open every day, including Saturdays and Sundays, between 9.30 am and 7.30 pm, from Easter to September.
It is closed from October to March. Visitors can walk round freely on their own or take a guided tour. No advance notice is needed. There is a small admission charge.

51 Pottery and Hand-Weaving

Pennant Crafts
Betws-y-Coed Potters and Weavers
The Pottery, Betws-y-Coed, Gwynedd
Tel: Betws-y-Coed 224

This is a small family business run by T. A. and M. G. Edward, producing earthenware pottery and small woven goods in wool, mohair and acrylic. Visitors can see all the pottery processes and weaving on single width power looms. The shop sells their own products and those of other craftsmen.
Practical details: The shop is open Monday to Friday from 9.30 am to 6 pm and Saturday 9.30 am to 5 pm. Organised parties cannot be catered for, due to the size of the premises, but other visitors are welcome without prior notice.
The pottery is on the A5 to Capel Curig.

52 Slate Caverns

Quarry Tours Limited
Llechwedd Slate Caverns
Blaenau Ffestiniog, Gwynedd LL41 3NB
Tel: Blaenau Ffestiniog 306

'Thought provoking . . . educational . . .

unique . . .' say the advertisements. 'Take a tram-ride into a bygone age, and the vast underground slate quarries of Llechwedd.' At the quarries visitors climb aboard four-seater passenger cars, pulled by battery-driven locomotives, to tour the network of tunnels and caverns built in 1846. The tram takes you past the first abortive trial excavations to the new vein, stopping several times by tableaux of mining activities with the original machinery, or to admire vast caverns.
The guide accompanying the tram has worked in the slate mines and he explains what you see. One of the highlights of the tour are the spectacular cathedral-like caverns, where the guide turns off the lights, so that you can imagine how it felt to be a miner working by candlelight.
Using pillaring techniques pioneered three thousand years earlier in King Solomon's mines beneath Jerusalem, the miners made tier upon tier of these caverns. Visitors see only one of the sixteen floors — real mining takes place two floors below. Incidentally, the underground temperature stays constant at about 50°F (10°C) so take a cardigan or jacket with you in summer.
Demonstrations of slate cutting are often given to visitors and your guide explains the techniques. The word slate comes from the old French word *esclater*, meaning to split, and the blue-grey slate can be split into as many as thirty-six to forty sheets per inch. Slate was used for roofing tiles in every continent until the first world war when cement took over much of the market.
When the mine was opened to visitors in 1972 it was awarded both the Welsh Tourist Board's Festival of Wales Trophy and the British Tourist Board's Come to Britain Trophy — a unique double for a tourist attraction.
Practical details: In the summer season, March to October, the caverns are open seven days a week from 10 am to 6 pm. The last tram into the mines leaves at 5.15 pm. During winter the caverns can be opened for booked parties by prior arrangement only.
Morning visits usually offer the advantage of lighter traffic.
There is an admission charge, which includes

tramway fares, with reductions for pensioners and children under fourteen. Special rates apply to booked groups. Prices available on application.

The Llechwedd Slate Caverns are by the A470, half a mile north of Blaenau Ffestiniog. A free car park, cafe and gift shop are on the site.

53   Handmade Decorative Candles

Celmi Candles
Cynfal House, Ffestiniog
Gwynedd LL41 4ND
Tel: Ffestiniog 2675

Most visitors on entering the showroom of Celmi Candles comment on the pleasant aroma, which is due to the different candle perfumes in the atmosphere. From the showroom visitors can look through a glass

Down into the Llechwedd Slate Caverns

partition into the workshop.

Candles will be at different stages of manufacture. You may see the candlemakers setting up moulds, fixing wicks and pouring wax into the moulds. Or you might see them taking set candles out of moulds and polishing, wrapping and packing finished candles. Not all of these processes will be seen at any one time.

Celmi Candles manufacture a variety of candles in many shapes, colours and perfumes. Yellow beeswax candles are made with a distinctive honeycomb finish. They sell candles, candle-holders, pottery from two local potteries and slate goods. Seconds of candles and pottery are on sale

Practical details: Individuals are welcome any time during opening hours — Monday to Friday 9 am to 5 pm. Celmi Candles is closed at weekends and on bank holidays. Parties of more than ten people should make arrangements in advance.

54　Welsh Love Spoons

Charles Jones Woodcarving Workshop
Criccieth
Tel: Criccieth 2833

Mr. Jones is a carver of the traditional Welsh
love-spoon, which used to be carved on long
winter evenings by poor young men who
wanted to create a love token which cost
nothing. The intricacy of the carving
indicated the degree of devotion of the young
man.

Mr. Jones is self-taught. He turned his hobby

into a business to supplement his income
when pensioned off from the GPO, after
injuring his back. He carves from hardwoods
of fruit-bearing trees such as pear, lime, apple,
elm and sycamore. He still carves the
traditional symbols, the wheel meaning 'I
work for you', the heart meaning 'I love you',
the bells symbolising marriage, and the links
indicating the number of children the couple
hope to have.

He describes his work as a 'hobby gone mad'.
Orders are received from all over the world,
and Mr. Jones' wife and son are pressed into
helping with polishing the finished spoons
with beeswax.

Should you buy a spoon from Wales you have
a truly Welsh souvenir. And even if you cannot
carve yourself, but want initials and date
added so that you can present a spoon to your
sweetheart, you are following a time-
honoured Welsh tradition.

Mr. Jones also carves Welsh spinning and
prayer stools to customers' own designs.

Practical details: The workshop is open seven
days a week at most times of year except the
occasional day off. The workshop is adjacent
to the East Promenade car park.

55　Weaving Shed

The Weaver's Loft
Things Welsh Limited, Jubilee Road
Barmouth, Gwynedd LL42 1EF
Tel: Barmouth 280779

The weaving shed is housed in a converted
coachhouse and visitors can see bobbin-
making, warping and weaving. There are four
looms. The cloth is made from pure new wool
and woven in eighteen colour combinations.
The adjoining shop sells clothes made from
the mill's cloth, plus a vast and varied
selection of other craft work.

Practical details: The weaving shed is open
Monday to Thursday from 8 am to 5 pm and
on Friday from 8 am to 3 pm. The shop is open
daily in summer from 9 am to 9 pm, and in
winter from 9 am to 5 pm. All kinds of visitors
are accepted, including groups.

SEE THE NORTH AT WORK

Cheshire, Greater Manchester
Lancashire, West Yorkshire
South Yorkshire, Humberside
North Yorkshire, Cleveland
Durham, Tyne and Wear
Northumberland, Cumbria
Isle of Man

1   Vehicle Manufacturers

Fodens Limited
Elworth Works, Sandbach
Cheshire CW11 9HZ
Tel: Sandbach 3244

The company is an engineering firm which
started 120 years ago, before the dawn of the
day of the motor vehicle. Now it makes not
only commercial vehicle chassis and cabs but a
large proportion of component parts. Axles,
gearboxes and the like are cast, forged and
machined from the basic materials. The range
of vehicles covers two, three and four axle road
vehicles, two and three axle dump-trucks for
the construction industry, and other specialist
vehicles for industrial and military use.
Practical details: The vehicle plant is open all
year except for two weeks in August. Write to
A. Stubbs, the senior education and training
officer to make an appointment.

2   Oil-fired Power Station

Ince 'A' Power Station
Elton, Chester CH2 4LE
Tel: Thornton le Moors 351

Where you see that a power station is called 'A'
or 'B' it indicates that the 'B' station is of more
recent construction. The newer plant is more
efficient and invariably the machines are of
much greater output capacity. Ince 'A' is a 240
megawatt station having four 60 megawatt

Final finishing at Fodens Limited

units, whilst Ince 'B' is a 1,000 megawatt
station comprising two 500 megawatt units.
Ince 'A' is a brick building. Separate from it is
its one cooling tower. Water enters about half
way up and falls through a labyrinth which

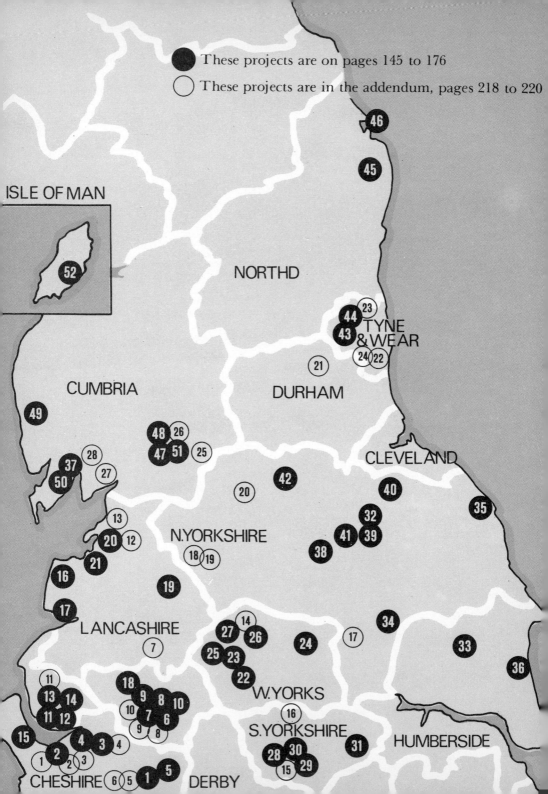

These projects are on pages 145 to 176

These projects are in the addendum, pages 218 to 220

ISLE OF MAN

52

NORTHD

CUMBRIA

46

45

23
44 TYNE
43 & WEAR
24 22

21

DURHAM

49

48 26
47 51 25

CLEVELAND

42

40

35

20

N.YORKSHIRE

32
41 39
38

28
37 27
50

13
20 12
21

18 19

19

16

17

LANCASHIRE

7

14
27 26

25 23

22

24

17

34

33

36

11

13 14

11 12

18
9 8
10 7 6
9 8
10

W.YORKS

16

S.YORKSHIRE

HUMBERSIDE

15

2

1 2 3

4 3 4

6 5 1 5

CHESHIRE

DERBY

28 30
15 29

31

Massive cooling towers at Fiddler's Ferry

breaks the water into rain-like spray which is cooled by the updraught of air.

Ince 'B' is a bright metal-clad building with one cooling tower — the only draught assisted cooling tower in the country (with a ring of special fans around the base). It looks the same size as the cooling tower by Ince 'A' but it is capable of handling four times as much water. The first unit of Ince 'B' station will come into operation in late 1978. The station should be completed in 1979.

Practical details: To see Ince 'A' write to the station manager a fortnight in advance. The time of tour is by arrangement between 9 am and 5 pm Monday to Friday throughout the year excepting bank holidays. Groups of ten to thirty people are accepted. Individuals who write a fortnight or so in advance could be attached to a group if such a visit has already been organised. Toddlers are not accepted. School parties and children supervised by parents are accepted. Ince 'B' is separately managed.

3   Coal-fired Power Station

Central Electricity Generating Board
Fiddler's Ferry Power Station
Widnes Road, Cuerdley
Near Warrington, Cheshire WA5 2UT
Tel: 051-424 2020

Fiddler's Ferry is the largest power station in the North West Region of the CEGB and has an output of 2,000 megawatts. The striking features of the station include the 650 foot high chimney, the eight massive cooling towers, the eighty-nine foot high turbine hall and the two hundred foot boiler house. Electricity is made by burning coal to produce steam to power turbo-generators. Some stations use oil or a nuclear reaction to produce the steam.

Coal is delivered to Fiddler's Ferry by British

A visiting group in the control room

Rail. Approximately twenty trains per day, which carry 1,000 tons, are received. The coal is discharged whilst the train is travelling at half a mile per hour over the track hoppers. Some of the coal is then transferred to stock by conveyor belts and the coal needed immediately is fed to the boiler house.
In the boiler house the coal is ground to a powder in pulverising mills. It is then mixed with air and blown into boilers where it burns in a similar manner to gas. The heat given off is used to turn the pure water which is circulating in tubes lining the boilers into high pressure steam.
There are four independent boilers at the station, each of which is capable of providing sufficient steam for one of the 500 megawatt turbo-generators. The steam from the boiler drives the turbine which is connected to the generator. The generator provides the electricity by rotating a sophisticated version of a magnet in coils of wire. Each one of the boiler/generator units, which can provide sufficient electricity for a city the size of Liverpool, is controlled remotely from the control tower room.
Having expended all its energy in the turbine the steam must then be converted back into water. This is done by passing the steam over thousands of brass tubes cooled by a separate circuit of cooling water. The temperature of the warm cooling water leaving the condenser

is reduced in the cooling towers so that it can be reused again, with only topping up supplies needed from the nearby river.
The cooling towers create a draught which passes through the warm cooling water as it sprinkles down a lattice inside the base of the tower. This produces some water vapour and it is this (and not smoke) which can be seen coming from the top of the towers. These towers are characteristic of inland power stations. By the coast, sea water can be used for cooling purposes — this is a much cheaper system.

Practical details: Contact the station manager by post or telephone 051-424 2020. Groups of up to twenty-one are preferred; the maximum number is twenty-eight. Conducted tours start at 2 pm and 7 pm by previous arrangement. No visitors are accepted at weekends or bank holidays. There is a·charge, depending on the size of the party, which includes tea and biscuits at the end of the visit. School parties free of charge.

4 Shellcraft and Driftwood Sculpture

Kay and Karen Wilson
Mary's Cottage, Vicarage Lane
Frodsham, Cheshire WA6 7DX
Tel: Frodsham 33375

Kay makes a wide range of shell animals and birds, abalone and mother-of-pearl jewellery, and modern collages made of shell and natural materials found on the sea shore. Her speciality is her jewellery, trinket and cigarette boxes and shell pictures, made as they were in the Victorian era.
Karen Wilson (Kay's daughter) carves in driftwood. Apart from abstract sculptures, her range includes bracelets, scarf rings, cuff-links, napkin rings; also walking sticks and love spoons completely hand carved in traditional woods. Although Karen now lives in Surrey a selection of her work is always available at Mary's Cottage and she will welcome visitors at her Surrey home if they write enclosing a stamped addressed envelope for an appointment (evenings only). (175

Croydon Road, Caterham, Surrey CR3 6PH.
Tel: 01-224 8670.)
Practical details: From Whit Sunday to the
end of September visits can be made between
11 am and 4 pm every day except Monday and
Thursday. Individuals should telephone in
advance; groups of up to twenty people should
write enclosing a stamped addressed envelope,
giving a choice of dates and two weeks' notice.
No children.
A group visit, for which there is a charge of
£3.50, includes a talk by Kay Wilson entitled
'Shells, their use and influence through the
ages', seeing Kay's wide collection of Regency
and Victorian shell work and of course a cup
of tea or coffee. There is always a selection of
shellcraft for sale.
Mary's Cottage is three-quarters of a mile from
the traffic lights in Frodsham, on the B5152.

5 Jodrell Bank

Jodrell Bank
Lower Withington
Macclesfield
Cheshire SK11 9DL
Tel: Lower Withington 339

Jodrell Bank's 250 foot radio telescope is still
one of the largest of its kind in the world. It is
driven by electric motors controlled by a
computer. Closed-circuit demonstrations,
photographs and diagrams show the
investigations of the astronomers and visitors
can steer a smaller 25 foot radio telescope
which picks up radio signals from the sun.
There are several working models.
The changing night sky is depicted on the
undersurface of the planetarium's dome and a
recorded commentary explains the
movements of the stars and planets.
Practical details: Jodrell Bank is open seven
days a week, 2 pm to 6 pm from Good Friday
to October 31st and from November 1st to
Easter at weekends only, 2 pm to 5 pm. It is
closed at Christmas and New Year. There is an
admission fee.
For further details write or telephone the
director, Mr. R. G. Lascelles.

6 Manchester Airport

Manchester International Airport
Manchester M22 5PA
Tel: 061-437 5233 Ext: 3712

Manchester International Airport is Britain's
second airport and it can handle more than
five million passengers a year. The airport
opened in 1938 and dealt with 4,500
passengers in its first year. It now handles the
same number in an hour!

The airport claims that more aircraft are
diverted to it than from it on account of bad
weather. The runway has been overlaid with a
porous friction course which improves its
characteristics in wet weather, and enables
aircraft to operate in higher crosswinds.
Airfield lighting is remotely controlled from
the control tower. There are two rows of light
bars on either side of the runway, and when the
aircraft descends at the correct slope (3°) the
pilot sees the nearer bars as white and the
distant bars as red. If he is too high both sets
appear white, if he is too low both sets appear
red.
In future the number of passengers is expected
to rise again, though less aircraft will be in use
because of the capacity of the latest planes.
The smaller planes seat about one hundred
passengers, but the new Lockheed 1011 Tristar
takes four hundred and the Boeing 747 'Jumbo
Jet' seats nearly five hundred people. You
should be able to spot a couple of the new
wide-bodied aircraft on your tour of the
airport.
Practical details: The airport is open every day
of the year and individuals and parties of any
size who do not want a guided tour may visit
the spectators' terraces. These are open from
dawn to dusk and no notice is required. Entry
to the terraces is by tokens, which can be
bought for a small fee from the kiosk at the
entrance. Groups who advise the airport
authority of their proposed visit in advance
can get a ten per cent discount, and parties of
retired people who are visiting midweek
(except on public holidays) can get in free.
Conducted tours are free and are booked up
well in advance. The airport director needs to

know the number of people in your group, dates and times of the proposed visit and alternative dates. There are two tours each day, for up to twenty-five people at a time, starting at 10.30 am, 2.30 pm or 7.30 pm. Tours cover the check-in hall, concourse, flight information control room and domestic lounge. The tours are general, not technical, and are suitable for children aged eight or over. There are no tours from midday Friday to midday Monday, nor on public holidays. Tours take about forty-five minutes, and afterwards you can eat and drink in the airport's restaurants and licensed bars.

7   Terry Towelling Weavers

W. M. Christy & Sons
Courtaulds Household Textiles
Terry Division, Fairfield Mills
Droylsden, Manchester M35 6PD
Tel: 061-370 3403

Fairfield Mills became famous for Terry towel weaving in the early 1850s after this unusual fabric was discovered in Turkey. Today the company employs about 475 people and Terry fabric is used for baby wear, beach clothes, dressing gowns, curtains, hospital blankets, tea towels and bar mats.
Processes include winding, creeling, sizing the ground warps, weaving on looms — some of which have attachments for Jacquard patterns, inspecting and side sewing, making up — including putting in labels, folding, shrink-wrapping, boxing and the final despatch of the completed towel.
Practical details: Christy's tours take place on Wednesday starting at 2 pm and ending at 4 pm. Groups of people up to thirty in number can be accepted, and as tours are usually fully booked several months ahead you should write to the personnel officer well in advance. There are no arrangements for individuals.

8   Manchester Stock Exchange

The Stock Exchange
6 Norfolk Street
Manchester M2 1DS
Tel: 061-833 0931

London has no monopoly on stock exchanges: others are found in Liverpool, Glasgow, Sheffield, Leeds, Newcastle, Birmingham and Manchester.
The only people allowed on the stock exchange floor are the brokers, jobbers and stock exchange staff, so visitors look down on the floor from the visitors' gallery, where there is a large computer screen showing a minute

Britain's second airport at night
Right: Huge weaving loom at Christy's

by minute record of prices. Casual visitors may pick up a leaflet and go up here by themselves, but it is better to arrange to join a group and hear an explanation of the proceedings. School parties are given a simple explanation of how the stock exchange works, what brokers and jobbers do and how to invest money. If sufficient notice is given, groups such as technical students, chartered accountants and bank employees can be given specialised talks relating to their particular interests.

For the layman it is fascinating enough to hear about 'bulls', 'bears', brokers and jobbers. The 'bull' (think of a bull in a china shop) is the optimist who expects the market to rise. He buys low before prices rise and sells when prices are high — hopefully just before they fall. The 'bear' (think of him as a grizzly misery of a pessimist) thinks the market will fall. He sells and hopes to buy back stocks and shares later when prices are low.

Practical details: The visitors' gallery is open from 10.15 am to 3.15 pm. Parties of up to twenty people who have booked in advance see the stock exchange trading floor, are shown a film (entitled 'My Word is my Bond'), and hear a talk from the guide. All groups are welcome,

particularly school parties. Individuals may join pre-arranged groups if they book in advance. Contact Miss Gillian Freeman for a suitable date.

9   Reproduction Coal Mine

The Salford Museum of Mining
Buile Hill Park
Eccles Old Road, Salford M6 8GL
Tel: 061-736 1832

As so many real mines are not open to the public, this museum, which contains a reproduction coal mine, provides an excellent opportunity for people who might not otherwise have the chance to see how a mine works.
Practical details: The two reproduction coal mines are generally open throughout the year, Monday to Friday. At present, the museum is only open to organised groups, and the group's leader must organise the guide, or lecture. Advance booking is essential. However, further galleries are being constructed, and they hope to be open to the general public by April 1979.

10   Port of Manchester

The Port of Manchester
Manchester Ship Canal Company
Ship Canal House, King Street
Manchester M2 4WX
Tel: 061-872 2411 Ext: 3188

The launch Silver Arrow II takes visitors round the Manchester Docks. There is a tour round the largest dock in the complex, which is over half a mile long. Visitors see the container terminal, which serves the Manchester-Montreal and Mediterranean services, and the 40,000 ton capacity grain elevator. The launch then enters Mode Wheel Locks and is lowered thirteen feet into the next section, where it passes the waterside oil refineries, an ore-discharging terminal, and factories in the Trafford Park Industrial Estate. The launch then goes to Barton Swing

Silver Arrow II touring Manchester Docks

Aqueduct and the road bridge.
The tour lasts about two hours and is accompanied by a guide.
Practical details: Tours take place from mid-February to November 30th, Monday to Saturday (except bank holidays), starting at 10 am and 2 pm.
The cost of tours is 40p per person. Afternoon tea is served in the Dock Office dining-room at the end of the tour and must be booked and paid for in advance. No refreshments are provided on morning or Saturday tours.
Group bookings can be made for no more than fifty-five people, and small groups and individuals are joined to existing parties when vacancies occur. Children under nine years of age must be accompanied by adults. Allow several weeks for making group arrangements as bookings are heavy in the holiday season,

and after booking dates have been confirmed
one month must be allowed for the issue of a
permit to enter the docks.
Envelopes of letters of application should be
marked Tours in the top left-hand corner, and
Mrs. Taylor, of the public relations
department, is the person to whom you should
apply.

11   Liverpool Law Courts

St. George's Hall, Liverpool

Members of the public can attend court
sessions and are welcome at the recitals held in
the main hall.
St. George's Hall itself is of great architectural
interest and experts have described it as the
finest example of Greco-Roman building in
Europe. Today it is used primarily as the
City's Law Courts — there are seven courts of
law — and concerts and exhibitions are
occasionally held here.
Practical details: The courts are in session and
open to the public Monday to Friday, 10.30 am
to 1 pm and 2.15 pm to 4.30 pm.
To obtain details of recitals and possible
private visits during public holidays
contact St George's Hall direct. Tel:
051-709 3752.

12   Liverpool Airport

Liverpool Airport
Liverpool L24 8QQ
Tel: 051-427 4101

Liverpool Airport started operations in 1930.
Scheduled flights operate within the UK and
Ireland, and holiday flights to resorts in
Europe. The main runway is 2286 metres long
and is highly developed to give 97% usability
allowing for a 20 knot crosswind.
Practical details: Guided tours of the airport
are available for organised parties. A written
application to the Airport Director is
necessary. The spectators' balcony is open to
all from April to September each year.

13   Municipal Government

The Town Hall
Liverpool L2 3SW
Tel: 051-236 5181

Public debates take place in the City
Council Chamber and from the public gallery
you will see that the chamber is divided, with
the controlling party to the left of the Lord
Mayor and the opposition to the right. Each
member's seat is equipped with microphone
and speaker, controlled from a panel behind
the dais. The ninety-nine members have had
many marathon sittings including one in 1968
which lasted thirteen hours. The building
itself has a splendid classical facade and the
amazing chandeliers and golden decorations
of the ballrooms are of great interest.
Practical details: Visitors must make prior
arrangements to attend Council Day which is
on a Wednesday. The exact times can be
checked by a telephone enquiry. No notice
need be given to visit during the two weeks
in August when attendants are on duty and a
thirty-minute tour is given.

14   Motor Car Manufacturers

Ford Motor Company Limited
Halewood, Liverpool L24 9LE
Tel: 051-486 3900

This famous factory produces more than one
thousand cars every day, and is the only car

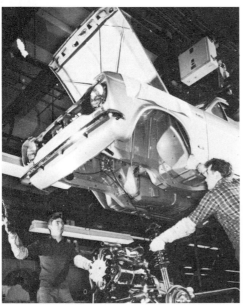

Making car seats and cushions at Fords

Above: The metal assembly area at Fords

Left: A Ford body is 'married' to its engine

factory in the country where complete cars are produced under one roof. Visitors can watch the whole process of manufacture, from the introduction of the sheet steel into the building, right through to the despatch of shiny new cars to showrooms all over the world.

Naturally you will not be able to see the progress of any one particular car as it takes twenty-five hours to build one from start to finish, but you will be able to see each separate process in operation. These include the panels of steel being beaten into shape, the several coats of paint, the engines going into the body shells, the wheels, seats, controls and such like being fitted.

Eventually come the stringent tests that cars undergo before being allowed out of the factory. Ford of Halewood are currently producing Ford Escorts only.

Practical details: Contact Mr. G. Stubbs on extension 6291 to arrange an appointment. Tours operate Monday to Friday starting at 9.30 am and 1.30 pm, and it is essential to book well in advance, as they are booked up as much as six months ahead. When writing it is advisable to give alternative dates. Individuals and all types of parties are accepted, but there is a lower age limit of twelve years, and a maximum of twenty-five people per party. Light refreshments are served free of charge during the two-hour tour.

Visitors should report to Number One gate. The factory is on the main Liverpool to Widnes road.

15 Soap Factory and Employees' Village

Lever Brothers Limited
Port Sunlight, Wirral, Merseyside
Tel: 051-645 2000 Ext: 8326

There is a choice of tours at Lever Brothers. One can firstly see the factory which is the largest of its kind in the world. Here soap and detergents are produced and packed.

The soap factory was founded by the first Lord Leverhulme, who had a vision of creating a village community where 'our workpeople

will be able to live and be comfortable. . . .'. It is this award-winning community scheme that one sees on the village tour.

About three thousand employees and older people live in the nine hundred houses, flats or maisonettes.

There is a dell with trees and flower beds, a ballroom, hotel and restaurant, school, library, theatre and training centre.

Practical details: Anyone interested in factory tours should apply to Mr. J. E. Threadgill at the above address. Tours are usually held on Tuesday, Wednesday and Thursday afternoons.

Organised groups of up to twenty people are accepted. Individuals can arrange to join smaller groups but should apply in advance. For village tours contact Mr John Wakefield at UML Ltd., Lever House, Bebington, Wirral, Merseyside. Tel: 051-645 2000 Ext: 217.

Soapmaking plant at Lever Brothers

16 Pottery at Thornton

Thornton Pottery
Potters Barn, 2 Fleetwood Road North
(Four Lane Ends), Thornton
Cleveleys, Blackpool, Lancashire
Tel: Cleveleys 5045

Potters Barn is more than 250 years old. The building now has a studio, kiln room, store room and two display galleries.

The pottery is hand-made in porcelain, stoneware and high fired earthenware. There should be something new to see every year, because the potters experiment to produce new and original finishes when the pottery is closed to the public during the winter. They believe that experimental work is one of the main functions of the studio potter.

The kilns are fired by electricity to temperatures between 1120°C to 1280°C in an oxidising atmosphere. These temperatures ensure the durability of the pottery. Candles are also made here, and all the goods can be bought on the premises.

The pottery's trade mark is a mill. You might look out for the windmill at Thornton. It is one of the few left in England which is in perfect condition.

Practical details: The pottery is open to individuals and small parties from 2 pm to 5 pm every day from June to Christmas, and closed from Christmas until Whitsun. It opens at other times by appointment. Parties of between twenty and thirty are shown the process of pottery making in the mornings and evenings.

Potters Barn is on the corner of the A585 to Fleetwood and the B5412 at Cleveleys. It is only five miles from Blackpool.

17   Premium Bond Office—ERNIE

Department for National Savings
Bonds and Stock Office
Lytham St. Anne's, Lancashire FY0 1YN
Tel: St Anne's 721212

A talk is given and a film about ERNIE is shown, followed by a demonstration of ERNIE in action. ERNIE is probably the best-known piece of electronic equipment in Britain. It is the Premium Bond draw machine at Lytham St. Anne's on the Lancashire coast. Every month ERNIE, whose initials stand for Electronic Random Number Indicator Equipment, pays out millions of pounds in Premium Bond prizes. Constant checks are made to ensure that ERNIE remains strictly impartial and that each eligible bond unit has an equal chance of winning a prize. Since the scheme began in 1956 more than £500 million

ERNIE — electronic equipment extraordinary!

has been distributed in prizes. Hundreds of civil servants work at the Bond Office and they notify winners by post of their good fortune. Premium Bonds differ from ordinary investments in that the distribution of prizes takes the place of interest or dividends. In addition, holders can always be sure of getting a pound for pound repayment of the money they have invested. There are twenty-one million holders of Premium Bonds, and as the pound is worth less every year anyway, they probably think that they might as well leave the money there and hope for a win.

Practical details: The office is open for visits Monday to Friday except Christmas, New Year, Easter and bank holidays. Visits start at 2 pm and last about two hours.

Parties of up to sixty people can be accepted, and the minimum booking is for twenty-five people. Individuals are welcome if they book in advance and are prepared to fit in with a pre-booked group. Educational groups of older children are also accepted. Visits are by appointment only and are so popular that there is a twelve month waiting list.

18   Weaving Museum

Tonge Moor Textile Museum
Tonge Moor Library, Tonge Moor Road
Bolton, Lancashire
Tel: Bolton 21394

Tonge Moor Textile Museum houses a

collection of important early textile machines including Crompton's Spinning Mule, Hargreave's Spinning Jenny and Arkwright's water frame. It illustrates the history of the development of the fine cotton spinning industry.

The museum leaflet covers early spinning and weaving, the revolutionary eighteenth century inventions and twentieth century inventions, including man-made fibres.

Practical details: The museum is open to the public on Monday to Saturday excluding bank holidays: on Monday, Tuesday and Thursday from 9.30 am to 7.30 pm; on Wednesday from 9.30 am to 1 pm; on Friday from 9.30 am to 5 pm and on Saturday from 9.30 am to 12.30 pm. Groups should telephone in advance. There is no guided tour but the museum's leaflet is given to school parties.

19   Green Slate Workshop

Lake District Green Slate Co. Limited
Fence Gate, Fence, Near Burnley, Lancs.
Tel: Nelson 66952

Slate comes in various colours — blue, black, purple and brown, but here in the Lake District it has a greenish tinge. The local slate, excavated from Coniston and Elterwater, about eighty miles away, is brought to the slate workshop in ten ton loads.

A craftsman at Lake District Green Slate

Six or seven of the workforce of ten can be seen at any one time making the slate into fancy goods and gifts. You will see slate being cut with diamond saws and made up. If slate is used as a mount for a clock or thermometer the object being mounted is glued on. The slate is finished with a sealant which stops it getting dirty and gives it a slight eggshell glaze. Some of the slate is made into house signs — names and numbers are engraved with a hammer and chisel. Holidaymakers can order house signs and have them sent on by post a week later. Other pieces of slate are made into parts for DIY fireplaces.

Products are sold in the shop by the entrance.

Practical details: The workshop can be visited at any time of year except Christmas week by individuals and groups of up to ten people. Workshop and shop are open Monday to Friday from 8 am to 5 pm and on Saturday until 4 pm. Visitors are welcome to walk in and look around without prior notice. There is no charge.

The workshop is on the A6068 Padiham-Nelson by-pass.

20   Large Popular Pottery

Hornsea Pottery (Lancaster)
Wyresdale Road
Lancaster LA1 3LA
Tel: Lancaster 68444

This spotless new pottery, with its 42-acre leisure park, is a branch of the famous Hornsea Pottery at Hornsea in Yorkshire, and offers similar varied entertainment for all the family.

The original Hornsea Pottery was started by two hard-working brothers with a second-hand kiln. They decided that their huge Hornsea site had been developed to capacity. So they looked for a second site. Lancaster was chosen because of the encouragement they received from the City Council, and this enabled the brothers to 'link the white rose and the red'. (In the 15th century Wars of the Roses the Lancastrian emblem was the red rose.)

Production started at the pottery in 1974 and it was opened to the public in 1976. In 1977 the pottery received an estimated 640,000 visitors.

The Lancaster products are manufactured by an entirely new ceramic process, with kilns operating at infinitely higher temperatures. The end product is a range of tableware which is fully vitrified, rock hard, chip resistant, oven, dishwasher and freezer safe. Production at Lancaster began with 'Contrast' oven-to-tableware which won the 1975 Design Council Award and gained a place for posterity in the Victoria and Albert Museum. The name is apt because the white glazed surfaces contrast with the rich, brown, pebble-smooth finish of the remainder. The range also includes new patterns called 'Impact', 'Contour', 'Pastoral' and 'Palatine' — all of which are Design Council Approved. The pottery also makes a wide variety of mugs including special commemorative mugs.

'Contrast' emerging from the kiln at Lancaster

'Young Lovers' mugs are a striking range made in the vitrimic body. A set of twelve designs depicts young lovers pursuing their courtship in a whimsical yet romantic manner.

The absorbing factory tour shows the whole production process from claymaking to firing.

Practical details: Everything in the factory and immediately around it is on one level, so the outing is very suitable for the elderly. The landscaped parkland has a picnic area, cafe, tea garden and children's playground.

Miniature golf and a small children's farmyard have been added to entertain the children, and by 1979 a Rare Breed Survival Farm will be established on the hillside above the factory.

The pottery is open all year round except for one week at Christmas. At Easter and spring bank holiday from 10 am to 6 pm. In summer during July to the first week in September, Monday to Saturday from 10 am to 6 pm, and on Sundays 10 am to 7 pm. During the rest of the year the opening hours are from 10 am to 5 pm each day, every day of the week.

For party bookings write to: The Visits Organiser, Hornsea Pottery Company Limited (Lancaster), Wyresdale Road, Lancaster LA1 3LA. There is ample free parking for cars and coaches. The factory is just off the M6 motorway.

21   Nuclear Power Station

Heysham Nuclear Power Station
Heysham, Morecambe, Lancashire
Tel: Heysham 53131

Building work on Heysham nuclear power station began in October 1970. Members of the public can watch the construction of this technological project from a hilltop observation tower on site. The two large square main buildings are more or less completed and in 1979 the station will start to generate electricity from nuclear power for the national grid. Meanwhile, construction is still in progress and the workforce is being trained.

Construction at Heysham Power Station

It is estimated that the project will have cost over £200 million by the time it is finished.

Practical details: The tower is open daily from 10 am to dusk from Easter to the end of September. Admission is free. Approved parties of between ten and thirty people can visit the station itself by prior arrangement in writing with the station manager. Smaller numbers can write in to ask if they can join a group which has already booked. Children under fourteen years cannot be taken on tours of the station building.

22   Quality Garment Factory

Kagan Textiles Limited
Gannex Mills, Elland, West Yorkshire
Tel: Elland 3371

Many clothes-conscious people will be familiar with the Gannex label. Gannex garments are made from top-quality blends of fabric, including pure wool, mohair and mink, pure alpaca and cashmere. Gannex

rainwear is pressure-waterproof, windproof
and air-insulated.
Visitors see all the cloth processing
departments. At the garment factory they see
the cutting, sewing, inspection and passing
departments, and also the customer service
department.
Practical details: The factory is open from
9 am to 5 pm and daytime visits are arranged at
all times of year except bank holidays, the last
three weeks in July and the second week in
September. Parties of schoolchildren or adults
are accepted, preferably in groups of about
thirty people. Individuals are welcome to join
smaller groups. Contact the company by letter
a month in advance.

23   Stoneware Pottery

Shelf Pottery Limited
Brooklands, Brighouse Road
Hipperholme, Halifax, West Yorkshire
Tel: Halifax 202366

Shelf pottery produces a range of stoneware
pottery, including oven-to-tableware, lamp
bases and decorative flower vases — all
produced in a variety of attractive stoneware
glazes. The lamp bases and vases are designed
to match each other and are made in many
shapes and sizes.
The pottery is run by two partners and their
wives, and a number of people are employed
both on a full-time and part-time basis.
Practical details: The pottery is open all year
round, Monday to Friday from 9 am to
6.30 pm and on Saturday and Sunday from
9 am to 11 am.
Individual visitors are welcome to look round
the pottery during these times. Unfortunately
no provision can be made for group visits.
The pottery produced here is normally sold
through retail outlets. However, a selection
of seconds are sold to visitors in the
showroom.
In their attempt to assist other small craft
producers Shelf Pottery also sells a range
of horse-nail jewellery, wood burnings,
macrame and basket ware.

24   Theatre

Leeds Playhouse
Calverley Street
Leeds LS2 3AJ
Tel: Leeds 42111

Leeds Playhouse is West Yorkshire's only
professional repertory theatre. It presents a
wide variety of plays, occasional concerts and
film shows on Saturdays and Sundays. It has
its own Theatre-in-Education team who
perform in schools throughout the country.
Practical details: Small parties seeing a
production at the Playhouse can sometimes be
given a tour of the theatre. For further details
telephone the assistant administrator at Leeds
42141.

25   Pot Luck Pottery

Pot Luck
'The Old Fire Station', Cragg Road
Mytholmroyd, Hebden Bridge
West Yorkshire HX1 5EG
Tel: Calder Valley 3651

Pot Luck Pottery is owned by Mr Edward
Underhill, a friendly, talkative man, who
worked in silk-screen printing for six years
before taking a degree in ceramics as a mature
student. You will see him and his four or five
part-time staff at work.
Groups of twelve to fifteen people can visit
the pottery by appointment. Mr Underhill
shows them all the processes, including high-
speed industrial methods, how to use plaster
moulds, slip casting and so on, plus printing
on tiles. There is a fixed charge for a group
visit, and coffee is served.
The pottery made here ranges from domestic
and kitchenware to ornamental and
decorative pieces. Most of it has on-glaze
decoration. Mr Underhill designs and hand-
prints tiles, which can be used for bathrooms,
kitchens or coffee tables. These are sold in
the shop. He also welcomes commissions,
making limited editions of commemorative
pieces and presents.

The pottery produces both earthenware and stoneware. For their commemorative pieces they buy china produced in Stoke-on-Trent which they then decorate. For example, in 1976 they depicted the Piece Hall (cloth and wool exchange) in Halifax, 6 miles away. In 1977 they decorated a Jubilee plate with the places in Yorkshire visited by the Queen during her reign, and in 1979 they will probably decorate another plate to show the Piece Hall for its bicentenary.

Other goods are displayed in the shop.
Practical details: The shop is open from Monday to Friday, 10 am to 6 pm, and on Saturday and Sunday from 2 pm to 6 pm. Visitors can see the workshop only by prior arrangement. Coach parties are not accepted. Mytholmroyd is on the main A646. The pottery is on the B6138.

26   Industrial Museum

Bradford Industrial Museum
Moorside Mills, Moorside Road
Bradford BD2 3HP
Tel: Bradford 631756

Bradford Industrial Museum is housed in a typical worsted spinning mill. You can see working machines used to convert raw wool into lengths of worsted material. It shows development from prehistoric times to the days of the huge mills. There is a stationary steam engine, a working waterwheel, the last surviving Bradford tram and a trolley bus.

Exhibits at Bradford Industrial Museum

In the grounds is the home of the mill owner which is furnished to show the life of a middle-class family in late Victorian times.
Practical details: The museum is open from 10 am to 5 pm seven days a week, including bank holidays, but with the exception of Christmas Day and Good Friday. All visitors are welcome. School parties should obtain the school booking form from the curator. The recommended maximum size of groups is forty people. There is no admission charge, and a car park is available.

27   Hand-loom Weaving

Bronte Tapestries
Ponden Hall, Stanbury, Near Haworth
West Yorkshire BD22 0HR
Tel: Haworth 44154

Bronte Tapestries is a co-ownership which fluctuates between four and ten people. It was started in 1962 by Roderick Taylor and only recently moved to Ponden Hall. Ponden Hall was built in 1560 and was made famous as 'Thrushcross Grange' in Wuthering Heights. Demonstrations of weaving are given.

The *showroom* is situated at Ponden Mill which was originally a corn mill. There is a demonstration hand loom here also, and many of the products made at the studio are displayed.
Practical details: The studio at Ponden Hall is open to visitors at anytime but it is inaccessible to coaches. There is a small admission fee. The *showroom*, at Ponden Mill (same address and telephone number) is open from 9.30 am to 5 pm. Admission is free and coaches are welcome.

28   Hand Tool Manufacturers

Record Ridgway Limited
Parkway Works, Sheffield S9 3BL
Tel: Sheffield 449066

Hand tools are manufactured here under the brand names of Record, Ridgway, Marples

Record Ridgway—vices near completion

and Gilbow. The group is a large public company employing about 1,800 workers in seven factories.
Practical details: Organised trade groups are accepted, but arrangements must be made in advance.

29   Scythe and Steelworks

Abbeydale Industrial Hamlet
Abbeydale Road South, Sheffield
South Yorkshire S7 2QW
Tel: Sheffield 367731

Here on the River Sheaf you will see a restored waterpowered scythe and steelworks dating from the late eighteenth and early nineteenth century with associated domestic housing. Souvenirs are available from the museum shop.
There are special events such as working days, children's working days and an annual craftsman's fair.
Practical details: Abbeydale Industrial Hamlet is open Monday to Saturday from 10 am to 5 pm and on Sunday from 11 am to 5 pm with extended hours till 8 pm (daily)

from spring bank holiday Monday to summer bank holiday Monday. It is closed on Christmas Eve, Christmas Day and Boxing Day. There is a small charge but pensioners are admitted free. A small charge is made for parking. A cafe is open during summer.
A charge is made for a pre-booked guide, but teachers can take a one-day course which will enable them to take their classes around. They are advised to read the Hamlet guide and museum information sheets as pre-visit teaching aids.
(Also enquire about Shepherd Wheel, Whiteley Wood, Sheffield. A waterwheel drives two cutlery grinding systems. It is open until 5 pm Wednesday to Sunday and on bank holiday Mondays and Tuesdays. It is closed on Christmas Eve, Christmas and Boxing Day and between 12.30 and 1.30 pm. Individuals are welcome and groups must contact Abbeydale Industrial Hamlet first.)

30   One-man Pottery

Pear Tree Potteries, Firbeck Lane
Laughton, near Sheffield
Tel: Dinnington 4788

Mr. Newman makes pots in the traditional manner — he decorates, glazes and does everything himself — even sweeping up! He gets a large number of overseas visitors in summer.
The pottery is in a 180-year-old chapel — a lovely old building.
Practical details: The pottery is open seven days a week from 10 am to 5 pm, including bank holidays. At weekends visitors can see pottery being made all day at the wheel. Mr. Newman tells us that as he doesn't employ labour, so he can only make the pots at weekends because of having to spend time on other processes.
School children are accepted by prior arrangement. Evening visits for groups can be arranged by appointment and include a talk on pottery, a demonstration on the wheel and a chance for one or two people to have a go themselves.

31   Unusual Jigsaws

Puzzleplex
Stubbs Walden, Doncaster
South Yorkshire DN6 9BY
Tel: Doncaster 700997

Puzzleplex is run by Peter and Dinah Stocken
who specialise in three dimensional jigsaws,
devised by Peter. The puzzles are very difficult
to put together as the average number of pieces
is about thirty and each piece interlocks in
every direction!
Most people take more than two hours over the
puzzles, though the occasional puzzle
genius has been known to assemble a puzzle in
twenty minutes.
The usual size of the jigsaws is three and a
half inches across, and one and a half inches
deep. Simple shapes include a heart, a
diamond and a circle.
There are also complex shapes such as a four-
leaf clover, a whale, an elephant or a bus.
Care is taken to select woods with an attractive
grain and in the case of home grown woods the
Stockens even choose a tree which is still
standing. The woods which they use include
English beech, red Paduak, yew, walnut
and holly.
Precious woods include Indian laurel, Indian
rosewood and olivewood.
Jigsaws are popular with people of all ages
and here at Puzzleplex they make jigsaws to
fascinate even those who are not jigsaw fans,
and jigsaw enthusiasts will be amazed and
delighted.
Prices range from £9 for a simple shape in
a basic wood to more than £70 for a complex
adults' puzzle in rare ebony wood, complete
with velvet lined presentation case bearing
a brass plaque giving the name of the
owner.
Practical details: Peter and Dinah Stocken
welcome individuals and small parties but not
groups. Visitors will see the making of
handmade puzzles. Goods can be ordered, or
purchased when in stock.
Puzzleplex is 'impossible' to find, they say,
so get directions from them before you set
off.

32   Country Furniture Workshop

Treske Ltd
Station Works, Thirsk
North Yorkshire YO7 4NY
Tel: Thirsk 22770

This furniture workshop uses one wood —
Yorkshire grown ash, and is probably the only
workshop in the country specialising in
English ash. The modern workshops are in an
imaginatively converted 150-year-old
maltings. Machine work is done on the
ground level, where the old quarry-tiled floor
has been preserved. Pillars support an upper
floor in the centre of the building, where hand
craft work is carried out. Around the upper
floor a 300-foot gangway has been built
specifically to enable visitors to walk around
watching work at both levels.
When the timber has been sawn at local mills
it is stored on the premises to dry out. If wood
is not thoroughly dried it shrinks and warps
later, particularly in centrally-heated homes.
Ash has one great advantage. It takes only six
months to a year to be dried out. At Treske's
they make a wide range of tables, chairs,
dressers, sideboards and chests; also smaller

items such as bread and pastry boards, napkin rings, children's building blocks and book ends. The two showrooms and the illustrated walkway enable you to see every aspect of the processes — wood being sawn and planed, mortice and tenon joints being made, high speed Router work (cutting at 24,000 revolutions per minute) — right through to the final polishing.

Ash is a porous wood, and to get a smooth finish they have perfected a method of sealing it with cellulose and coating the surface with clear melamine. This is more expensive than using polyurethane, but produces a softer feel and a more durable finish. Tables treated this way are heat-resistant and do not need table mats.

Ash is a hard wood, and their standard range is all solid wood — no veneer. Dining tables include round, rectangular or refectory styles and there are chunky solid-looking rockers as well as upholstered dining chairs. The light-coloured ash, which looks not unlike stripped pine, suits modern homes. Ash comes in a variety of colourings — white, brown, tan and olive. It can also be stained. Some stained black ash furniture is sold in a major department store under the house brand name, but most of Treske's products are sold here, direct to the public. The majority of their sales are to farmers and others living in the area. The firm also make up furniture to individual requirements. They aim to appeal to English taste though they use intenationally known designers for the main lines, and have exported to an Arabian place or two. Traditionally, oak is used in churches, but Treske's are trying to get ash accepted in modern churches. Photographs in their display show where ash has been used. About ten people work here full-time and an unusual feature of the place is that it is residential. The manager and his wife, and the apprentices live at the old kiln end of the factory, so it is open to visitors at all times.

Practical details: Treske Ltd is a mile from Thirsk and buses and trains stop beside the workshops. Groups should give a few days' notice. Tea can be provided by arrangement. There is no charge. Individuals can walk in unannounced. The name Treske is from the Anglo-Saxon spelling of Thirsk.

33   Oak Furniture and Workshops

Oak Rabbit Crafts
Wetwang, Driffield
North Humberside YO25 9XJ
Tel: Driffield 86257

Oak Rabbit Crafts was established in 1970 and all the articles are made in English oak and bear the registered trademark of a carved rabbit. There are no specific talks or demonstrations but visitors can look around the three showrooms and the workshop.

In the first showroom visitors can see small articles ranging from ashtrays to nests of tables. The main showroom displays dining furniture and small pieces, all with an adzed finish. The third showroom is for bedroom furniture.

In the workshops craftsmen can be seen carving the rabbit which is on each piece of furniture, or carving lattices for dining-chair backs, or perhaps turning fruit bowls, and making up furniture.

The locally produced oak can be seen stacked on the premises where it is seasoned for years before it is ready for use.

Practical details: The workshops and showrooms are open Monday to Friday from 8 am to 5 pm, and most weekends from 10 am to 5 pm. Individuals and groups are welcome but parties should book well in advance to arrange a suitable time. If they wish to see work being done, visits must be arranged during the week before 5 pm, although evening visits can be made by prior arrangement.

Visitors may purchase goods.

34   Edwardian Street and Craft Workshops

Castle Museum
York YO1 2RY
Tel: York 53611

The most famous part of the Castle Museum is an Edwardian cobbled street of tiny shops, their windows and shelves crammed with old-fashioned goodies. The museum sets out to show how people have lived and worked in Yorkshire during the last four hundred years. Parents enjoy this nostalgic scene even more than the children.

The museum has period rooms, a tithe barn interior and Victorian streets. The debtors' prison to the right of the entrance hall has a military collection, costumes and toys, the Edwardian street and craft workshops. Outside the museum is the working water-driven cornmill.

Practical details: The museum is open to everyone all year on Monday to Saturday, from 9.30 am to 6.30 pm (closing at 5 pm from October to March); and on Sunday from 10 am to 6 pm (closing at 5 pm in winter). The turnstiles shut half an hour before closing time. The museum is closed on Christmas Day, Boxing Day and New Year's Day but open on other bank holidays from 9.30 am to 6.30 pm. Prior booking is required for school parties in May, June and July — send an s.a.e. for application forms. Evening visits can be arranged.

As well as extensive teaching materials, the museum sells a variety of books, guides, transparencies and postcards.

35   RNLI Life-boats

Royal National Life-boat Institution
Life-boat Museum, Pier Road, Whitby
Tel: Whitby 2001

At Whitby you can see the old and the new — perhaps the best RNLI Museum in the country and a modern life-boat station. The main feature of the Whitby Life-boat Museum is the last life-boat to be pulled by oars in this country — used as recently as 1957! The old life-boat house was turned into a museum in 1955 by Mr. Eric Thomson and displays hundreds of photographs, line-throwing guns, anchors and all sorts of paraphernalia connected with life-boats. Mr. Thomson, who is now semi-retired, repairs and renovates the museum models in his workshop and his son Peter, mechanic of one of the Whitby life-boats, has painted a scene showing how in 1881 the Whitby life-boat was hauled overland through deep snow to Robin Hood's Bay. There is a full page account from the Whitby Gazette of February 1861: 'Loss of the crew of the Whitby life-boat'. The north coast of England is closely associated with the development of life-boats. The first life-boat station in Britain was started in Bamburgh — the birthplace of Grace Darling — in 1786.

The oldest life-boat still in existence in the world, the Zetland, can be seen at Redcar (approximately twenty miles north of Whitby). By way of contrast there is also a modern life-boat at Redcar which can be seen when the boathouse is open during the holiday season.

On the opposite bank of the river to the Whitby Museum, about two hundred yards away, you can see an example of one of today's RNLI sea-going boats. (You might also see the inshore life-boat, if it is called out or goes on an exercise.)

The Whitby life-boat is typical of one of the boats based on latest American designs. These are built of steel, not wood. They have seats fitted with car-type seat belts to keep you anchored in rough weather. Their technical equipment includes radar, VHF/UHF radio, and an intercom between the after cabin and the wheelhouse, so that the helmsman and radio operator can communicate. Another of these modern boats can be seen at Hartlepool. Several life-boat stations in Britain open for visitors. As at Whitby, they make no charge, but sell souvenirs such as tea towels, head scarves, key-rings and note-pads.

Practical details: Whitby Life-boat Museum is open at weekends from Easter to Whitsun, and daily from Whitsun to the end of September. There are no set times but opening hours are roughly 10.45 am to 5 pm. The museum can be opened specially out of season for school parties and even individuals. There is no charge. Parties can write to Mr. Eric Thomson, 4 Wentworth Crescent, Whitby. Tel: Whitby 2001.

If you are interested in visiting another life-boat station, send a stamped addressed envelope to Mr. Andrew Gould, RNLI, West Quay Road, Poole, Dorset (Tel: Poole 71133) and he will send you the address of the secretary of your nearest life-boat station.

36   Large Popular Pottery

Hornsea Pottery
Hornsea, Yorkshire HU18 1UD
Tel: Hornsea 2161

The Rawson brothers started the pottery in their home with a tiny second-hand kiln. They had no experience but their success has been phenomenal. Hornsea Pottery now employs about three hundred people and produces four

Packing kiln trucks at Hornsea Pottery
The RNLI—launching for a practice run

million pots a year.

Hornsea is noted for its modern designs and for its special decorative effects. All Hornsea tableware is Design Council accepted and is safe for use in freezers, ovens and dish-washers.

The absorbing factory tour (30 minutes) shows the production process right through from clay making to glazing and firing. Hornsea Pottery has broken away from traditional methods of decorating tableware by perfecting their own method of screen-printing onto pots, with a specially formulated (and patented) ink. The results are unique after firing — a contrast between the colour of the glaze and the pattern, and between the texture of the smooth and glass-hard glaze and the matt decoration.

The pottery is popular, and provides plenty of entertainment for a family day out. It is set in a twenty-eight acre landscaped leisure park featuring a lake, playground, picnic areas, pony rides, aviary and mini-zoo for the children, and a tea garden. There is a gift shop and a large country craft centre selling house plants, kitchenware and a range of speciality foods and wines.

The magnet for most visitors, however, is the famous pottery shop stocked with Hornsea's selected seconds where you can browse at leisure and pick up a basketful of bargains. A new model village is being constructed and is planned to open in 1979.

Practical details: The pottery is open all year round except for one week at Christmas. At Easter and spring bank holiday from 10 am to 6 pm. In summer, during July to the first week in September, Monday to Saturday from 10 am to 6 pm, Sundays until 7 pm. During the rest of the year opening hours are from 10 am to 5 pm each day, every day of the week.

For party bookings write to the Visits Organiser. There is ample free parking for coaches and cars.

37 Designer/Screen Printer

Wendy Todd Textiles
Corn Mill Galleries
The Old Town Mill
Ulverston, Cumbria
Tel: Ulverston 55456

Wendy Todd works in a 17th century corn mill which has been converted into a large workshop for hand printing textiles. The galleries display silk scarves and ties, fashions, cushions, table linens, unusual greetings cards on linen, and dress and furnishing fabrics produced here. Also exhibited are paintings and craftwork including jewellery, silverwork, ceramics, glass and weaving. The textiles are all designed by Wendy, and she wholesales to other shops and undertakes commissions.

Practical details: Corn Mill Galleries and workshop are open from 9.30 am to 5.30 pm Tuesday to Saturday. Visitors are welcome to watch the printing at any time during opening hours. Demonstrations can be arranged for parties of up to 50 people, by appointment. The waterwheel and corn-grinding machinery should be in operation by 1979/80.

Silk screen printing at Wendy Todd Textiles

38 Spinning and Weaving

Malcolm McDougall weaving fine worsteds

Grewelthorpe Handweavers
Grewelthorpe, Ripon HG4 3BW
Tel: Kirkby Malzeard 209

The main output of the workshop is cloth
made from Botany yarn for exclusive evening
skirts and dresses. Other articles made here
include dolls, tapestry belts, bell pulls, drink
mats, doll and drink mat kits, collage kits,
fudge, spinning spindles and french knitters.
Grewelthorpe Handweavers run a lecture-
demonstration which lasts about forty
minutes. For the average adult group Mr. and
Mrs. McDougall explain and demonstrate the
principles of spinning and weaving. As their
system dates from 1750 (immediately before
the industrial revolution) they can follow the
historical theme (for schools, for instance), or
show how the craft workshop is adapted for
today's conditions (for students or other
career-minded groups).
For handicapped children they concentrate on
realistic basic skills — spindle weaving, braid

weaving and so on.
The business is a husband-and-wife team with
occasional help from their three children who
do bead weaving and corn dollies.
Practical details: The workshop is open to
visitors seven days a week during July and
August and at other times of the year Tuesday
to Sunday, from 9 am to 6 pm (closed
Monday), but they are always open on bank
holidays and other holidays. Specific lecture-
demonstrations for groups of up to fifty
people (schools, women's institutes and so on)
are arranged by prior appointment, in the
evenings if required.

39 Oak Carvings and Furniture

Robert Thompson's Craftsmen Limited
Kilburn, York YO6 4AH
Tel: Coxwold 218

The trademark of Robert Thompson's is the
mouse. Robert Thompson, who died in 1955,

Carving the famous mouse at Thompson's

never intended to advertise, but it has become a very successful advertising symbol.
Thompson used to describe how he thought of the idea. 'I was carving a beam on a church roof when another carver, Charlie Barker, murmured something about us being as poor as church mice, and on the spur of the moment I carved one. Afterwards I decided to adopt the mouse as a trademark, because I thought how a mouse manages to scrape and chew away the hardest wood with its chisel-like teeth, working quietly with nobody taking much notice. I thought that was maybe like this workshop hidden away in the Hambleton Hills. It is what you might call industry in quiet places — so I put the mouse on all my work.'
Robert Thompson loved English oak and succeeded in reviving the craft of oak carving. His work was to be seen in seven hundred churches, including Westminster Abbey and York Minster, as well as in numerous schools, colleges, official buildings and in homes throughout the country.
His work is now continued under the direction of his two grandsons and his timber frame cottage has been converted into a showroom. The workshop itself is relatively modern.
Every year hundreds of visitors go to Kilburn hoping to buy something with a mouse carved on it. In addition to domestic furniture, ranging from grandfather clocks to rocking chairs and carvings, small articles can be ordered or bought from stock. These include book-ends, bowls and cheeseboards — all adorned with the mouse.
Practical details: The workshop and showroom are open Monday to Friday from 8 am to 12 noon and 12.45 pm to 5 pm, and on Saturday from 10.30 am to 12 noon.
Individuals are welcome to arrive without prior notice and walk around the workshop and showroom. No coach parties or school parties are allowed. Conducted tours are not arranged.

40   Stoneware Clay Figures

Manor Farm Studio
Stokesley, Middlesbrough
Cleveland TS9 5AG
Tel: Stokesley 710267

Mrs. Sheila Kirk specialises in hand-carved stoneware clay figures of old country folk and craftsmen. She has studied the methods, tools and clothes of these folk and each figure is made individually, without using a mould, for fine and accurate reproduction. They are finished with a simple oatmeal glaze.
Sheila Kirk also makes the usual variety of pots, bowls, dishes, vases and lamps, as well as flower-arrangers' pots, wall reliefs and ceramic sculpture, but concentrates on one-off pots rather than repetitive design. Pots can be made to customer's requirements and, indeed, are often made to the customer's own design. Inspiration for decoration and form often comes from natural objects and the cultures of past civilisations. Another interesting idea which you will see formulated here is the creation of composite pots combining different methods of construction.
The wide variety of wares together with a range of glazes ensures changing displays in the tiny showroom.
Practical details: This is Sheila Kirk's home and you may call any reasonable time, but telephone first if you are making a special journey to check that she will be in. The workshop is small so large parties cannot be accommodated.

Clay figures, hand-modelled by Sheila Kirk

41   English Oak Furniture Maker

Albert Jeffray
Sessay, Thirsk YO7 3BE
Tel: Hutton Sessay 323

There is usually a small amount of finished
work in the showroom and visitors are
welcome to look round the workshop. Ninety
per cent of the work is furniture made of
English oak but other woods are used when
specified by customers.
Carvings and furniture are produced to
customers' requirements. Items include
dining, occasional and church furniture.
Small items, such as fruit bowls, ash trays,
bread and cheese boards, trinket boxes, table
lamps, book racks and leaf dishes are also
made here. Albert Jeffray is a member of the
Guild of Yorkshire Craftsmen.
Practical details: The workshop and
showroom are open to visitors in all daylight
hours. It is advisable to make an appointment
for visits at weekends and on bank holidays.
Sessay is two miles off the A19 between Thirsk
and Easingwold.

42   Dollmaking and Herb Products

Carlton Crafts
The Tiring House, Carlton
Richmond, North Yorkshire
Tel: Piercebridge 461

Heather Bates makes herb sachets, lavender
bags, herb pillows, brides' pillows stuffed
with lavender for scenting linen, and
Yorkshire character dolls whose bases are
stuffed with sweet-scented herbs. The herbs
used are lemon balm, eau de Cologne, mint,
hyssop, rosemary and applemint.
She also sells herb doll kits and pot pourri in
bags for filling pot pourri holders.
Visitors will see herbs growing from May to
September/October and being dried and
made into herb products from June/July until
October/November ready for the Christmas
gift market.
Practical details: Individuals and groups of up

Huge storage tanks at Tyne Brewery

to ten people can telephone for an
appointment any day, including bank
holidays, during daylight hours until 7.30 pm
on the long summer evenings. The best time to
call is at the weekend until 4 pm. There is less
to see in winter as the herbs are not growing,
but before Christmas herb products can be
seen. You can ask to see a demonstration of
making up dolls — particularly interesting if
you are considering buying her kits. Carlton is
one and a half miles from Aldbrough St. John
(the nearest village) and five miles from Scotch
Corner on the A1.

43   Ale-Brewing and Bottling

Scottish and Newcastle Breweries Ltd.
Tyne Brewery, Gallowgate
Newcastle-upon-Tyne NE99 1RA
Tel: Newcastle 25091

Visitors are given a conducted tour of the Tyne brewery, where the famous Newcastle Brown Ale and other 'Blue Star' ales are brewed. You will see the step-by-step process of making beer, from the hop store where the hops are kept ready for selection and blending before being added to the coppers, right up to the bottling and despatching of the beer in delivery tankers. At the end of the tour you are given an opportunity to sample the ales.
Practical details: The brewery is open to visitors Monday to Friday at 2.30 pm. Up to twenty people can be accepted in a group, but you must book well in advance with the brewery guide, in the public relations department. Individuals are also welcome to join groups and need usually only give a few days' notice.

44   Bread and Cake Bakery

Greggs of Gosforth
Christon Road
Gosforth Industrial Estate
Newcastle-upon-Tyne NE3 1XH
Tel: Gosforth 841411

All through the visit you will notice the delightful aroma of freshly baked bread and cakes. The hour-long tour starts with an outline of the history of the company. Visitors then see the production stages, from dough in a mixing bowl to a loaf being sliced and packed ready for despatch. Bread, ferments, confectionery and savoury goods are produced. You may buy products in the small shop.
Practical details: Visits take place on Tuesday afternoons, starting at 2.30 pm. Normally organised groups of up to only sixteen people are accepted, and local groups are booked up to twelve months in advance. However, parties can occasionally be accommodated at short notice. Individuals are welcome if they book six months in advance. There is no age limit, and no charge for the tour.
The bakery is about three-quarters of a mile off the A1, near Gosforth High Street.

45   Kipper Curers

L. Robson & Sons Limited
Haven Hill, Craster
Alnwick NE3 66K
Tel: Embleton 223

The process of curing kippers will be explained to visitors and it is interesting to note that this has not been changed for more than a hundred years. The original smoking-houses which were built in 1856 are still being used. Kippers are available in the factory shop, but this depends on herring catches, so there is no guarantee that you will be able to buy them every day.
Practical details: The factory is open from

The traditional method of kipper curing

June to mid-September, excluding bank holidays. Working hours are Monday to Friday from 9.30 am to 5 pm (closed for lunch from 12 noon to 1 pm), and on Saturday from 9.30 am to 12 noon. The factory is not always working in the opening times stated above, as these depend on the herring catches. However, someone is always available to explain the processes which take place there. Individuals are welcome to arrive without prior notice and walk around the works. Large parties and schools must give notice.

46　Lindisfarne Liqueurs

The Lindisfarne Liqueur Company
St. Aidan's Winery
The Holy Island of Lindisfarne
Northumberland
Tel: Holy Island 230

The managing director of this most unusual company tells us that due to Customs & Excise restrictions visitors are not actually allowed into the working area of the winery. However, they are welcomed into the winery showroom, where groups can have the processes explained. Every visitor over the age of eighteen is allowed to sample the famous Lindisfarne Mead. People under this age may sample Lindisfarne Liqueur Honey,

Lindisfarne Liqueur Marmalade, Strawberry preserve with Lindisfarne Liqueur and their famous lemon curd with Lindisfarne Advocaat.

The recipe for the mead is still a closely guarded secret, but it is safe to say that fermented grape juice, water from an artesian well on the island, honey and locally gathered herbs are used.

Practical details: The Lindisfarne Liqueur Company is open from Easter 10 am to 5 pm, seven days a week, including all bank holidays.

All visitors are accepted into the showroom. However, it will be appreciated that if school parties are brought into the showroom, ten people at a time will be the maximum, and they should be under strict supervision.

47　Industrial Museum

Museum of Lakeland Life and Industry
Abbot Hall, Kendal
Cumbria LA9 5AL
Tel: Kendal 22464

The museum was the first winner of the Museum of the Year Award in 1973 and is well worth seeing. Farming is illustrated by a display of equipment and photographs show the implements in use. A farm-house parlour is furnished as it would have been in the last century. Other sections show printing and weaving.

Upstairs there is a fascinating display of blacksmiths', wheelwrights', mechanics', painters', brewers', miners' and bobbin-makers' equipment. Children will be particularly interested in a classroom from Kendal's Old Grammar School, displaying early toys and games.

Changing exhibitions show the activities of present-day local industries such as K Shoes and the Abbey Horn Works.

Practical details: Open 10.30 am to 12.30 pm and 2 pm to 5 pm on weekdays and 2 pm to 5 pm on Saturdays and Sundays. Closed from December 17th to January 2nd and Good Friday.

Peter Hall—polishing an oak stool

48   Craftsman-built Furniture

Peter Hall Woodcraft
Danes Road, Staveley
Kendal, Cumbria LA8 9PL
Tel: Staveley 821633

Peter Hall makes solid oak and mahogany furniture, dining-tables and chairs, joint stools, sideboards and Welsh dressers, coffee tables and bookcases. Visitors can see the making of furniture throughout its different stages, and some particular pieces which are designed to the customer's individual requirements. **Practical details:** Open to individuals and small groups during normal working hours throughout the week but closed on Sunday.

49   Nuclear Power Station and Re-processing Plant

Calder Hall Nuclear Power Station
Windscale and Calder Works
British Nuclear Fuels Limited
Sellafield, Seascale, Cumbria CA20 1PG
Tel: Seascale 333 Ext: 220

The Windscale and Calder works are on the same site. Between them they have five reactors. Calder Hall was the first nuclear power station large enough to produce electricity on a commercial scale and it was opened by the Queen in 1956. A visit consists of an illustrated talk followed by a tour of the reactors and turbine hall. Windscale re-processes nuclear fuel and any electricity generated which is surplus to the plant's own requirements is passed on to the national grid. **Practical details:** Visits are arranged by appointment at 10 am and 1.30 pm Monday to Friday, excluding bank holidays. Parties of up to forty people are accepted for the two-hour tour and the minimum age limit is twelve years. Write to the visits liaison officer two months in advance.

50   Reproduction Antique Glassware

Cumbria Crystal Limited
Lightburn Road
Ulverston LA12 0DA
Tel: Ulverston 54400

Cumbria Crystal came into being because five collectors of antique glass decided that the beautiful old English designs should be preserved. The company started in 1975 and it makes reproduction glass based on seventeenth and eighteenth century designs. One characteristic of eighteenth century glassware is the variety of forms in the stems. About thirty people work here including eleven glassmakers. You will see men blowing glass and making wineglasses and decanters. The shop sells glasses, decanters, animal figures and coloured glass paperweights. The most popular purchase is a glass swan.

Work with molten glass at Cumbria Crystal

Children like to buy pieces of cullet — waste glass cut from shaped items, which is normally melted down again.
Practical details: The glassworks' hours are 9 am to 4 pm Monday to Friday. In June to September it is open on Saturday morning from 9 am to 12 noon. It is closed during Christmas week but open at Easter. All visitors including children are welcome. Individuals can be shown around. Notice would be preferred for parties of more than thirty people. There is no charge but they like visitors to have a look around the shop.

51   Snuff Makers

Illingworth's Tobaccos Limited
Aynam Mills, Kendal, Cumbria
Tel: Kendal 21898

Visitors are usually given a sample of snuff and are told about the history of snuff taking in general and about this particular firm. Snuff-taking had its heyday during the Regency times in the reign of George IV, when the tobacco came into the ports on the west coast of Britain from the West Indies. At one time there were snuff factories all over Kendal, now there are very few left. This particular factory was founded in 1867, and the original grinding and mixing machinery is still used every day. Mr. Edmondson, the director of Illingworth's, tells us that there are now only three firms left here in Kendal and two in Sheffield which still grind their own snuff. These five factories supply blenders, who add their own perfumes to previously ground tobacco. He estimates that there are about half a million snuff takers in Britain, of whom forty per cent are women. Snuff can be bought by visitors in sets of a dozen tins at reduced prices. There is a choice of a dozen perfumed snuffs, including wallflower, rose, jasmine and patchouli. There are also six medicated snuffs, including menthol, menthol and eucalyptus, and camphor. The snuffs are made from tobacco, ground into perfumed and medicated brown powders, some in dainty pill-box size tins.
Practical details: The factory is open Monday to Friday, but closed on bank holidays. Telephone or write to Mr. K. Edmondson, the director, a fortnight in advance. Individuals and groups of up to about ten people are welcome, and children aged twelve years and over. The free tour takes about an hour.

52   Handloom Mill

St. George's Woollen Mills Limited
Laxey, Isle of Man
Tel: Laxey 395

Holiday-makers are invited to see the handloom being operated and turning out pure wool Manx tweeds and travel rugs. The mills were founded in 1881 by the Oxford scholar, John Ruskin. In the showroom you can buy the products made here such as Manx tweeds, Mohairs, deerskin and suede products, ties, socks, scarves, stoles, capes, skirts, car coats, sports jackets and knitwear.
Practical details: The handloom unit and showrooms are open Monday to Friday from 10 am to 5.30 pm. On Saturday the showroom only is open from 10 am to 5 pm. These times apply to the summer season, May to October, and the mills are open on bank holidays. Individuals and groups are welcome but school parties must telephone or write in advance for confirmation.

1   Gem Rock Workshop

Creetown Gem Rock Museum
Old School, Creetown by Newton Stewart
(Wigtownshire)
Tel: Creetown 357

Creetown's local beaches, especially those
facing west, provide a rich hunting ground for
the gem-stone collector. You can pick up agate
and jasper, and displays in the museum show
you where to look.
The Craig family have a world-wide network
of rock-collecting friends and enthusiasts who
send them stones and examples of specialist
cutting. They claim that their collection is one
of the largest of its kind in the British Isles.
The exhibits show the gem-stones from the
source rocks and the processes they go through
to become finished jewellery. Visitors will be
interested in watching the process of cutting
the stones, then polishing them in readiness
for setting into beautiful and unusual
jewellery.
Practical details: The museum and walk-
around workshop are open Monday to
Saturday from 9.30 am to 6 pm and on Sunday
from 2 pm to 6 pm. During October to May
they close for lunch from 1 pm to 2 pm. Joe
and Mary Craig and family only require notice
from large parties who wish to have a
conducted tour in the height of the season or
in the evening. School parties are welcome.
There is a small entrance charge and the
complex includes a cafe and rest areas.
The souvenir shop sells the jewellery made on
the premises. You may also buy rock and
mineral samples, text-books on rocks, fossils
and sea-shells, jewellery fittings and kits — in
short, all you need for collecting and
identifying and processing gem-stones.
One-day courses on cutting cabochons
(polished stones) are held throughout the year
and organised groups can arrange to learn
about local geology, gem-stones, lapidary
processes, local mining and historical stones.
The large oak-panelled hall provides a lovely
setting for conferences and evening outings.
You may also wish to visit the Tidemark Sea
Shell Collection at Stranraer, which is a
branch of this museum. The museum is
signposted from the A75 opposite Creetown
Clock Tower.

2   Hydro-Electric Power Station

Tongland Hydro-Electric Power Station
Near Kirkcudbright
Kirkcudbrightshire
Tel: Kirkcudbright 30114

Parts of the Tongland reservoir and gorge can
be seen from the road but visitors on the
Tongland tour can take a closer look, not only
at the interesting engineering of the power
station and dam, but also at the impressive
scenery.

Edward Iglehart—individual glassware

Tongland Dam is sharply curved against the pressure of the water and measures nearly three hundred metres along the top. It rises more than twenty metres above the river bed and creates a reservoir of twenty hectares in area. Below the dam the spectacular gorge is accessible because some of the water is diverted. Visitors will also see one of Scotland's famous fish ladders, which curves round the eastern side of the gorge in a series of stepped pools.

Each summer the salmon return from their Atlantic feeding grounds to mate and spawn in the fresh water: they can be seen leaping up the ladder or resting in the top pool before entering the reservoir. The salmon are counted electronically and in a good year about four thousand pass through the system of ladders.

The power of the water turbine depends upon the volume of water which flows through it and the height or 'head' from which it is piped. The engineers manage the dam and reservoir so that there is enough water at a sufficient height to produce electricity.

Hydro-electric power stations have the great advantage that they can start up quickly to meet an unexpected demand. In summer, when the water supply may be limited, they are used mainly at times of peak load to supplement the output of other power stations. In winter, when the demand for electricity is high, the heavier rainfall enables the hydro-electric power stations to work longer hours.

Practical details: The Tongland tour is run from the end of June to late September. Visitors should telephone the tour centre to reserve a place. Parties of up to twelve people are met at the Information Kiosk in Kirkcudbright, and are driven in a minibus to the power station. At the tour centre next to the power station buildings visitors are given a short talk.

They are then taken by bus to the dam, where there is an observation area with seats, tables and information panels. From here the guide leads the party across the dam and down the side of the fish ladder. An audio-visual presentation is laid on when the weather is bad. Visitors who do not wish to view the ladder and prefer to enjoy the scenery from the dam can do so.

3   Glass Craftsman

North Glen Gallery
Palnackie, Castle Douglas
Kirkcudbrightshire
Tel: Palnackie 200

Half-a-mile up a narrow farm lane from the small port of Palnackie, stone buildings, sheep, free-range hens and coastal scenery provide a retreat for a former research scientist, Edward Iglehart. He has developed his own methods of glass working, including making his own colours and decorative materials. Molten glass is rolled in a combination of oxides and colourants, mixed in the fire, and drawn into rods, which are used to shape and form hollow pieces. No fixed range is produced, because all Mr Iglehart's work is original — but bottles, vases and drinking vessels are usually well represented.

His eventual aim is to produce glassware made entirely of local materials, fired using methane from an organic composter, which also provides the fertilizer for the vegetable

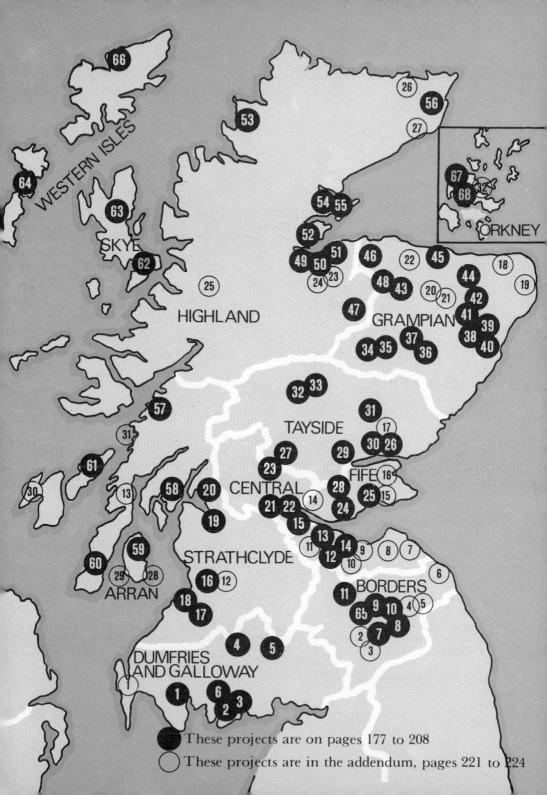

These projects are on pages 177 to 208

These projects are in the addendum, pages 221 to 224

garden. This, by the way, is where you should search if there is no-one in the workshop.

Practical details: The gallery is open from 10 am to 6 pm Monday to Saturday and at other times by arrangement. Individuals or groups should telephone in advance, when arrangements can be made for them to watch steel being cut and welded into sculpture, or glassblowing.

4   Spinning Wheel Maker

H. Pouncey
The Stables, Craigdarroch
Moniaive, Thornhill, Dumfriesshire
Tel: Moniaive 230

The stable workshop is a one-man craft shop situated in the grounds of Craigdarroch House, former home of Annie Laurie, immortalised in the Scottish song.
Mr. Pouncey produces a range of spinning wheels to meet the needs of all kinds of spinners. They are all made to traditional designs used in Scotland, Scandinavia, Saxony, Holland, Finland and Austria.

Practical details: The workshop is open Monday to Saturday, from 9 am to 5 pm and limited numbers of visitors are welcome, although not in parties. Please write or telephone in advance.
Craigdarroch is two miles west of Moniaive on the B729.

5   Wrought Ironwork

E. Martin and Son
Closeburn, Thornhill, Dumfriesshire
Tel: Closeburn 267

The Martins do all kinds of general blacksmithing in these premises and the wrought-iron work is only one aspect of their business. They also do horse-shoeing and other related iron-forging assignments.
Practical details: Contact Mr. E. Martin before

paying them a visit as the wrought-iron forging is done only on specific orders and is not, therefore, a continuous process.

6   Stoneware Pottery

John Davey
Davey Pottery, Bridge of Dee
Castle Douglas, Kirkcudbrightshire
Tel: Bridge of Dee 239

At his workshop in the small village of Bridge of Dee, John Davey produces stoneware pottery. He is an artist craftsman with long experience in ceramics, who works with two assistants, making a wide range of practical domestic stoneware.

His range includes casseroles, soup bowls, mugs, ovenware and butter-dishes. Each piece is hand-thrown. The items are decorated in wax resist and oxides and finished with glazes, mixed in the workshop to the potter's own recipes, in shades of green, blue and brown, which reflect the inspiration of the country environment.

Practical details: Visitors who would like to view the workshop should telephone for an appointment, as the pottery receives about four hundred people every day, and not everyone can be accommodated. There is a small entrance fee and the opening hours are 9 am to 5 pm Monday to Friday. Parties of up to ten people at a time will be taken on each tour, which start 11 am, 11.30 am, 2.30 pm and 3 pm, and last about twenty minutes. In the showroom domestic ware, plant-pots, large ceramic sculptures and other items are on sale.

7   Industrial Weaving

Trow Mill Weavers
Trow Mill, Hawick
Roxburghshire TD9 8SU
Tel: Hawick 2555

This most picturesque of mills produces Hawick Honeycomb Gold Medal cellular blankets, tweeds and travel rugs, which are all available direct to the public at mill prices. Visitors can enjoy a free cup of tea or coffee in the showroom or on the lawn, and browse among the beautiful tweeds, Shetland and lambswool knitwear, scarves, stoles and knitting wools.

The technically minded can visit the mill itself with a guide, going through the various stages of tweed and blanket manufacture.

Practical details: The mill and showroom are open Monday to Friday from 8 am to 5 pm. The showroom alone is open on Saturdays 9 am to 5pm and in winter from 2 pm to 5 pm; other times by arrangement.

The mill receives a large number of visitors so coach parties must book at an early date. The tour of the mill lasts about forty-five minutes and they are well prepared for groups. There is a snack bar where light refreshments may be purchased and, in addition, they have arranged with hotels in Hawick to provide lunch or high tea. The mill is 2½ miles from Hawick on the A698.

8   Embroidery

Mrs. Mary Johnstone
Palace, Crailing
Near Jedburgh, Roxburghshire
Tel: Crailing 225

Visits are completely informal and visitors can see any work that is in progress such as gold embroidery, canvas work and many other types of embroidery. Mrs. Johnstone makes small decorative panels using gold or silver threads and silk, to her own designs, and she accepts church commissions. She also makes patchwork quilts or cushions, in traditional patterns, and uses canvas work both for cushions and small pictures in abstract designs. She will sell her handwork or take orders for similar pieces.

Practical details: Mrs. Johnstone is open at any reasonable time to visitors interested in embroidery, provided that a day or two's notice is given. The studio is not large so it is only suitable for individuals and small parties.

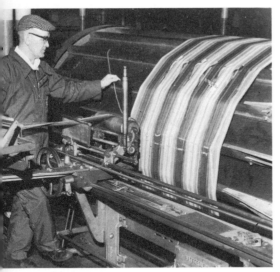

9   Weaving Mill

Abbotsford Mills
Huddersfield Street
Galashiels
Selkirkshire TD1 3BE
Tel: Galashiels 3364

This is a weaving mill where yarn is brought
from the spinners, and woven into cloth.
After weaving, any broken threads are
invisibly mended before the cloth goes to the
finisher who washes, dries, presses and
examines the cloth ready for the customer.
Practical details: Telephone the retail
manager, Mr. S. Henderson. Individuals or
groups of up to about twenty people can be
shown around the mill, preferably by
appointment, though occasionally
individuals may be accepted without making
prior arrangements. The opening hours are
9 am to 12 noon and 2 pm to 4 pm, Monday to
Friday and the mill is closed on public
holidays. Tours last half an hour. There is no
charge.
Yarns, tweeds, furnishing fabrics, ties and
knitwear are on sale at the mill shop, which is
open Monday to Friday from 9 am to 5 pm and
Saturday from 10 am to 4 pm. Goods are sold
at direct-from-mill prices.

10   Costume Doll Maker

Anne Carrick
The Pendstead, Melrose, Roxburghshire
Tel: Melrose 2573

Anne Carrick makes costume figures with
wire and fabric. Each one is individually
made, sometimes based on a portrait of an
historical character, sometimes drawn from
imagination. Most work is commissioned but
a few items are on sale in the gallery.
Practical details: The house-cum-studio is
open every day. Up to twenty people can be
accommodated at one time. A telephone call is
vital because she plans to move to Kelso
during 1978.

11   Tweed Manufacturers

D. Ballantyne Brothers & Co. Limited
March Street Mills
Peebles EH45 8ER
Tel: Peebles 20146

The mill employs four hundred people, and
visitors may observe all the manufacturing
processes involved, from preparation of the
yarn to weaving and finishing. Around 450
pieces of tweed are produced here every week.
Practical details: The mill is open Monday to
Thursday 9 am to 4.30 pm. Contact Mr.
Roland Brett by phone or letter. Groups of
twenty to forty-five people should give at least
a week's notice. Individuals are welcome with
children aged five years or older. Tours last an
hour.

12   Cut Crystal Glassware

Edinburgh Crystal Glass Company
Eastfield, Penicuik
Midlothian EH26 8HB
Tel: Penicuik 72244

Visitors see all the processes of making
Edinburgh Crystal in this ultra-modern and

Potter John Davey — see page 181

efficient factory. Particularly fascinating are the glass-blowing and cutting which turn the molten glass into the beautiful crystal articles.
Practical details: The factory is open all year except for four weeks, at Christmas, spring, mid and late summer holiday times. Tours are arranged for groups of ten to twenty-five people, Monday to Thursday at 2.00 and 2.15 pm, and they last over an hour. Telephone at least two weeks in advance and make an appointment. Individuals, however, should ring a day or two before and arrangements will be made for them to join a group of fewer than twenty-five people. Children under ten years of age are not accepted and children over this age must be accompanied by two adults. Seconds may be purchased in the visitors' shop which is open only to people taking this tour.
You will find the factory about ten miles south of Edinburgh.

---

13   Whisky Blending and Bottling

Wm. Sanderson and Son Limited
27 The Loan, South Queensferry
West Lothian
Tel: 031-331 1500

Visitors may watch the blending and bottling of Vat 69 and The Antiquary de luxe whiskies for the United Kingdom and all export markets. The Company's bond is operated under surveillance of HM Customs and Excise and no shop is allowed to sell the products on the premises.
Practical details: The plant is open Monday to Friday from 7.30 am to 5 pm, except on Friday afternoons. Bookings should be made by telephone or letter — large parties two to three weeks in advance — and individuals three to four days. Thirty-five to forty people can be accepted at one time. They do not usually take parties of school children. However, they do not object to children accompanied by parents. There is a car and coach park on the premises and admission is free.
The plant is situated on the Firth of Forth between the Forth road and rail bridges.

14   Modern Brewery

Scottish & Newcastle Breweries Ltd.
Abbey Brewery, Holyrood Road
Edinburgh EH8 8YS
Tel: 031-556 2591

Scottish and Newcastle Breweries' New Fountain Brewery is one of the largest and most automated complexes in the world. On the tour you see the complete brewing process, including a look at the high-speed canning line. You may try a sample of the end product in the visitors' room at the end of the tour.
Practical details: Tours are held on Monday to Thursday at 10.30 am and 2.30 pm and on Friday at 10.30 am, and the brewery is closed on all bank holidays. Individuals and groups of up to twenty people are accepted, also children and school parties. Visitors should write or telephone in advance as visits depend on time available.
The ninety-minute tour is physically demanding, which is something club leaders should bear in mind.

---

15   Rocking Horses

Peter Walmsley
18 Main Street, Larbert
Stirlingshire
Tel: Larbert 4030

When visiting Peter Walmsley at his workshop you will have to take a chance as to what you will see. Sometimes he will be merely cutting up pieces of wood, but at other times he may be working on an intricate and detailed carving. A rocking horse may be 'on the blocks', or finished and waiting delivery, or not even started. However, he likes a chat and may offer you a cup of tea.
Practical details: Usually open Tuesday to Saturday 10 am to 5 pm, but phone first to make sure he is there. Individuals and small groups up to five please.

Peter Walmsley carving a rocking horse

16   Whisky Blending and Bottling

John Walker & Sons Limited
Kilmarnock, Ayrshire KA3 14D
Tel: Kilmarnock 23401

'Johnnie Walker' is the brand name of the
world's largest selling Scotch whisky — see
the Guinness Book of Records. Whisky from
all over Scotland is brought here for
blending and bottling.

The tour starts with an exhibition
demonstrating how Scotch whisky is made
and a film is shown. Visitors then travel to
Barleith to see whiskies being blended. Fifty
coopers can be seen at work, repairing the oak
casks which store the whisky, by hand. Back at
Kilmarnock, visitors tour the bottling halls
and taste a wee 'dram'.

Practical details: Visiting parties must make
prior bookings. The tour, which lasts about
two hours, is not suitable for very young
children or the elderly as there is a fair amount
of walking and a number of steps to climb.
Telephone or write to Mr W Gammie at the
above address.

Individuals and small groups may come along
and join larger groups on tours at 10 am or
2.15 pm. Again, prior booking is needed.

17   Hornwork

St. Inan (Products) Limited
Ayr Road, Dalmellington, Ayrshire
Tel: Dalmellington 265

Here you will see all aspects of hornwork such
as the shaping or moulding of the horn, the
cutting and grinding processes and finally the
polishing and assembly into fancy goods.

Practical details: The workshop is open from
8 am to 4.30 pm. Visitors should write or
telephone Mr. Charles Fairns in advance, and
he will accept parties of up to twenty people,
or, of course, individuals.

18   Aircraft Manufacturing

Scottish Aviation Limited
Prestwick International Airport
Strathclyde, Ayrshire KA9 2RW
Tel: Prestwick 79888

Scottish Aviation (a British Aerospace
Company) is located on an eighty-six acre
site at Prestwick Airport. Over one thousand
employees produce light transport and
training aircraft, major airframe assemblies,
precision machining of engine components
and overhauling complete engines.
Practical details: Visitors are accepted
infrequently because of security and other
reasons, therefore requests for visits must be
made well in advance and are accepted only
from recognised organisations.

19   Vacuum Cleaner Manufacturers

Hoover Limited
Somervell Street, Cambuslang
Glasgow G72 7TZ
Tel: 041-641 5111

Lady guides dressed in tartan uniforms take
visitors round the factory and answer
questions. The factory produces all models
from the Hoover range, including the vacuum
cleaners, and the small products like kettles,
toasters and irons.
Practical details: Schools, colleges, women's
organisations and other specialist groups may
visit the Hoover factory. Requests should be
made in writing to J. Valentine at least three
weeks in advance of the proposed visit. Hoover
do not cater for individual visitors.

20   Knitwear Factory

Lomondside Knitwear
Lomond Industrial Estate
Alexandria, Dunbartonshire
Tel: Alexandria 52517

At this small modern factory visitors can see
the manufacture of fully-fashioned knitwear
through all its processes from the yarn to the
finished article. A large mill shop sells goods
at factory prices and also Scottish-made crafts
and tartans.
Practical details: The factory is open Monday
to Friday from 9 am to 5 pm, and opens at
9.30 am on Saturday and 11.30 am on Sunday,
closing at 5 pm. Visitors, including coach
parties, are welcome during these times
without prior notice.

21   Hand-thrown Stoneware

Barbara Davidson Pottery
Muirhall Farm, Muirhall Road
Larbert, Stirlingshire FK5 4EW
Tel: Larbert 4430

The pottery is usually visited by people who
are interested in seeing the manufacture of
hand-thrown stoneware .
There are two potters and two apprentices at
work making coffee sets, mugs and bowls.
The showroom is situated in the farm's byre
(cowshed) and there is always an interesting
selection of pottery for sale.
Practical details: Pottery-making can be seen
in progress Monday to Friday.
The showroom is open Monday to Saturday
from 9 am to 5.30 pm, and also on Sundays
from 2 pm to 5.30 pm. All members of the
public are welcome to watch the potters at
work and browse in the showroom.
There is no entrance fee and ample car
parking space is provided.
Muirhall Farm is on the A876 twenty-six miles
from Glasgow.

22   Knitting Wool Factory

Messrs. Patons & Baldwins Limited
Kilncraigs Factory
Alloa, Clackmannanshire
Tel: Alloa 723431

Visitors see wool and other yarns being spun,
dyed and finished — from the arrival of yarn

tops to the completion of balls of yarn which
are banded and packed. Hand-knitted
garments are displayed and there is a talk
about how to block and press hand-knitted
garments.
After the talk tea is served and visitors can buy
seconds.
Practical details: Tours take place on
Wednesday and Thursday starting at 2.15 pm
and lasting until about 4.30 pm. Groups of
between twenty-five and forty people, aged
over fifteen, are accepted. Individuals will be
joined to a group. Write to Miss A. B. Govan
giving six weeks' notice. No charge is made.

23   Weaving of Tweeds and Mohair

D. C. Sinclair & Son
Clock Mill, Tillicoultry
Clackmannanshire
Tel: Tillicoultry 419

There is no actual guided tour here but you
can happily spend between thirty minutes and
an hour wandering around watching the
weaving of Scottish tweeds, authentic tartans,
mohair scarves and so on. Some of the other
goods produced are skirts, kilts, capes, tweed
tartan, travel rugs, stoles, blankets, cashmere,
lambswool, Shetland knitwear, pottery,
jewellery, clan maps and books.
Practical details: The mill is open Monday to
Friday from 8 am to 5 pm and the shop alone is
open on Saturday from 9 am to 12 noon.
Telephone T. P. Sinclair in advance. Articles
are sold at direct-from-factory prices and a
small coffee lounge provides refreshment.
Individuals and small groups are welcome.

24   Small Pottery

Anne Lightwood
57 Main Street
Lower Largo, Fife KY8 6BN
Tel: Lundin Links 320686

Anne Lightwood makes pottery for domestic
use — such as mugs, soup bowls and casseroles

— and decorative stoneware pieces. She makes
a narrow stemmed vase, not unlike a flower,
with holes in the flared top to help you
arrange dried grasses. This is a studio pottery,
with only two people working in a small
converted cottage, so there is not always a great
deal to see. But all the processes are carried out
here, from preparing the clay to throwing,
turning, bisque firing, glazing and glost firing
in a gas kiln.
Practical details: Individuals and small
groups (not more than twelve people) may
visit by appointment only. Normally
demonstrations can be arranged. All finished
work is transferred to the shop which is open
daily, from 2 pm to 5 pm, from April to
December.

25   Mixed Craft Centre

Balbirnie Craft Centre
Balbirnie, Near Markinch
Fife KY7 6MR

Balbirnie Craft Centre, which is part of the
Balbirnie Park, is open to visitors daily and
you may wander round on an informal basis.
In order to pay a special visit to any of the
workshops it is advisable to make prior
arrangement by contacting the craftsmen
individually. The workshops are housed in
the eighteenth-century stable buildings of the
estate.
There are no catering facilities and large
parties cannot be accommodated, but
specialist groups may write to the secretary for
an appointment. There is no charge for
admission to the park and centre.
Contact each workshop separately as follows:
Stained glass artist—John Blyth
Tel: Glenrothes 756839
Practical details: Saturday 2 pm to 4 pm when
convenient. Work is on a commission basis.
Handloom weaver—Elizabeth Crawford
Practical details: Monday to Friday from
10 am to 6 pm when convenient.
Commissioned work only.
Reproduction furniture—Joe Chartris
Tel: Glenrothes 758273

John Blyth at the Balbirnie Craft Centre

Practical details: Saturday only. Commission basis only.
Pottery and ceramics—David Heminsley
Tel: Glenrothes 755975
Practical details: Monday to Saturday from 9 am to 6 pm, and Sunday from 2 pm to 6 pm. Articles are for sale.
Fashion designer—Marjorie Heminsley
Tel: Glenrothes 755975
Practical details: Monday to Saturday from 9 am to 6 pm, and Sunday from 2 pm to 6 pm. Garments for sale, and to order.
Furniture & woodwork — Donald McGarva
Tel: Glenrothes 758759
Practical details: Monday to Friday from 9 am to 6 pm, and Saturday and Sunday from 2 pm to 6 pm. Wooden objects are on sale but the furniture is made on a commissioned basis, with a standard range available.
Jewellery—Alison and Roy Murray
Tel: Glenrothes 753743
Practical details: Monday to Saturday from 10 am to 6 pm. Articles may be purchased.
Leatherwork—Ron and Susan Muir
Tel: Glenrothes 758759
Practical details: Monday to Sunday from 10 am to 6 pm. Articles may be purchased.

26   Computers and Terminals

NCR Limited
(Manufacturing Division)
Kingsway West, Dundee DD2 3XX
Tel: Dundee 60151

Visitors see all the latest in electronic technology. 'To those who know little of electronics it will be like opening a magic box,' they promise. There are electronic modules and machines being assembled, electronic accounting systems, electronic data terminals, system peripherals using the latest in micro-computer technology and computers.
Practical details: The factory is open Monday to Friday from 8.45 am to 4.15 pm. Groups of up to twenty people, aged over fourteen years, can be taken round the factory.
Contact the information liaison co-ordinator at least two weeks in advance to arrange a visit.
The guided tour, lasting over an hour, is free of charge.

27   Mouthblown Hand-made Glass

Strathearn Glass Limited
Muthill Road, Crieff, Perthshire
Tel: Crieff 2942

The glassware made is for the international prestige market and consists of ranges of modern and more traditional clear and coloured vases, bowls, table-lamp bases, ashtrays and candleholders. High quality paperweights, both modern and traditional millefiori, are a speciality, and doorknobs, too, are made in millefiori designs. Millefiori, Italian for thousands of flowers, looks like clusters of tiny pieces of edible rock. Most people recognise it when they see it, though they do not know the name.
The engraving department accepts special commissions for goblets, decanters and vases in full lead crystal and crystalline. Individual items or sets, engraved with monograms and

dates, are popular presents.
The glassworks is one of the most modern and
beautifully sited in the country.
Practical details: The factory is open Monday
to Friday from 9.30 am to 11.30 am and
1.30 pm to 4.30 pm. On Saturday the
showroom alone is open from 9.30 am to
11.30 am. Factory and showroom are closed on
public and local holidays.
Individuals and groups are welcome. Parties
of ten or more should make an appointment
one week in advance, when guides can usually
be arranged for them. There is no admission
charge.
The showroom shop sells 'seconds' at reduced
prices and takes orders for 'firsts'. The modern
building is set in landscaped grounds between
the A822 and the River Earn.

28   Leather Craftsman

Eddergoll Studios
Eddergoll House
29 Bonnygate
Cupar, Fife KY15 4BU
Tel: Cupar 4757

Raymond Morris of Eddergoll and his wife
Margaret have restored an early 18th century
Georgian house and workshop, and are
shortly adding a craft shop, in the centre of the
Royal Burgh of Cupar. Cupar is the county
town of Fife (once known as the Kingdom of
Fife). Raymond Morris is one of the few master
leather carvers left in Britain and produces a
wide range of items. One of his specialities is
reproduction targes, the circular shield of the
Scottish clans used during the 17th and 18th
centuries until the Battle of Culloden in 1746,
after which the English government banned
the use of all weapons in Scotland. The targe
could be an offensive weapon when a spike
was fixed to the centre. The targes you can see
and buy here have been meticulously copied
from historic originals. They are made of
wood covered with leather and decorated with
hundreds of press studs. Some have intricate
patterns tooled into the leather.
Chevalier Raymond Morris of Eddergoll (he is

Engraved glass from Strathearn Glass Ltd.

a Knight of the Military and Hospitaller Order
of St Lazarus of Jerusalem, which dates back
to the crusades) also specialises in heraldic art.
This can range from hand-carved or tooled
wall panels or heavy leather showing coats of
arms, either painted or left natural, to
medieval style jewel boxes, coffee tables,
table mats or coasters.
His three dimensional leather wall panels of
historical figures, heraldry or Celtic art look
most impressive and he makes them to order in
any size.
His other side lines are wood carving, enamel
work on copper, candle making and hand

Above: Whisky casks at John Dewars
Right: Targemaking at Eddergoll Studios

painting 8th century Celtic designs onto stoneware pottery which has been made elsewhere. He describes himself as 'a dedicated craftsman striving to keep alive traditional Scottish crafts to a high standard in the face of inflation and imported "Scottish souvenirs".'

Practical details: As they live on the premises the workshop is open every day from about 10 am. Individuals can call without giving notice. Groups should telephone prior to a visit. Cupar is 12 miles inland from St Andrews and is on the Edinburgh-Dundee railway line.

29   Whisky Blending and Bottling

John Dewar & Sons Limited
Inveralmond, Perth PH1 3EG
Tel: Perth 21231

Six guides are in charge of taking visitors round to see blending and bottling of Scotch whisky. All the processes are on view, from the receipt of casks from the distilleries to the despatch of cases of whisky to the markets of

the world. The plant, which cost two million
pounds to build, occupies twenty-four acres
and about eight hundred people are
employed. More than forty whiskies are used
to produce Dewar's blend. They are blended in
a huge vat, then transferred to oak casks, where
they mature. From there the whisky is pumped
to the automatic bottling plant which handles
more than a quarter of a million bottles a day.
Practical details: The warehouses are open
Monday to Friday throughout the year except
for the annual holiday fortnight during July,
plus the local and factory holidays — not
necessarily the same as bank holidays. Visitors
are received by prior arrangement only.
Individuals or small parties should write or
telephone at least twenty-four hours before
their intended visit. Groups of up to fifty
people can be accepted but large parties are
advised to write months ahead as the diary
soon becomes booked. Children under
eighteen are not admitted. Parties should
arrive at 10.15 am or 2.15 pm. The warehouses
close at 4.15 pm. The person to contact is Mr.
J. H. Conner, the visits organiser.
A sample of the product is usually provided
before visitors leave.
The Dewar warehouses are at Inveralmond,
one mile north of Perth on the A9.

30   Basket, Bedding and Brush Making

The Royal Dundee Institution for the Blind
59 Magdalen Yard Road, Dundee DD1 4LJ
Tel: Dundee 644433

About one hundred blind, partially sighted
and severely disabled sighted people work at
this factory using a blend of craftwork and
machine operations. They make baskets and
baby basinettes in cane and willow, as well as
mattresses, divans, continental quilts,
pillows, brushes, canetex furniture and
novelty pouffes. These products can be bought
on the spot and, if necessary, delivered or sent
to your home.
Practical details: The showroom can be visited
without an appointment from 9 am to
12 noon and 1.30 pm to 4.30 pm, Monday to

Dundee Institution for the Blind
Above: Whisky bottling at Dewars

Friday, except during annual and public
holidays. Individuals who wish to visit the
factory should give one day's notice. Parties of
up to ten people are accepted and they should
give two days' notice. The factory is in the west
end of Dundee, facing the north end of the Tay
railway bridge.

31 Farming and Fruit Picking

Rosemount Farms
Rosemount, Blairgowrie, Perthshire
Tel: Blairgowrie 3578

Rosemount Farms is a mixed arable-dairy-
fruit enterprise consisting of four farms.
The main attraction to visitors would be
during the fruit-picking season which starts
early in June with strawberries, then
raspberries and finally blackcurrants. Visitors
are welcome to participate by picking fruit for
themselves, or merely to watch.
Practical details: To fix an appointment for a
visit contact the farm manager, Mr. W. S.
Courts.
You will find Rosemount Farms on the road
to Balmoral Castle.

32 Power Station and Fish Ladder

North of Scotland Hydro-Electric Board
Pitlochry Power Station
Pitlochry, Perthshire
Tel: Pitlochry 2271

Pitlochry Dam fish ladder is a great tourist

attraction, visited by 500,000 people every
year. Through windows in an underground
room you can see salmon passing upstream to
spawn. Fish go upstream mainly in late spring
and early summer. An electric recorder counts
the salmon — distinguishing between fish
passing up and kelts passing down after
spawning — and between the smaller grilse
and the heavier mature fish. Inside the
Pitlochry Dam is a hatchery with
accommodation for a million salmon eggs.
Practical details: There is a hydro-electric
exhibition, including an audio-visual display,
open to the public daily from Easter to
October. There are working models of hydro-
electric sets, fish ladders and pump storage
schemes.

33 Tweed Weaving

A. & J. MacNaughton Limited
Woollen Manufacturers
Pitlochry, Perthshire PH16 5AF
Tel: Pitlochry 2432

Visitors see the making of tweed from raw
wool to finished cloth.
Practical details: The normal opening times
are 7.30 am to 4.30 pm, closed for lunch
between 12 noon and 1 pm, and the company
is also closed for a fortnight for annual
holidays.
Individuals and groups are accepted —
individuals by obtaining an entry card from
MacNaughton's retail premises at Station
Road, Pitlochry. Groups will be given a
conducted tour by prior arrangement. School
children of under sixteen years are not
permitted in groups.

34 Woodcarving

J. &. I. Crichton, Woodcarvers
Braemar, Aberdeenshire
Tel: Braemar 657

These woodcarvers make wooden moulds for
printing patterns on shortbread and butter.

One traditional design is the thistle. You can also watch them making tea-caddy spoons, spirtles (wooden sticks for stirring porridge), bread-boards and cheese-boards.
Practical details: Telephone for an appointment.

35   Hornwork

Glenroy Horncraft
Braemar, Deeside
Aberdeenshire
Tel: Braemar 614

Staghorn and cowhorn articles are made here, mostly from local horns.
Practical details: The workshop and shop are open Monday to Friday between the hours of 8 am and 5 pm.

36   Lavender Farm and Factory

Dee Lavender
Ingasetter Limited
North Deeside Road
Banchory, Near Aberdeen, Grampian
Tel: Banchory 2600

The smell of lavender hits you the minute you open the door of this small factory. The lavender grows in neat rows in a field at the back. Picking of lavender only takes place in July, so visitors are shown a short film covering all the processes, including distilling the lavender and making cosmetics.
A guide, often the chemist himself, in his white coat, takes you through the laboratory where the mixing takes place and the rows of test tubes are sniffed and watched for changes in colour. Distilling is done in a large vat. Containers are filled and packages are wrapped and despatched by women in an adjoining room. Products for sale include lavender water, lily of the valley hand-cream, cleansing cream, vitamin cream, aftershave, perfume and an insect repellent stick.
Practical details: Between March and October individuals and groups of up to forty-five people are welcomed. Tours are given Monday to Friday between 9 am and 5 pm starting every half hour, so there is no need to book. The tour itself lasts about half an hour. The shop remains open throughout the year.

37   Stoneware Pottery

Dess Station Pottery
Kincardine O'Neil, Aberdeenshire AB3 5BD
Tel: Kincardine O'Neil 254

The pottery occupies an old railway station, built in about the 1860s, on the former Royal Deeside line. The front area has been glassed in and forms the showroom. Casual visitors can look through the arched windows of the showroom to watch the potter at work. Stewart Johnston makes a range of stoneware including oven-to-table ware and teapots, coffee pots and jugs. The stoneware has quiet stone-like colours because high temperatures diminish the colours.

Mr. Johnston makes a variety of one-off decorative pieces such as vases, figurines and bottles. The bottles are square and slab-built. **Practical details:** The showroom is open to the public throughout the year. Mr. Johnston gives talks and demonstrations to groups by arrangement. He says that about fifteen to twenty adults is a reasonably comfortable crowd but he has, through a shift system, had groups of more than forty people. His fee is £5 and the session lasts an hour. Give him at least one week's notice. Individuals and small parties can join groups provided they are willing to book well ahead and fit in with the times arranged for a group visit.

Early morning at Aberdeen's fish market

38   Fish Market

The Fish Market
Aberdeen, Grampian
Tel: Aberdeen 52932

Although looking at dead fish is not everybody's idea of fun, there is an air of excitement in the market-place which is very infectious, and it is fascinating to find out how the fish you eat get from net to table.

The fish start arriving at Aberdeen market as early as 4 am. They are brought overland from smaller ports, as well as being unloaded directly from ships at Aberdeen. Aberdeen is Britain's third largest port, after Hull and Grimsby, and it handles more than seven million pounds worth of fish every year. The local fish speciality is haddock — you've

probably heard of Finnan haddock. You will
see all kinds of fish arriving packed in ice,
having been boxed that way at sea.
The catch is winched ashore in baskets,
weighed, and laid out in lines of boxes for the
buyers to inspect. Everything happens very
fast. Competition is keen, with two to three
hundred firms out to buy fish, and many of the
buyers radio news about prices back to their
offices.
The auctions start at 7.30 am and, on days
when there is a good supply of fish, they carry
on until midday. After the fish have been sold
they are whisked off in lorries to processing
plants in Aberdeen and elsewhere, or they
might be put on British Rail's daily express
fish train to London.
Practical details: The market is open Monday
to Friday from 7.30 am to 11 am. The best time
to arrive is 8.30 am.
After you have finished seeing the market the
ideal lunch or breakfast is, of course, fish! You
can eat a Scottish breakfast in the New Market
off Union Street. Or, take a tip from somebody
who has lived in Aberdeen and buy a whole
smoked salmon before leaving. It costs less
here and it ought to be the best you have ever
tasted.

39   Village Crafts

The Camphill Village Trust
Newton-Dee Community
Bieldside, Aberdeenshire AB1 9DX
Tel: Aberdeen 48701

Camphill communities, based on the work of
Rudolf Steiner, help mentally handicapped
adults to work within a sheltered and secure
community, developing their skills and
independence. The Newton-Dee village has
twelve houses where 150 people live. They
work in the houses, in the workshops or on the
land. The farm of more than a hundred acres is
a mixed one, producing crops such as oats, hay
and potatoes. There are also pigs and cattle.
Surplus from the land is sold locally.
Workshops include the bakery, dollmaking,
joinery and weaving. There are tie-and-dye,

One of the many crafts at Camphill

metal and rug-weaving shops. Goods which
you buy, and perhaps watch being made,
include pure silk squares in batik and tie-and-
dye patterns. There are pull-along wooden
toys made from hardwood, and African, Asian
and European rag dolls.
Practical details: The village is open Monday
to Friday from 10 am to 12 noon and 3 pm to
5 pm, and on Saturday from 3 pm to 5 pm.
Individuals and groups of up to fifty people
should give a week's notice of a visit to the
secretary. The workshops are closed on
Saturday afternoon but the shop and coffee bar
can still be visited.
The free tour lasts two hours, including time
for buying goods and for refreshments in the
coffee bar.

40   Creamery and Dairy Products

Aberdeen & District Milk Marketing Board
Twin Spires, Bucksburn, Aberdeen
Tel: Aberdeen 696371

The creamery is highly automated and
produces milk, milk powder, cream and butter
and a wide range of dairy products. It is
equipped with highly sophisticated
machinery and is one of the leaders in spray-
drying technology.
Practical details: Visitors are welcome by
appointment on two afternoons each week, in
groups of ten to twenty-five people. Mrs. A.
Hay requires three weeks' notice. Individuals
and small parties can join groups, by
appointment, provided they are willing to fit-
in with times arranged for a group visit. The
tour takes two hours.

41   Gemstone Cutting and Polishing

Lapidary Workshops Company
Garlogie School, Skene,
Aberdeenshire AB3 6RX
Tel: Skene 381

This is the home of Scotland's national
gemstone, 'The Cairngorm'. Interesting local
minerals and specimens from all over the
world are on display. You can watch
gemstones being cut, polished and drilled.
Most of the company's business is with
manufacturing jewellers and goods are on sale
to the public at the same price.
Practical details: The workshop is open to
individuals and small groups during normal
working hours.

42   Highland Whisky Distillery

Glengarioch Distillery
Oldmeldrum, Aberdeenshire
Tel: Oldmeldrum 235

Glen Garioch highland whisky is made from
barley which is malted (meaning soaked) in

Milk Marketing Board—quality control

local soft water, with nothing but the water
and peat smoke to give it colour and
flavouring. The result is a 'light, fragrant,
flowery whisky, not very smoky, and
surprisingly mild on the palate'. This
distillery is one of the few which still produces
its own malted barley.
One large building has a number of floors
where the malt is laid to germinate. If you
burrow into it with your hand you can feel the
heat that it generates. In another building the
malt is 'peated' for twelve hours with peat
smoke to give it flavour. After it has been
dried, the barley is sent through the malt mill.
The first mill removes the dust and the second
removes the roots and developing stems. Next
the malt is ground.
Then comes the mashing which dissolves the
sugar and takes seven hours. Several waters are
used and conditions have to be kept the same
every week, so that there is no variation in the
characteristic taste of the whisky.
The liquid is cooled, the yeast is added, and
during the fermentation a head comes up in

the huge vats — it looks rather like boiling milk.

After fermentation the malt is distilled. It is boiled to evaporate some of the alcohol, and after maturing water is added to dilute the whisky to the British standard for whisky. The whisky is matured in oak casks which have previously been used for storing sherry. The casks are sixty or seventy years old and the whisky is matured in them for eight years.

Practical details: Individuals can phone in advance and ask for Mr. J. Hughes. Parties should give two to three weeks' notice. Oldmeldrum is fifteen miles from Aberdeen, on the rural bus route, and the tour lasts 1½ to 2 hours. There is no age limit for visitors. The distillery is open all year except for one week at New Year and three weeks in the July and August period. Visitors can taste a tiny tot in the newly-built visitors' centre. The bus back to Aberdeen takes half an hour, just right for sobering up, and the scenery looks even nicer than on the ride out.

43   Whisky Distilling and Bottling

William Grant & Sons Limited
The Glenfiddich Distillery
Dufftown, Banffshire
Tel: Dufftown 375

At Glenfiddich you can see the distillation of a single malt whisky — made from malted barley and pure highland spring water — using the methods which have remained basically the same for 400 years.

The outstanding feature of this distillery is that you can watch the famous Glenfiddich Pure Malt Whisky being bottled in its characteristic green triangular bottles. Glenfiddich is the only highland single malt whisky which is 'chateau bottled'. At the end of the tour, they say, 'We like visitors to take a dram with us'.

Practical details: The distillery is open Monday to Friday throughout the year, except Christmas and New Year, from 10 am to 12 noon and 2 pm to 4 pm. Individuals and groups of up to twelve people can be accepted

without prior booking, although a telephone call is advisable in the 'off season'.

At least seven days' notice is required from groups of thirteen or more and the maximum that can usually be accommodated is about fifty. Children are welcome, although the tour is not really suitable for children under eight.

44   Hand-weavers

Russell Gurney Weavers
Brae Croft, Muiresk, Turriff
Aberdeenshire AB5 7HE
Tel: Turriff 3544

Russell Gurney Weavers are a cottage based

industry on a ten-acre croft and specialise in the production of handwoven ladies' and gentlemen's suitings, ties and evening-skirt lengths. Visitors are welcome to come and see them at work and will have the weaving process explained to them. Cloths are all woven in short lengths and patterns are never repeated.

For those interested in actually learning the craft a limited number of weaving courses is offered each year.

Practical details: The weavers are open Monday to Saturday from 9 am to 5.30 pm. They are seldom away, but a telephone call to D. R. Gurney will ensure their availability. Parties of up to twenty people are accepted, but these should make prior arrangement.

There is no charge for the handweaving demonstration, which lasts about half-an-hour. Goods may be purchased.

Brae Croft is 600 yards off the B9024 Turriff to Huntly road, 2½ miles from Turriff.

45   Marble Cutting and Polishing

Portsoy Marble Company
The Marble Workshop
Shorehead, Portsoy, Banffshire
Tel: Portsoy 404

The local serpentine stone, popularly called

Copper Pot Stills at William Grants

A lovely glass engraved by Harold Gordon

'Portsoy marble', which has lovely subtle green and red colouring was ordered by the Kings of France, who always had the best of everything. You will see it if ever you go to the Palace of Versailles.

The marble workshop makes and sells paperweights, penknives, pen-holders, desk thermometers, table lighters, brooches, pendants and other jewellery. You can watch the marble being polished and made up into useful articles. If the work interests you, you can buy lapidary equipment designed for the amateur lapidary enthusiast — tumblers, saws, grinders, instruction books and, of course, rough or polished stones and jewellery fittings.

Next door is Portsoy Pottery where you can see the potter at work making stoneware.

Practical details: The marble workshop is open every day except Sunday, from 8 am to 5.30 pm. Parties are not shown around but individuals are welcome to watch the work in progress.

46   Glass Engraving

Harold Gordon
Greywalls Studio
Forres, Morayshire IV36 0ES
Tel: Forres 2395

Harold Gordon works at Greywalls, a stone-built stable, which he bought and converted to provide studio and storage rooms after the last war. He now has a flourishing business engraving glass with copper wheels, which he makes himself. He has a stock of more than two hundred, ranging in size from pinhead to four inches. As you watch him at work, he moves the glass across the revolving wheel. Most of his work is done for people wanting designs for special occasions and anniversaries. He prefers not to clutter the glass with dates and inscriptions, but to use pictures and patterns which are meaningful to the people who will own them.

Practical details: Harold Gordon tells us that his studio is open to anyone from Monday morning till 12 noon Saturday, unless he happens to be on holiday which is usually July or early August. He cannot cope with large parties but can manage four to six people. He prefers visitors with a special interest. As he works alone it would be better to ring the studio beforehand.

47 Pottery at Aviemore

Castlewynd Studios Limited
Inverdruie, Aviemore
Inverness PH22 1QL
Tel: Aviemore 810645

Castlewynd Animals such as Highland cattle
and Black Faced Sheep have become part of
Scottish tradition. The pottery range includes
many shapes which are modern versions of
traditional Scottish vessels — saut buckets,
coggies and luggers. Descriptive leaflets are
supplied with each of the traditional pieces.
For example, saut (or salt) buckets were
originally large vessels used for salting down
meat or fish for use in winter. Later, small
pots, with the same characteristic side
opening, stood by the Scots kitchen stove and
held cooking salt.
Saut buckets are now made at the Aviemore
pottery in a variety of sizes and decorations.
Practical details: The pottery shop is open
9 am to 5.30 pm, with the exception of
public holidays.
Visitors can watch pottery-making on the
factory floor from a viewing window in the
showroom.
You will find Castlewynd Studios on the
A951.

Castlewynd Animals—almost a tradition

48 Popular Whisky Distillery

J. & G. Grant
Glenfarclas Distillery
Marypark, Ballindalloch
Banffshire AB3 9BD
Tel: Ballindalloch 245

The Glenlivet area has no fewer than thirty
distilleries bearing the name Glenlivet in their
title and we have chosen to feature Glenfarclas
distillery because it has such excellent
facilities for visitors. They are all cheerful,
friendly people here. 'See round the old
distillery' they say, 'We'll make you really
welcome'.
The Glenfarclas distillery has a reception
centre with an exhibition hall and a craft

shop. They stock booklets such as 'Hamish's
Guide to Glenfarclas Distillery' which
explains the processes with the help of a
cartoon character. Hamish also appears on
one of their tea-towels called DO-IT-
YOURSELF MALT WHISKY. The captions
to Hamish's antics read: '1. Take one sack of
good malt. 2. Grind into a flour. 3. Mix
thoroughly with boiling water. 4. Drain the
liquid and add a wee bit of yeast to it. 5. Stand
and allow to ferment. 6. Drain and distil. 7.
Leave to mature for fifteen years.
'NOTE: DON'T GET CAUGHT! You'll be
quicker and safer buying a bottle of
Glenfarclas Highland Malt Whisky.'
The distillery is on a hillside by the Spey River
and the combination of clear water, peat cut
from the hillside moorland, and locally grown
barley gives the distinctive flavour to whisky
made here. As in France, where wines from
neighbouring vineyards have different
characteristics, so it is with Scottish whiskies.
Glenfarclas Distillery was established in 1836
and the Grant family has owned and
supervised it since 1865. In the 1830s the
development of the patent still led to the
production of grain whisky (what the
Americans call Bourbon). For thirty years
malt and grain whiskies were distilled and
drunk as single whiskies. Then in the early
1860s the practice began of blending malt and
grain whiskies. 'Scotch' is made by blending
several malt whiskies from different

Grant's popular distillery

distilleries with grain whisky.

Since 1972 Glenfarclas has bought in malted barley from outside. You will see mashing, mixing the crushed malted barley with hot water to extract the sugar in a mash tun, fermenting the liquid (called worts) with the help of yeast, distilling twice in pot stills, and leaving whisky to mature in casks.

Practical details: The distillery is open Monday to Friday from 9 am to 5 pm. Individuals and groups of up to one hundred people are welcome and should give one day's notice to Mr. R. MacDonald.

49   Woollen Manufacturers

James Pringle Limited
Holm Woollen Mills, Inverness
Tel: Inverness 31042

The Holm Mill started in 1780 as a small country mill driven by water power, preparing the farmer's wool for home spinning and weaving. Nowadays modern machinery is at work in the old buildings and small farmers from the Shetlands, Orkneys and the Highlands, still send wool here to be spun into knitting wools and turned into goods.

On a tour you see raw wool being dyed, colours being blended, and carding — which is the combing of wools ready for spinning into thread. The single threads are used to make tartans, tweeds and travel rugs on high-speed automatic weaving machines.

In the warehouse you will see the wools, tweeds and tartans which are sold by the yard, as well as lambswool and knitwear, dresses, jackets, coats, cashmere knitwear, skirts, kilts, sports jackets, scarves, stoles and travel rugs.

Practical details: The woollen mills are open all the year Monday to Friday from 8 am to 5.30 pm, except during the first fortnight in July, the Christmas and New Year period. The

warehouse, where visitors can buy factory goods, is open all the year except for Christmas and New Year's Day, on Monday to Friday from 9 am to 5 pm and on Saturday from 9 am to 12.30 pm.
Visitors are welcome to arrive without notice and walk around individually or in groups. Children and school parties are welcome.

50 Targemaker

James McConnell
5 Friars Street,
Inverness IV1 1RJ
Tel: Inverness 30402

These reproductions of the ancient Scottish battle-shield known as the targe are made on a base of wood covered with animal skin and studded in traditional designs.
Each targe weighs about ten pounds, and is approximately twenty inches in diameter by one inch in width. Targes are covered in cowhide, suede, leather or stagskin according to the customer's order. The studs used are nickel, brass, bronze or antique finish. Some of the targes have steel spikes projecting from the centre — a perfect gift for the man who has everything and wishes to defend himself.
Practical details: Mr. McConnell's workshop is small so visiting parties are limited in number to twenty people, and the organiser should give seven days' advance notice. Individuals are welcome and may call during normal working hours.

51 Culloden Pottery

Culloden Pottery
Gollanfield, Near Inverness
Tel: Ardersier 2340

You can see a variety of pottery and pottery-making processes here — hand-thrown individual pieces and tableware, earthenware and stoneware.
Practical details: The pottery, shop and restaurant are open every day from 9.30 am

to 6 pm, all year round.
Individuals and groups of up to ten people wishing to see the pottery should telephone or write to Mr. Park at least seven days in advance.

52 Makers of Natural Stone Gifts

'The Stone House'
Avoch, Ross IV9 8PS
Tel: Fortrose 20665

Rob Henderson uprooted himself at fifty-five and started a new venture cutting stones. Years of illness and two steel hips caused him to rethink his future, so he and his wife Beryl sold their home in England and went first to Italy and then Malta, where instead of retiring and sitting in the sun, Rob learned stonecutting from local craftsmen.
He brought his skills back and settled in Scotland, choosing a base with the aid of geological maps. Rob's search for the ideal stone led him all over Britain until he eventually found a marble in the Hebrides with a varied and attractive veining.
At the Stone House you will see Scottish stone and agate turned into useful objects — cigarette boxes, table lighters, ashtrays, table lamps, clocks, letter racks, pencil holders, letter openers and paperweights.
Practical details: The Hendersons welcome visitors at all times of the year and every day except Sunday.
Avoch is on the main A382 from Inverness.

53 Art and Stone-Craft

Sutherland Gemcutters
Mr. Ian Yates
114 Achmelvich, Lochinver
Sutherland
Tel: Lochinver 312

The workshop is in a beautiful setting about one hundred feet above an inlet of the sea, Loch Roe, where terns nest on the small islands below. Local rock material is used by the workshop in jewellery, lamps, pen stands and so on. The tiny workshop also cuts precious and semi-precious gem materials from all over the world.

Visitors can have a polished face put on their own specimens while they wait: information is given on local collecting areas and rock types and a booklet is available detailing local walks for collecting polishable material.

Practical details: The workshop is open Monday to Saturday from 9.30 am to 5.30 pm. It is closed for lunch from 1 pm to 2 pm. Only small groups can be accommodated, but there is a large viewing window between the showroom and workshop. Children are not allowed into the workshop when machinery is running.

A wide range of goods is available here, or in their shop in Lochinver, from individually designed and hand-made silver and gold items, to small polished stone pendants. There are 'seconds' of other lines selling for as little as 30p. The Yates undertake special commissions and repair work during the winter months.

54   Cheese Making

Highland Fine Cheeses Limited
Blarliath, Tain, Ross and Cromarty
Tel: Tain 2034

The story of 'Highland Fine' began ten years ago when Reggie and Susannah Stone were milking cows on the spot where their colourful creamery now stands. He remarked that he remembered delicious home-made 'Crowdie', the fresh Highland cheese that he had eaten on oatcakes long ago. Susannah made some and, having too much for their own family, she took the rest to the grocer in Tain. He came back for more, and more, and they were in business.

One delicious cheese is 'Caboc', made from thick cream then rolled in toasted pin-head oatmeal. Its texture and taste is like butter — and it's curiously addictive. You might also try double cream cheese, Crowdie and Wild Garlic, Hramsa, and Galic — rolled in nuts

and large flaked oats.

Practical details: Anybody and everybody is welcome to visit this pleasant open-plan building with its background of piped music. In the summer the 'cheesery' has well over one hundred visitors each day and the staff are actively encouraged to talk to people in order to create a happy atmosphere, so you will find any one of them eager to answer any questions. There are also many opportunities to sample the various cheeses. The factory is open Monday to Friday from 10 am to 2.30.

55   Earthenware Pottery

Cromarty Design Workshop
Fishertown, Cromarty, Ross-shire
Tel: Cromarty 254

Old fishing cottages have been converted into pottery workshops and a shop. The pottery made here is hand-thrown or slab-built in terracotta clay, and often decorated with coloured slips which are either brushed or sprayed onto the pot. Sgraffito work is also done, which involves scratching a design through a layer of slip to reveal the clay underneath. Natural forms such as leaves and flowers are used for the design.

White slip-cast ware is made and hand-painted in various colours.

Practical details: The workshop and shop are open from 10 am to 6 pm, Easter to October. As the potters live on the premises they sometimes open at other times. Individuals and small groups are welcome to watch whatever work is in progress. Large groups should book.

56   Glass-Blowing and Engraving

Caithness Glass Limited
Harrowhill, Wick, Caithness
Tel: Wick 2286

Caithness Glass was founded in 1960 to provide employment in Caithness. Highly skilled craftsmen were brought in from the continent to train local apprentices. The company produces high-quality artware and tableware, using specially developed coloured glass which is cased in clear crystal glass. The colours, inspired by the local landscape, are peat, heather, moss green and twilight blue. The combination of these subtle colours with their elegant designs has given Caithness glass its very high reputation.

The engraving department has been so successful that it is now one of the largest of its kind in Europe and it caters for anything, from an individual one-off commission, to a limited edition of two thousand pieces.

Practical details: All visitors are welcome to the factory, which is open Monday to Friday from 9 am to 4.30 pm all year. The shop is open until 5 pm from September to May and also until noon on Saturday, and until 6 pm from June to August, as well as until 4.30 pm on Saturday. No advance notice is required as there are no guided tours and visitors can take their time looking around.

Seconds are sold at reduced prices. There is no charge for the visit.

57   Glassworks—Paperweights

Oban Glassworks
Lochavullin Industrial Estate
Oban, Argyll
Tel: Oban 3386

Paperweights are made here and you can see the complete paperweight-making process, from the first gather of hot glass to the beautifully shaped and hand finished article.

Practical details: The *factory* is open Monday to Friday from 9 am to 5.30 pm all year. The *shop* is open from 9 am to 5.30 pm May to September, Monday to Saturday and in October and April, from 9 am to 5 pm Monday to Friday. No advance notice is required as there is no guided tour and visitors may take their time looking around.

Should you be interested in buying a paperweight, the prices for seconds in the shop are very much reduced. There is no charge for the visit.

58   White Heather Farm

The Scottish White Heather Farm
Dunoon, Toward, Argyll
Tel: Toward 237

These extensive nursery gardens overlooking the Clyde contain a nursery section of dwarf heathers, trees, rhododendrons and azaleas. Next to the nursery is the 'Cottage' which displays British and continental cookware and jewellery. Visitors can watch white heather sprays and horseshoes being made up by Mr. and Mrs. Abercrombie.

White heather sprays are sent daily to all parts of the world. Orders range from a horseshoe for somebody in Alice Springs, Australia, to ten thousand white heather sprigs for a sales promotion campaign.

Practical details: The heather farm is open from 9 am to 6 pm every day except Sunday. Everyone, including coach parties, is welcome during opening hours, or at other times by prior arrangement, but as all the work is done by the husband-and-wife team, visitors are expected to walk round by themselves.

59   Sculpture and Pottery

Alasdair Dunn
Tigh-an-Droma
King's Cross, Brodick, Isle of Arran
Tel: Whiting Bay 323

The main output of the pottery is Alasdair Dunn's small 'wheel sculptures' which are thown on the wheel. The most popular are the bird shapes and the 'Arran Chuckie-Stanes'. The latter are inspired by local pebbles, and local clay and sand are used to give them an interesting surface texture. Each piece is different. After throwing each one is sculpted on the bench and fired to high stoneware temperature.

'In a tourist world of imported tartan gimmickry,' Mr. Dunn tells us, 'the word "souvenir" can have some gruesome connotations. In its best sense it means a work of high craftsmanship, designed and executed

Alasdair Dunn 'throwing' pots

in local materials, and sold in its place of origin. For the buyer or the recipient it should evoke a scene he loves and wishes to be reminded of.'

Practical details: Alasdair Dunn can be seen at work during the holiday season.

The workshop is at Tigh-an-Droma, which means house on the ridge, and is best reached on foot.

Alasdair Dunn's work can also be seen at 'Studio 4', the craft shop in the middle of Lamlash village, or on the mainland in Edinburgh at the Scottish Craft Centre.

60   Animal Skin Rugs and Grogbottles

Grogport Rugs
Grogport Old Manse
Carradale, Campbeltown, Argyll
Tel: Carradale 255

This is not a factory but a private house — the old wash-house having been turned into a tannery. The operation is carried out in large tanks and there is no smell!

The business specialises in skins of different colourings, but all are the natural colours of the animals, for nothing is dyed or tinted. Sheepskins are brown, black, grey, white, or brown and white spotted. Deerskin rugs are also made here from Red deer, Sika, Roe and the spotted Fallow deer.

All rugs are fully washable. They have been chosen for their character, processed with attention to detail, and each one is properly finished and brushed out. The result is something different.

At the other end of this same work-room is the squashed bottle business. Squashed bottles (Grogbottles) are wine bottles processed by heat into dishes and ashtrays. Each one is unique and is an example of waste re-cycling at its most simple.

Practical details: Mrs. M. F. Arthur tells us that visitors are welcome, though it is wise to phone first, as they also breed ponies and may not be visible if you call unexpectedly. They will accept all ages, but not in great numbers at one time. No charge is made and you can buy goods at reduced prices from the stock in hand.

Grogport Old Manse is just twenty miles from Tarbert on the road to Carradale.

61   Spinning and Simple Weaving

Susan Searight
Lealt, Isle of Jura, Argyll

The workshop is a very simple affair, with the emphasis on 'anyone can weave rugs like these'. Visitors can crowd into the small premises, and look around and ask questions. The workshop contains an upright simple frame for the weaving of floor rugs and wall hangings. There are also two spinning wheels on which she spins all her wool. All questions will be answered in this informal atmosphere and the processes are explained.

Practical details: Visitors may call without prior notice, any time of day, any day of the week, though there is no guarantee that the workshop will be open as Susan Searight is sometimes away and she has no telephone. In

general the workshop is open from July to
September, and people often drop in on their
way to the whirlpool, ten miles farther north.
Rugs and wall hangings are on sale.

62   Knitting Workshop

Muileann Beag a' Chrotail
Sgoil Dhuisdeil
Camus Croise (Camascross)
Isle of Skye, Scotland IV43 8QR
Tel: Isle Ornsay 271

The name of the company is Gaelic and means
'The little Crotal Mill'. You can usually see
ten to fifteen people knitting jerseys, scarves
and hats on hand machines.
The main product is traditional jerseys in
colours which were originally derived from
vegetable dyes. Jerseys and scarves can be
bought at mill prices in the little shop.
Iain Noble asked us to add a few words of
Gaelic: Tha sinn an comhnaidh toilichte ar
cairdean fhaicinn a seo. Tha Gaidhlig againn
uile, agus ma thig sibh bidh fios agaibh ma
tha an t-sean fhacal ceart 'Sleibhte riamhach
nam mnathan boidheach'.
No doubt he will translate it for you if you ask!
Practical details: The factory is open from
9 am to 5.30 pm and usually on Saturday
mornings in summer. Visitors are accepted
any time when the factory is open.

63   Traditional Weaving

Skye Wool Mill Limited
Portree, Isle of Skye
Tel: Portree 2889

Since the days of Bonnie Prince Charlie, there
has been a small woollen mill at Portree on the
Isle of Skye. Visitors to Portree can still see the
mills where weaving in the traditional
manner is carried on. In the large warehouse
tweeds and tartans made here are on sale —
and other goods supplied by the parent firm,
James Pringle Limited of Inverness.
Practical details: The warehouse, where
visitors can buy goods, is open all the year
round, except for Christmas and New Year's
Day, Monday to Friday from 9 am to 5 pm and
on Saturday from 9 am to 12.30 pm. Special
arrangements can be made to see the goods for
sale at other times by telephoning
the mill.

64   Hand-Woven Harris Tweed

Lachlan MacDonald
'Cnoc-Ard'
Grimsay, North Uist, Western Isles
Tel: Benbecula 2418

Harris tweed has been known for decades as
one of the warmest and most durable tweeds
and it is still a cottage industry in the
Hebrides, where it is woven on hand-looms by
individual weavers. Mr. Lachlan MacDonald
believes that his distinctive contribution to the
industry is that, as well as sporty menswear
colouring, he has produced very attractive
colourings for ladies' wear, generally not
associated with Harris tweed.
Island and Shetland knitwear is available and
he has an expanding mail-order trade for both
tweeds and knitwear.
Practical details: Lachlan MacDonald sends
this poetic invitation, 'Hiking over the
moorland, listening to the song of the birds,
the whisper of the breeze, you could also hear
the familiar click-clack, click-clack of the
loom and, of course, you are very welcome to

stop for a chat and see how it is all done.' You may also drive up to the gate (though public transport is very limited).

65   Weaving & Knitting

Bernat Klein Designs Ltd
Waukrigg Mill, Galashiels
Tel: Galashiels 4592

A permanent exhibition contains about one hundred of Bernat Klein's textile and other designs, from their early stages of conception to the finished article. Bernat Klein is well known for his fabric designs, and the materials are sold separately or made up into clothes so that the buyer can put together a co-ordinated outfit. There are Shetland and other tweeds, mohair voile (a 100% mohair in a loose see-through looped weave), and polyester prints in swirling colours to match. Before you visit the mill you might like to read Bernat Klein's book 'Design Matters' which has a few words to say about the Design Centre, the need for more design education in schools, and for changes in the attitudes of industry.
Practical details: The permanent exhibition is open seven days a week from 10 am to 4 pm. Individuals and groups can see it without an appointment.
Tours of the mill can be arranged for groups by appointment.
The mill shop is also open seven days a week, 10 am to 4 pm. It sells a wide range of fabrics and clothes, as well as 'seconds'.

66   Harris Tweed Weaver

John M. MacGregor
27 Garenin, Carloway
Isle of Lewis PA86 9AL
Tel: Carloway 257

Mr. MacGregor works alone in a small shed, weaving the soft colours of Harris Tweed on a foot-powered loom. He creates his own designs and he loves explaining to visitors the secrets of his trade. Many of Mr. MacGregor's

visitors have returned a second or third time, so that he regards them as friends.
So, *when* you get to the Isle of Lewis, you will find the shed one mile along the road leading from Carloway bridge to a small group of black houses, by the seashore at Garenin Bay.
Practical details: Mr. MacGregor's workshop is open all the year, but 'never on Sunday'. He welcomes individuals, families or carloads of about six people, as larger parties would find his shed too crowded.

67   Cheese Making

Swannay Farms Limited
Birsay, Orkney KW17 2NP
Tel: Birsay 365

Visitors see the making of various British cheeses including Swannay Farm cheese. The visit lasts about twenty minutes.
Practical details: The creamery is open Monday to Friday from 10 am to 12 noon. Individuals can visit the creamery by giving one day's notice to Miss E. Shearer. Groups of up to fifteen people can be accepted at one week's notice.

68   Silver and Gold Jewellery

Ortak Silvercraft
Hatston Industrial Estate
Kirkwall, Orkney KW15 1RH
Tel: Kirkwall 2224

Silver and gold jewellery is manufactured here in Nordic and Scottish traditional designs — also stone jewellery in modern designs.
Practical details: The *workshop* is open Monday to Friday from 9.30 am to 12.30 pm and 2 pm to 4.30 pm. The *showroom* is open Monday to Saturday from 9 am to 1 pm and 2 pm to 5 pm. Ortak Silvercraft is closed on the four local holidays and also during Christmas and New Year.
Visitors are allowed to walk around the workshop and the processes are demonstrated if requested.

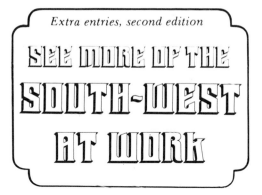

Extra entries, second edition

SEE MORE OF THE SOUTH-WEST AT WORK

Cornwall, Devon, Dorset, Somerset Avon, Wiltshire

1 *Geevor Tin Mines Ltd, Pendeen, Nr Penzance, Cornwall. Tel: St. Just 788662*
Visitors will see part of a producing tin mine. Tours of the tin treatment plant are arranged on weekdays. Tin mining museum is open daily April to October from 10 am to 5.30 pm.

2 *The Leach Pottery, St Ives, Cornwall. Tel: St Ives 6398*
Famous pottery set up by the influential Bernard Leach (now retired). Professional potters can visit the workshop. Public welcome at showroom, weekdays 9 am to 5 pm and summer Saturdays 9 am to 12.30 pm. Closed bank holidays. Suitable for the disabled.

3 *Plymouth 'B' Power Station, Prince Rock, Plymouth, Devon. Tel: Plymouth 63062*
Situated on the River Plym which provides the water for cooling. Burns 60,000 tonnes of oil a year, and can produce 217 megawatts. Contact the station administration officer to arrange evening visits. Age limit 12+.

4 *East Yelland Power Station, Fremington, Barnstaple, Devon. Tel: Instow 860522*
An older-type station. Specially small coal is fed into the furnace on an endless steel belt, and boilers produce steam to turn the turbines. Water from the River Taw condenses the steam for re-use. Contact the station

administration officer for a visit.

5 *Little Creech Animal Centre, RSPCA, West Hatch, Taunton, Somerset. Tel: Hatch Beauchamp 384*
For sick, injured and orphaned wildlife and domestic animals. Oiled Bird Unit. Interesting for children. Open Monday to Saturday 9 am to 4.30 pm and Sunday 9 am to 12 noon, except bank holidays. Casual visitors welcome. Suitable for the disabled.

6 *The Hinkley Point 'A' and 'B' Nuclear Power Stations, Hinkley Point, Nr Bridgwater, Somerset. Tel: Bridgwater 652461*
Two power stations of different design — the 'A' is of the earlier Magnox design, while the 'B' has two advanced gas cooled reactors and can produce enough electricity for a city three times the size of Bristol. Contact the administration officer for visits.

7 *Admiral Blake Museum, Blake Street, Bridgwater, Somerset. Tel: Bridgwater 56127*
A museum of the now defunct brick and tile industry. Also display of local boat building and shipping history. Open Tuesday to Saturday 10 am to 5 pm. Closed bank holidays. Individuals welcome, groups of 10 or more phone in advance.

8 *Brympton d'Evercy, Yeovil, Somerset. Tel: West Coker 2528*
Stately Home with the Priest House Country Life Museum. Vineyard, extensive gardens, tea room in old stable and picnic area. Open May to September, Saturday to Wednesday from 12 noon to 6 pm. Individuals and groups welcome (party rates).

9 *Mr N de M Godden, The Pilton Manor Vineyard, The Manor House, Pilton, Shepton Mallet, Somerset. Tel: Pilton 325*
Vineyard open all year for sales of wines and vines. Also Sunday open-days from end of August to end of September, including bank holiday. Refreshments in the wine bar or medieval gardens. Groups (minimum 20) in summer by appointment. Send sae for leaflet giving current details.

10 *Bridport Museum, South Street, Bridport, Dorset. Tel: Bridport 22116*
Not strictly 'modern Britain at work'. Local factories now make nets from rotproof synthetics and have donated to this museum their old tools and machinery for making hemp and flax ropes, nets and fishermen's lines. Museum open June to September, 10.30 am to 1 pm and 2.30 to 4.30 pm, Monday to Saturday except Thursday and Saturday afternoons. Open in morning during winter.

11 *Woodart, Dreadnought Works, Magdalen Lane, Bridport, Dorset. Tel: Maiden Newton 317, evenings and weekends*
Models of rural vehicles are made and sold here. Open Monday to Friday 9 am to 4.30 pm and weekends by appointment. Up to 10 people accepted.

12 *Cerne Valley Forge, Duck Street, Cerne Abbas, Dorset. Tel: Cerne Abbas 298*
Hand-forged ironwork designed and made here. It is displayed in the adjoining craft shop, from which the forge can be seen. Open Monday to Saturday 9 am to 5 pm. Handicapped people welcome.

13 *Leslie Gibbons A.T.D., The Owl Pottery, 108 High Street, Swanage, Dorset*
One-man business producing hand-made, highly decorative earthenware pottery. Workshop can be seen from shop. No parties, but educational visits arranged for a charge. Closed Sundays and Thursday afternoons.

14 *Bennett Ironwork (Dorset) Ltd, 45 Nuffield Road, Fleetsbridge, Poole, Dorset. Tel: Poole 6146*
Blacksmithing and wrought ironwork. Open Monday to Friday 10 am to 4 pm, and weekends by arrangement. Appointments advisable to ensure that work can be seen. Up to 10 people accepted.

15 *Poole Power Station, Rigler Road, Poole, Dorset. Tel: Poole 2663*
Cost £22 million to build. Burns 50,000 tons of oil a year, which is delivered by tanker from a nearby oil refinery, and produces 320 megawatts. Contact the station administration officer for weekday visits (over age 11).

16 *Stoney Down Pottery, Lytchett Matravers, Nr Poole, Dorset. Tel: Lytchett Minster 2392*
Stoneware and porcelain. Dorset 'Owl' cider flagons, pitchers, tankards, goblets, wine and water sets, bowls, vases and planters. Up to 20 people accepted, including the handicapped. Open nearly every day.

17 *The Wimborne Pottery, 6 West Borough, Wimborne Minster, Dorset. Tel: Wimborne 887613*
Hand spun and woven garments, hand thrown and decorated pottery, corn dollies, wood ware and basketware on sale. Hand spinning and weaving workshop in the attic. Hand printed and tie and dye clothes on sale. Open Monday to Saturday 9.30 am to 5 pm. Handicapped people welcome.

18 *Puxey Pottery, Prospect House, 45 Bridge Street, Sturminster Newton, Dorset. Tel: Sturminster Newton 72234*
Pottery, basketry, woodware and leatherwork are made and sold here. Up to eight visitors accepted.

19 *Guild Crafts (Poole) Ltd, Fontmell Magna, Shaftesbury, Dorset. Tel: Fontmell Magna 597*
Pottery, woodwork and leatherwork — workshops open 9 am to 5 pm. Also an exhibition of traditional craft tools and bygones. Small charge. Up to 40 people accepted. Coach/car parking space. Products on sale.

20 *Lackham Agricultural Museum, College of Agriculture, Lacock, Chippenham, Wiltshire. Tel: Chippenham 3251*
Not 'modern Britain at work' but old farm machines, tools and wagons, thatching and smithy items, reconstructed granaries, dairy section and donkey-wheel. Open on the first Sunday of May and October, from 2 pm to 5 pm. Other times for groups or individuals by appointment. Small charge for adults, children free. Suitable for the disabled.

21 SS *Great Britain, Great Western Dock, Gas Ferry Road, Bristol. Tel: Bristol 20680*
Brunel's revolutionary ship, the first ocean going ship to be built of iron and driven by a propeller. Now being restored. Individuals and groups welcome, 10 am to 6 pm. Admission charge. Souvenirs on sale. Also see Brunel's striking suspension bridge at Clifton, nearby.

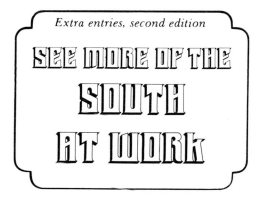

Extra entries, second edition

SEE MORE OF THE SOUTH AT WORK

**Essex, Kent, East Sussex
West Sussex, Surrey
Greater London, Hertfordshire
Bedfordshire, Buckinghamshire
Oxfordshire, Berkshire
Hampshire, Isle of Wight**

1 *Mr S W Greenwood, New Hall, Purleigh, Essex, Tel: Purleigh 343*
Dry white wines can be sampled and bought in the old farmhouse cellar. Open every day. For viewing of winery and for large groups please phone for appointment.

2 *Chart Gunpowder Mills, Westbrook Walk, Faverham, Kent. Tel: Faversham 4542*
Oldest gunpowder mills in the world which made powder for Wellington and Nelson. Open by arrangement to groups. Schools welcome. No post at mill, so write to Arthur Percival, Fleur de Lis, Preston Street, Faversham.

3 *Haxted Mill, Watermill Museuem, Edenbridge, Kent. Tel: Edenbridge 862914*
Built in 1680, a watermill with grinding machinery in working order, and a Wealden iron industry display. Open Easter to September 12 noon to 6, at weekends and on bank holidays. Children must be accompanied and school parties must book. Ground floor only suitable for the disabled.

4 *Christian Barbotin, Brighton & Hove Engineering, off Nevill Road, Hove, East*

Sussex. Tel: Brighton 559583
Huge horizontal engine, models of steam
railway engines, and steam boats, full-size
steam roller, fire engines coal furnaces and a
giant 200-foot beam engine. Static on
weekdays, steaming at weekends. Pre-visit
booklets. Public welcome, for small
admission charge. Guided tour on request.

5 *Pestalozzi Children's Village, Sedlescombe,
Battle, Sussex. Tel: Sedlescombe 444*
Children from developing countries get
practical secondary education, grow food, and
build houses, farm equipment and furniture,
eventually returning home. Guided tours of
workshops, shop etc by appointment for
individuals or groups. Open daily in July.
Small charge.

6 *Michelham Priory, Upper Dicker,
Hailsham, Sussex. Tel: Hailsham 844224*
Restored watermill last used for grinding corn
·in 1928. Now grinds wheat. Moated medieval
priory open Easter to mid-October. Guided
tours available with reductions for groups
who book. Also see ancient fishponds, forge
and wheelwright's museum. Occasional
exhibitions of working craftsmen.

7 *Merrydown Wine Co Ltd. Horam Manor,
Horam, Heathfield, E. Sussex. Tel: Horam
2254*
Vineyard tour and English wine and cider
sampling. Open summer — phone first.
Groups up to 40. Accompanied children over
12 accepted. Admission charge.

8 *Bluebell Railway Ltd, Sheffield Park
Station, Nr. Uckfield E. Sussex. Tel: Newick
2370*
Full size steam railway running for 5 miles to
Horsted Keynes. Send sae for timetable.
Suitable for the disabled.

9 *The Craftsman, 18 The High Street,
Ditchling, Sussex. Tel: Hassocks 5246*
Visitors may see Jill Pryke making green-
glazed earthenware pottery in her workshop.
She also makes named mugs and christening
plates to order. Open Monday to Saturday 10

am to 5 pm, closing 1 pm on Wednesdays.
There is a sales and information centre for
Sussex craftsmen here.

10 *The Horsham Museum, Causeway House,
9 The Causeway, Horsham, Sussex. Tel:
Horsham 4959*
Part of a 16th century timber-frame house has
been converted into old-time shops — a
wheelwright's, saddler's and blacksmith's.
Open Tuesday to Friday 1 pm to 5 pm, and
Saturday from 10 am to 5 pm. Other times by
arrangement. Admission free. Suitable for the
disabled, on the ground floor only. Closed on
public holidays.

11 *Earls Court & Olympia Ltd, Earls Court
Exhibition Centre, Warwick Road, London
SW5 9TA. Tel: 01-385 1200*
The Press Office has a fixture list of
exhibitions open to the public, including the
well-known Daily Mail Ideal Home and
Handicrafts & DIY exhibitions. Also the Boat
Show, Motor Fair, Audio Fair and Royal
Smithfield Show & Agricultural Machinery
Exhibition. Plus numerous specialised trade
exhibitions.

12 *Thamesmead Information Centre, Harrow
Manor Way, London. Tel: 01-318 5223*
This large development will eventually be a
large 'New Town' to house 45,000 people.
Visitors will see examples of town planning
and architecture which won the Abercrombie
Architectural Award in 1961, and also areas
currently under construction and plans for the
future. Film shows, talks and guided tours can
be arranged.

13 *National Museum of Labour History,*

Limehouse Town Hall, Commercial Rd, London E14. Tel: 01-525 3229
Historical documents on the struggle for the vote, suffragettes, trade unionism, the fight for improved working conditions and better wages, and the co-operative movement. Open Tuesdays, Thursdays and Fridays, 11 to 4.30 and Wednesdays until 6.30. Groups phone first. No charge.

14 *The Times, New Printing House Square, Gray's Inn Road, London WC1X 8EZ. Tel: 01-837 1234*
Visits take place on Monday to Thursday evenings, starting at 8.15 and ending at 10.30, for parties up to eight. Applications should be made to the visits secretary (Ext: 6108), bearing in mind that tours are usually booked six months in advance.

15 *Fuller, Smith & Turner Ltd, Griffin Brewery, Chiswick, London W4 2QB. Tel: 01-994 3691*
Fullers is one of the two remaining independent breweries in London. All their beers are brewed by traditional methods. Waiting list for group visits. Individuals can occasionally join groups — apply in writing.

16 *Kew Bridge Engine Trust, Kew Bridge Road, Brentford, Middlesex. Tel: 01-568 4757*
Engines which supplied west London with water until 1944, including the world's largest Cornish beam pumping engine. Also a museum. Open at weekends 11 am to 1 pm and 2 to 5 pm. School visits by appointment. Small charge.

17 *Musical Museum, 368 High Street, Brentford, Middlesex. Tel: 01 560 8108*
Restored instruments (with glass panels to show workings). Automatic pianos, organs, musical boxes and phonographs. Individuals welcome. Groups (minimum 40) by arrangement. Tours last one hour and there is a charge. Open Saturdays and Sundays, 2 to 5 pm, April to October. Closed bank holidays. Not suitable for young children.

18 *Luton Airport, Luton, Bedfordshire. Tel:*

Luton 36061 Ext 33
Casual visitors can watch from Spectators' Enclosure. Groups may have a guided tour — give a month's notice.

19 *The Cottage Craft Shop, Chipping Warden, Banbury, Oxfordshire. Tel: Chipping Warden 200*
Display of work by 200 craftpersons — everything handmade. During the summer, demonstrations of corn-dolly making, lace-making, macramé, crochet and leatherwork arranged on request. Phone for details.

20 *Reading Head Post Office, Friar Street, Reading, Berkshire. Tel: Reading 55868 Ext 249*
Visitors see letters and parcels being sorted, and the delivery sections. Local groups and schools welcome for a tour at 2 or 7 pm.

21 *Bartley Heath Pottery, North Warnborough, Odiham, Hampshire. Tel: Odiham 2163*
Handthrown stoneware pottery — mugs, jugs, ovenware, moneybanks and vases. Open Monday to Saturday 9 am to 8 pm, and some Sundays (phone to check). Up to 16 people can watch the potters, when convenient.

22 *Peter Ingram, Limes End Yard, High Street, Selbourne, Nr. Alton, Hampshire. Tel: Selbourne 312*
Mr Ingram builds, restores and decorates living-waggons, and restores horse-drawn vehicles of all kinds to show condition. Showroom of gypsy life. Open to visitors most weekends, or during the week by arrangement. Small charge. Items for sale.

23 *Tichborne Pottery, Tichborne, Nr. Alresford, Hampshire. Tel: Alresford 2825*
Visitors can watch work in hand in this one-man pottery. Up to 12 people are accepted, but phone before calling. Handicapped welcome.

24 *Roger Powell, The Slade, Froxfield, Petersfield, Hampshire. Tel: Hawkley 229*
Specialist bookbinding, conservation, repair and rebinding of early manuscripts, printed

books and documents. Decorated binding for collectors. Visitors (maximum 10) with a specific interest in the subject can see work in progress, by appointment.

25 *Old Forge Pottery Ltd, 37 Durrants Rd, Rowlands Castle, Hampshire. Tel: Rowlands Castle 2632*
A range of wheel-thrown stoneware pottery — dinner services, coffee sets, ovenware, wine bottles, goblets and individual pots. Open daily 9 am to 5 pm and Sundays 2 to 5 pm. If work is in progress visitors can watch. Up to 10 people accepted, if more than 8 please phone first.

26 *HMS Dolphin, Fort Blockhouse, Gosport, Hampshire. Tel: Portsmouth 22351 Ext 41868*
Visitors see the submarine base, submarine, midget submarine, church, memorial chapel and Royal Navy Submarine Museum. Groups only, entrance free. Book in advance. Souvenir shop.

27 *Overstone Pottery, 260 Brook Lane, Sarisbury, Southampton, Hampshire. Tel: Locks Heath 84474*
Hand-thrown pottery. Demonstrations can be given for up to 14 people.

28 *Max Factor & Co, Francis Avenue, West Howe, Bournemouth, Hampshire. Tel: Bournemouth 25541*
A one-hour tour, walking round the factory, for local secondary schools and colleges. One month's notice needed.

29 *The Island Pottery Studio, Avenue Rd, Freshwater, Isle of Wight. Tel: Freshwater 2356*
Traditional father and son craft pottery. Individuals and groups of up to 10 people are shown all the stages of production. Children must be accompanied. Phone a day ahead for details.

30 *Calbourne Watermill, Calbourne, Nr. Newport, Isle of Wight. Tel: Calbourne 227*
16-foot iron watermill (still in use) which drives millstones, then rollers, to grind flour.

Also a museum. Picnic place. Open April to October. Small charge. Families walk in. Groups please book.

31 *Steam Railway, Havenstreet, Ryde, Isle of Wight. Tel: Wootton Bridge 882204*
Steam trains from the late 1800s run regularly on Easter and Spring bank holidays, on Sundays from May to September, and on Thursdays in July and August. Phone for details. Summer show in August. Special group rates. Suitable for the disabled.

32 *Isle of Wight Studio Glass Ltd, Old Park, St Lawrence, Ventnor, Isle of Wight. Tel: Ventnor 853526*
No formal tour but you can watch the glassmaking. Open all year to individuals, groups in winter only when a week's notice is necessary, small charge.

**Suffolk, Norfolk, Lincolnshire
Cambridgeshire, Northamptonshire
Leicestershire, Nottinghamshire
Derbyshire, Staffordshire
West Midlands, Warwickshire
Gloucestershire
Hereford and Worcester, Salop**

1 *B T Ambrose, Nether Hall, Cavendish, Sudbury, Suffolk. Tel: Glemsford 280221*
Elizabethan manor house with vineyard. Open daily. Visitors welcome. Groups by appointment. Picnic place. Small charge. Send sae for details.

2 *Bressingham Gardens & Live Steam Engine Museum, Bressingham, Diss, Norfolk. Tel: Bressingham 386*
Steam train trips in open-sided coaches. 40 engines on wheels, plus old threshing equipment, stationary engines, steam roundabout and an organ.

3 *Pye Business Communications Ltd, Cromwell Rd, Cambridge. Tel: Cambridge 45191*
Small groups may see how they market communications equipment such as private automatic telephone exchanges, PABX public address intercom, paging, staff location and closed circuit TV systems.

4 *Waterways Museum, Stoke Bruerne, Nr. Towcester, Northants. Tel: Northampton 862229*
Comprehensive collection of relics from canal life and industry, including a full size reconstruction of a butty boat cabin fitted out and decorated traditionally, brasses, traditional clothing and cabinware. Open daily in summer from 10 am to 6 pm, and in winter 10 am to 4 pm (except Mondays). Closed on Christmas and Boxing Day. Groups by arrangement. Small charge.

5 *Dodyke Pumping Station Preservation Trust, c/o Bridge Farm, Tattershall, Lincs*
Working equipment rather than people at work — machinery once used for draining the Fens, demonstrating four types of power. Open to public in summer, in steam first Sunday in each month. Groups by arrangement.

6 *Major Alan Rook, Stragglethorpe Hall, Lincoln. Tel: Loveden 72308*
Vineyard, winery and gardens at a wine merchant's house. Open to all on August Saturday afternoons from 2 to 5.30 pm. Reductions for children and groups. Suitable for the disabled.

7 *The Old House Museum, Cunningham Place, Bakewell, Derbyshire. Tel: Bakewell 2378*
Leadminers', saddlers', wheelwrights' and cobblers' tools. Farming equipment, costumes and a Victorian kitchen. Open daily on summer afternoons to individuals. 2.30 to 5 pm. Groups must book.

8 *Cheddleton Flint Mill, Cheddleton, Leek, Staffordshire*
Water-powered mills used for grinding flint, stone and bone. Display of working machinery. Individuals welcome on weekend afternoons, all year. Groups send sae to Mr F Underwood, 4 Cherry Hill Avenue, Meir, Stoke-on-Trent to arrange daytime visits, or to Mr E Royle, 5 Caroline Cres, Brown Edge, Stoke-on-Trent for evening visits.

9 *Chapman Sheepskin Ltd, The Old Mill, Tutbury, Burton-upon-Trent, Staffordshire. Tel: Burton 814067*
Tours of the tannery on Wednesday and

Thursday afternoons from 2.30 to 4 pm, April to October, for parties up to 30 by prior arrangement. Small charge. School groups and children under 14 not accepted. Finished products on sale.

10 *Information Bureau, National Exhibition Centre, Birmingham. Tel: 021-780 4141*
Fixtures list of exhibitions open to the public, such as the International Furniture Show; Boat & Leisure Life Show; and Kitchen & Bathrooms International. Plus trade shows including Communications Equipment; Printing Machinery; Environmental Pollution Control; and Building & Construction.

11 *The Avoncraft Museum of Buildings, Stoke Heath, Bromsgrove. Tel: Bromsgrove 31363*
Open-air museum with buildings varying from a fully operational windmill and chainmaking workshop to the great 14th century Gueston Hall Roof from Worcester. Open March to mid-December daily 10.30 am to 5.30 pm (or dusk if earlier). Admission charge. Reductions for groups by arrangement. Refreshments and picnic site.

12 *Berkeley Power Station, Berkeley, Gloucester. Tel: Berkeley 431 Ext 38*
Cost £50 million to construct and was the first commercial nuclear power station to start operating in the UK, in 1962. It burns 100 tonnes of imported uranium a year. Contact the station warden for visits. Supervised coach parties accepted (age over 15), evening visits possible.

Extra entries, second edition

SEE MORE OF WALES AT WORK

**Gwent, South Glamorgan
Mid Glamorgan, West Glamorgan
Dyfed, Powys, Clwyd, Gwynedd**

1 *Welsh Industrial & Maritime Museum, Bute Street, Cardiff. Tel: Cardiff 371805*
On a large site in Cardiff's dockland, this Museum has restored to working order pumping, winding and driving engines from various industries — coalmines, iron and steel works, tinplate mills, gas and electricity generating plants. Open daily all year, except Sunday mornings. Admission free.

2 *Aberthaw 'A' and 'B' Power Stations, Nr Barry, Glamorgan. Tel: St Athan 271*
See stations using coal pulverised in mills which grind the coal finer than face powder. For visits contact the administration officer.

3 *Haverfordwest Pottery, Haroldstone House, Clay Lane, Haverfordwest, Dyfed. Tel: Haverfordwest 2611.*
Hand-made and mechanically-made stoneware, fired in electric kilns. Shop open Monday to Friday. Closed bank holidays. Small groups accepted, give 3 weeks' notice.

4 *Penybont Pottery, Penybont, Nr. Llandrindrod Wells, Powys*
Resident potter makes earthenware and stoneware tableware, and sculpture. Antique pottery and porcelain also on sale.

5 *Wylfa Power Station, Cemaes Bay, Anglesey, Gwynedd. Tel: Cemaes Bay 471*

One of the world's largest nuclear power stations — 1,000 megawatt output — it is sited on Anglesey's rugged north-west coast. Nature trail, and an observation tower overlooking the power station and countryside (open from 10 am). Station tours for groups by arrangement with the station manager. Schools free (age 14+).

6 *Bryn Coch Pottery, Nr Penygroes, Nebo, Caernarfon, Gwynedd. Tel: Penygroes 367*
Mugs with handles in the shape of fish, seals etc. Animal studies, dishes and other one-off items. Potters can usually be seen daily 11 am to 7.30 pm. Closed Saturdays and Sunday mornings.

7 *John Davies, The Pottery, Nr Fourcrosses (Y Ffor), Pwllheli, Gwynedd. Tel: Pwllheli 2932*
Pots thrown on a kick-wheel. Local materials used and wood-fired domestic stoneware produced. Workshop visits by written appointment. Showroom open weekdays and Saturday mornings.

8 *Porthmadog Pottery, The Mill, Snowdon St, Porthmadog, Gwynedd. Tel: Porthmadog 2785*
Vases, sandwich trays and cruets are made by various methods, and hand-decorated. Open weekdays, 10.00 am to 4.30 pm. Groups must book. Visitors may try using the potters wheel and enter the "pot of the week" competition. Seconds shop.

9 *Trawsfynydd Power Station, Trawsfynydd, Blaenau Ffestiniog, Gwynedd. Tel: Trawsfynydd 331*
First nuclear power station to be built inland — in Snowdonia National Park — it was completed in 1965. Lake water used for cooling. Follow the nature trail and see the CEGB's trout farm. Station tours by arrangement with the station manager. Schools free (age 14+).

10 *Penmachno Woollen Mill, Penmachno, Gwynedd.*
Large woollen mill on the banks of the River Conwy. Weaving Monday to Friday. Shop open every day in summer. Picnic site and walks.

11 *Harlech Pottery, Ffordd Pentre Refail, Harlech, Gwynedd. Tel: Dyffed 397*
Individually modelled sheep, bulls and badgers. Also flower and candle holders and domestic pottery. Showroom open Monday to Saturday. Throwing demonstrations for groups by appointment, and holiday courses.

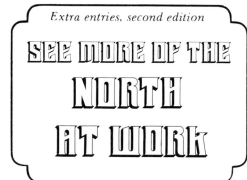

Extra entries, second edition

SEE MORE OF THE
NORTH
AT WORK

**Cheshire, Greater Manchester
Lancashire, West Yorkshire
South Yorkshire, Humberside
North Yorkshire, Cleveland
Durham, Tyne and Wear
Northumberland, Cumbria
Isle of Man**

1 *The Abbey Green Scene, The Workshop, Abbey Green, Chester. Tel: Chester 319181*
Showrooms and workshops. See them making pine furniture, sculpture, painted silks, appliqué, painted furniture and screen printed fabric. Open Monday to Saturday. Individuals and small parties welcome.

2 *Mr Alan Marmion, Art Centre, Northgate Street, Chester.*
Can supply a list of Cheshire crafts workers who accept visitors.

3 *Peter Cooper Saddlery, Northgate Street, Chester*
Mr Cooper will show you saddles and let you know when you can see them being made.

4 *Hylyne Rabbits Ltd, Woodacre Farm, Statham, Lymm, Cheshire. Tel: Lymm 3005*
Commercial rabbit breeding farm producing rabbits for meat and fur. Tour lasts 1 hour and is suitable for the handicapped. Individuals and parties (maximum 20) preferably on Wednesday, Thursday or Fridays. Book at least one month ahead. No admission charge.

5 *Overton Hall Cheshire Cheese Dairy, Nr.*

Malpas, Cheshire. Tel: Malpas 297
Visits by arrangement with the Publicity Officer, Town Hall, Chester. Small admission charge.

6 *J W Wycherley & Son, Church Street, Malpas, Cheshire. Tel: Malpas 316*
Makes saddles and harnesses for supply to shops, riding schools and stables. Open weekdays 8 am to 6 pm (not Wednesday afternoons). Closed for lunch 1-2 pm.

7 *Bury Transport Museum, Castlecroft Rd, Bury, Lancashire. Tel: 061-764 7790*
Steam locomotives, preserved buses and a steam roller. Loco in steam on the last Sunday of each month, March to September. Phone or send sae for details.

8 *Ordshall Hall Museum, Taylorson Street, Salford. Tel: 061-872 0251*
No people at work, but period rooms and a Victorian kitchen. Schools and other organised groups must book. Open Monday to Saturday 10 am to 5 pm, and Sunday afternoons.

9 *Salford Museum & Art Gallery, The Crescent, Peel Park, Salford, Lancashire. Tel: 061-736 2649*
No modern workers, but a street of reconstructed shops from about 1900. Clogger's shop, chemist's, milliner's, blacksmith's forge etc. School and other organised groups please book. Open Monday to Saturday, 10 am to 6 pm (winter until 5 pm) and Sunday afternoons.

10 *Monks Hall Museum, 42 Wellington Road, Eccles, Manchester. Tel: 061-789 4372*
Static industrial machinery — steam hammer, gas engine, steam engine etc — especially James Nasmyth's inventions. Open Monday to Saturday. Schools and the disabled please book.

11 *The Pilkington Glass Museum, Prescot Road, St Helen's, Merseyside. Tel: St Helen's 28882 Ext 2499*
Industrial museum which illustrates the

evolution of glassmaking and the various applications of glass. Open on weekdays 10 am to 5 pm, Wednesdays (March to October only) until 9 pm, weekends and bank holidays (not Christmas or New Year) 2 pm to 4 pm. No charge. Groups must book.

12 *Kathy Cartledge, Bentham Pottery, Oysterber Farm, Low Bentham, Lancaster. Tel: Bentham 61567*
Individuals and small groups welcome — parties need to book. Workshop open 9 am to 5 pm Monday to Friday. Shop also open at weekends in summer.

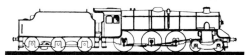

13 *Steamtown Railway Museum Ltd, Warton Rd, Carnforth, Lancashire. Tel: Carnforth 4220*
Restored steam engines. Flying Scotsman and other famous locos exhibited. Model railway, rides and coaling plant operating on some Sundays in summer. Museum open every day, except Christmas. Please phone first, to arrange a guide for groups.

14 *Damart Thermawear (Bradford) Ltd, Bowling Green Mills, Bingley, W. Yorkshire. Tel: Bingley 7071*
Factory not seen, but a film of their extra-warm clothing being worn on expeditions, demonstration of clothing and sale of garments at reduced prices. Individuals can join booked groups, Monday to friday 2 to 4.30 pm.

15 *Rabone Chesterman Ltd, Pomona St, Sheffield. Tel: Sheffield 660044*
The manufacture of various tape measures and rules can be seen. Educational groups, consumer associations and other interested groups can tour the works by day, or see a few processes in the evening, by appointment.

16 *Wood Brothers Glass Co Ltd, Brough Flint Glass Works, Pontefract Road, Barnsley, South Yorkshire. Tel: Barnsley 203637*

Manufacturers of the 'Cascade' collection including spaghetti jars, jelly moulds and piggy banks. Also cosmetic bottles, scientific, laboratory and industrial glassware. Tours for adults only, by appointment. Souvenirs.

17 *The Ark Museum, Kirkgate, Tadcaster. Yorkshire. Tel: Tadcaster 2091*
Run by John Smith's brewery. Brewing bygones — cooper's tools, beer pumps, spirit jars and bottles. Open midweek afternoons. Groups please book.

18 *George Leatt Industrial & Folk Museum, High Corn Mill, Chapel Hill, Skipton, N. Yorks. Tel: Skipton 2883*
Waterwheels drive pairs of mill stones, grinders, winnowers and haychoppers. A water-powered turbine makes electricity to light the mill, and there's a treadmill, blacksmith's shop and historic scenes. Open most summer Sunday afternoons to the public. Groups write to Mr Leatt, Albert Street, Skipton, for other dates.

19 *Craven Museum, High Street, Skipton, N. Yorkshire. Tel: Skipton 4079*
Small museum with static lead ore crushing machine, farming and domestic items. Closed every Tuesday, and on Sundays in winter.

20 *W R Outhwaite & Son, Ropemakers, Town Foot, Hawes, North Yorkshire. Tel: Hawes 487*
Visitors will see ropes made by the traditional method. Ropes, twines, cords and related craft items, including macrame and netting on sale. Open in working hours for individuals and families. Group visits by arrangement (sae please). No charge. Children's playground.

21 *Beamish Museum, Beamish Hall, Nr Stanley, Co Durham. Tel: Stanley 33580*
An open-air museum showing the way of life in the north-east at the turn of the century. It includes a colliery with steam winder, coal wagons and pit cottages, a farm with horse-drawn carts and implements, and furnished shops and workshops. Craftsmen demonstrate potting, printing with an old printing press,

coir mat making, proggy mat making and bread baking in a coal-fire oven. Reduced rates and worksheets for schools. Open April to September daily except Mondays. Phone for winter opening hours.

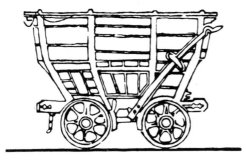

22 *Vaux Breweries Ltd, Sunderland. Tel: Sunderland 76277*
Guided tour to see brewing and bottling of ale, and the horses used for local deliveries. Groups only. Tours can be arranged any time Monday to Friday. Suitable for the disabled.

23 *Newcastle Chronicle & Journal Ltd, Thompson House, Groat Market, Newcastle upon Tyne. Tel: Newcastle 27500*
See the printing and production processes, every Monday throughout the year (except bank holidays). Afternoon or evening visits last 1½ hours. Parties (9 to 15 persons) must book 6 months ahead, through the promotions department.

24 *Washington Studio Pottery, Old Hall Smithy, The Green, Washington Village, District 4, Tyne & Wear.*
Stoneware pottery evolved from the English medieval tradition. Also tiles, murals and sculptural items. Commissions are accepted for individual designs. Open Monday to Saturday 9.30 am to 5 pm, and Sundays 1 pm to 5.30. Groups up to ten people.

25 *Dent Glass, Risehill Mill, Dent, Sedburgh, Cumbria. Tel: Dent 323*
All stages of hand prepared sandblast engraving can be seen. Open Monday to Friday 9 am to 4 pm, all year. Also weekends

July to September 10 am to 4 pm (no production). Groups up to 20 by arrangement.

26 *The Brewery Arts Centre, The Old Brewery, Highgate, Kendal, Cumbria. Tel: Kendal 25133*
Converted brewery housing jewellery, lapidary, and screen printing workshops, darkroom and TV studio where video-recordings are made. Theatre, photographic gallery, snack bar and bar. Open to all, day and evening (not Sundays).

27 *The Old Smithy, Cavendish St, Cartmel, Nr Grange-over-Sands, Cumbria. Tel: Cartmel 362*
300-year-old smithy which operated until 1968, with all tools and equipment still intact. Craftwork on display and for sale. Closed Sundays.

28 *Lakeside & Haverthwaite Railway, Haverthwaite Station, Nr Ulverston, Cumbria. Tel:Newby Bridge 594*
Steam trains in action at Easter, and then daily from early May to October. They run from Haverthwaite Station on the A590 near Newby Bridge to Lakeside Station on Lake Windermere, where connections can be made with Sealink steamers. Parties welcome.

Extra entries, second edition

SEE MORE OF SCOTLAND AT WORK

Dumfries and Galloway, Borders Lothian, Strathclyde, Central Fife, Tayside, Grampian, Highland Orkney, Western Isles

1 *Tidemark Sea Shell Collection, Tidemark Shellcrafts, 1 Charlotte Street, Stranraer.* World-wide shell collection includes killer cones, murex shells used for dyes, and money cowries. Hand painting of local beach pebbles is done on the premises, and during the summer demonstrations of enamelling, doll-making and painting are given. Open 9.45 am to 12.30 pm and 2 to 5.30 pm. Closed on Wednesdays and Sundays. Admission free.

2 *Wilson & Glenny Ltd, Langlands & Ladylaw Mills, Bath Street, Hawick, Roxburghshire. Tel: Hawick 2241* Free one-hour tour of the mill to see yarn being spun and the dying of yarn and wool. Monday to Friday 8 am to 5 pm. Individuals welcome. Groups give a week's notice. Shop with tweeds, wool and knitwear also open on Saturday till 4.30 pm.

3 *Wellwood Weavers Craft Shop, Wellwood, Selkirk. Tel: Selkirk 21201* Craft shop in a converted stable, with various crafts in the making. Open Easter to Christmas 9 to 6.30 pm, other months 9 am to 5.30 pm, including Sundays (Sunday afternoons only, in November and December).

4 *Mr Macdonald Scott, The Pendstead, Melrose, Roxburghshire. Tel: Melrose 2573*

Decorative wall-hangings for churches and homes, tapestry hand-woven in wool on cotton warp. Subjects abstract, symbolic or as commissioned. Art gallery, and work for sale. Room for up to 20 people. Phone call preferable, but not necessary.

5 *The Kelso Pottery, The Knowes, Kelso, Roxburghshire. Tel: Kelso 2027.* Domestic pots in high-temperature stoneware, decorated with brightly coloured slips. Piggy-banks, bowls and plates carry the symbol based on the Pictish Eye. See pots thrown on the wheel, 10 am to 1 pm, 2 to 5 pm. Closed Sundays.

6 *Edrom Nurseries, Coldringham, Eyemouth, Berwickshire. Tel: Coldringham 284* Alpine plants, heathers, woodlands and shrubs. Individuals can walk in Monday to Friday (closed noon to 1.30 pm). Groups booking a week ahead can have a 1 -hour guided tour.

7 *Leonard & Patricia Hassall, 'The Hand' Pottery Studio, Woodbush Brae, Dunbar, East Lothian. Tel: Dunbar 63724* A variety of individual pieces — vases, flower ladies, chess sets, goblets, plaques and plates. Often, throwing on the wheel can be seen from the shop area. Open all year 10 am to 5 pm, Monday to Saturday. Seconds usually available.

8 *James Mitchell, Lammermoor Woollens, Mitchell's Close, Haddington, East Lothian. Tel: Haddington 2207* A one-man business. This former woollen designer now makes his own exclusive high fashion ladies' tweeds using up to 24 coloured

yarns in one pattern. Hours variable, so phone first.

9 *National Museum of Antiquities of Scotland, Queen Street, Edinburgh. Tel: 031-556 8921*
The archive, useful to teachers, writers, journalists and film-makers, is open 9.30 am to 5 pm on weekdays. It contains photographic and documentary information.

10 *The Scotsman Publications Ltd, 20 North Bridge, Edinburgh. Tel: 031-225 2468 Ext 254*
See the printing, editorial and tele-ad departments of the Evening News. Individuals and groups welcome. Book a week ahead for afternoon tours. Children and the disabled welcome.

11 *George Garson, 1 Newhouses Road, East Burnside, By Broxburn, West Lothian. Tel: Broxburn 852808*
Mr Garson (Head of Murals, Glasgow Art School) makes murals in mosaic, concrete, paint and brick, and also stained glass. He does small size commissions at home. Interested individuals (eg art students) welcome. Phone first.

12 *Blackwood Morton & Sons Ltd, BMK, Burnside Works, Kilmarnock, Strathclyde.*
Organised groups are given a weekday afternoon tour, to see a film, and preparation, weaving and finishing of Axminster, Wilton and tufted carpets. Free brochure, and a question and answer session. Book one month ahead.

13 *Ann R Thomas Gallery, Harbour Street, Tarbert, Argyll. Tel: Tarbert 390*
Harbour-front gallery selling paintings and printed products. Open 10 am to 8.30 pm in the holiday season, other times until 5.30 pm. Printing can be seen when in progress in the workshop behind the gallery.

14 *Tron Shop, Culross, Fife. Tel: Newmills 271*
Many Scottish crafts, with the family specialising in patchwork, hooked rugs and

Ann R. Thomas

screen printing. Also dulcimers and bodhrans made to order. Open shop hours and Sunday afternoons.

15 *George L Thomson, The White Cottage, Balgrie Bank, by Leven, Fife.*
He writes scrolls and illuminated addresses, books published in facsimile, and carves on wood and stone. See his work at the Scottish Craft Centre, or his hilltop farm home — 'difficult access, no telephone, toilets or tours'.

16 *Reedie Hill Farm, Auchtermuchty, Fife. Tel: Auchtermuchty 369*
First commercial red deer farm in Britain, with domesticated deer. No dogs allowed. Individuals and groups welcome Monday to Friday, but give one day's notice by phone. Admission charge covers informal guided tour. Suitable for the disabled.

17 *Sidlaw Industries Ltd, Meadow Place Buildings, Bell Street, Dundee, Tayside. Tel: Dundee 23161*
The company is involved in jute and other textiles, hardware, packaging, engineering and oil servicing. Local schools and student groups welcome to see spinning and weaving. PR department will forward information and product samples.

18 *Patrick & Dorothy Forsyth, Craft Shop, 16 Broad Street, Fraserburgh, Aberdeenshire*
Woodturning demonstrations daily from mid-June to the end of September. Children may

try to make a small item. Open to individuals and groups, Monday to Saturday from 9 am to 5 pm. Also Sundays by arrangement for coach parties. Suitable for the disabled.

19 *Scotcrafts, Station Road, Peterhead, Aberdeenshire. Tel: Peterhead 4669*
Making ships — and getting them into bottles! Also hand-knitting in traditional Arran patterns. Open Monday to Saturday for individuals and groups. Give two days' notice for a demonstration. Suitable for the disabled.

20 *Colonel W A D & Mrs Innes, Innes Weavers, The Old Manse of Marnoch, Huntly, Aberdeenshire. Tel: Bridge of Marnoch 273*
Handwoven tweeds, ties, shoulder bags and bedside rugs are made here and on sale. Individual visitors welcome, but phone first.

21 *William Teacher & Sons Ltd, The Glendronach Distillery Co Ltd, Forgue, By Huntly, Aberdeenshire. Tel: Forgue 202*
Distillery tour lasting 1½ hours. Open Monday to Friday from 10.30 am to 2.30 pm, by appointment only. Individuals and groups of up to 50 people accepted at one day's notice.

22 *Chivas Brothers Ltd, Strathisla Distillery, Seafield Avenue, Keith, Banffshire. Tel: Keith 2636*
See the distillation and storage of 12-year-old Chivas Regal, and the Rolls Royce of whiskies Royal Salute (21-years-old). No coaches or small children please. Tours Monday to Friday, mid-June to mid-September, 10 am, 11 am, 2 pm, 3 pm and 4 pm.

23 *Hector Russell (Highland Industries) Ltd, 49 Huntly Street, Inverness. Tel: Inverness 31713*
Above the retail tartan shop you can see kilts being made. Display of spinning wheels, looms, military kilts and the original Culloden battlefield map. Open to individuals Monday to Friday 9.30 to 11.30 am and 3.30 to 4.30 pm. Groups give one day's notice.

24 *The Isle of Skye Handloom Co Ltd, 20*

Homnahurich Street, Inverness. Tel: Inverness 36333
Handloom weaving of original tartans and colourful tweeds. Mill open Monday to Friday from 9 am to 5 pm (closed 12.30 to 2). Just walk in — no restrictions on numbers. Shop also open on Saturdays. Suitable for the disabled.

25 *Marquesa de Torre Hermos, Garve Society, Strathbran, Achnalt, Garve, Rosshire. Tel: Garve 202*
Call at any time to see deerskin articles and enquire where you can see them being made.

26 *UK Atomic Energy Authority, Dounreay, Thurso, Caithness. Tel: Thurso 2121 Ext 656*
Exhibition open Monday to Saturday, May to September, from 9 am to 4 pm. Also daily visits to the prototype fast reactor, for a limited number of people who must book in advance at the Tourist Information Centre, Riverside, Thurso.

27 *Lybster Pottery, Lybster, Caithness*
Visitors will see slip casting, litho decoration and hand decoration. Open Monday to Friday 9 am to 12.30 pm and 1.30 to 4.30 pm. There is a large seconds shop.

28 *Mrs Lindsay H Hamilton, School House, Kildonan, Isle of Arran. Tel: Kildonan 254*
See pots being made on the wheel and watch pots being trimmed, biscuit fired and glazed. The kiln is gas-fired. Open summer weekdays and sometimes in winter. Phone first.

29 *The Scottish Milk Marketing Board, Torrylinn Creamery, Kilmory, Isle of Arran. Tel: Sliddery 240*
Individuals and groups can see the small Arran Dunlop cheese being made, Monday to Friday. Give three days' notice.

30 *Islay Creamery Co Ltd, Port Charlotte, Isle of Islay, Argyll. Tel: Port Charlotte 229*
Individuals and groups can see the various stages in cheese making. Give one week's notice.

31 *Old Rectory Design, Longhouse Buttery,*

Gallery & Workshop, Cullipool, Isle of Luing, by Oban, Argyll. Tel: Luing 209
See the design and packaging of graphic material. Open to individuals daily from 10.30 am to 5.30 pm, all year. Gallery and restaurant. Phone first in winter.

32 Halmatic (Scotland) Ltd, Hatston Industrial Estate, Kirkwall, Orknay. Tel: Hatston 2390
See work on glass fibre fishing vessels and commercial craft up to 54' in size. Small groups welcome for an afternoon visit. Book two weeks' in advance.